WHITEWASH TO WHITEWASH

Daniel Brettig had been a journalist for eight years, first with *The Advertiser* and then AAP in Adelaide and Sydney, when he joined ESPNcricinfo in March 2011, starting just in time for Ricky Ponting's resignation as Australian captain. Those roles have taken him on tours to all the major cricket nations save for Pakistan and Zimbabwe, and a few others besides. Among other publications, he has written for *Wisden Australia*, *Wisden*, *Inside Edge*, *The Cricketer* and *Sports Illustrated India*.

WHITEWASH

Australian Cricket's Years of Struggle and Summer of Riches

TO

WHITEWASH

DANIEL BRETTIG

VIKING
an imprint of
PENGUIN BOOKS

VIKING

UK | USA | Canada | Ireland | Australia
India | New Zealand | South Africa | China

Penguin Books is part of the Penguin Random House group of companies
whose addresses can be found at global.penguinrandomhouse.com.

Penguin
Random House
Australia

First published by Penguin Group (Australia), 2015

1 3 5 7 9 10 8 6 4 2

Design by John Canty © Penguin Group (Australia)
Cover photography by Phil Hillyard/Newspix (top image);
Ryan Pierse/Getty Images (bottom image)
Typeset in Adobe Garamond Pro, 12/16pt by Samantha Jayaweera, Penguin Books (Australia)
Printed and bound in Australia by Griffin Press, an accredited ISO AS/NZS 14001
Environmental Management Systems printer.

National Library of Australia
Cataloguing-in-Publication data:

Brettig, Daniel
Whitewash to whitewash : Australian cricket's years of
struggle and summer of riches / Daniel Brettig.
9780670078424 (paperback)
Subjects: Cricket – Australia – History.
Cricket matches – Australia – History.

796.3580994

penguin.com.au

For Mum and Dad, who were always there.
And for Phil, Peter and Phillip,
three we lost along the way.

CONTENTS

PREFACE

My first cricket tour was to Malaysia in 2006 for the DLF Cup, a little-remembered triangular limited-overs series between Australia, India and the West Indies. Compared with the assignments ahead, including an ODI Champions Trophy and then a home Ashes series, this two-week sojourn in Kuala Lumpur seemed minor. But Ricky Ponting's team were in full battle mode. They had recently undertaken a boot camp and were intent on charging through every opponent between that September and the fifth Ashes Test in Sydney the following January. Ponting's intensity was palpable, with that of Matthew Hayden, Andrew Symonds and Glenn McGrath not far behind.

My colleague Ben Dorries got on the end of a pointed rebuke from Ponting after we both wrongly assumed that he was about to be suspended by the International Cricket Council (ICC) for a third dissent charge inside twelve months. But there were also moments when this all-conquering collective had the sorts of issues common to any team or business. It was possible to laugh at a short-lived attempt to enforce team discipline by ordering every member of the squad to do twenty push-ups whenever an error occurred in training. It was inevitable that people would gawk at the coach John Buchanan as he engaged in a long phone call to Shane Warne, who had been quoted at a book launch as saying, 'I'm a big believer that the coach is something you travel in to get to and from the game!' And it was sensible to conclude that successful teams don't always have to get along.

At the end of the tournament, I found myself drinking with Glenn Connley, then of ESPN, in the hotel all the journalists and teams were sharing. When Glenn turned in, I sat finishing my drink and watching the Australian players celebrate their win in a corner of the bar. After a few minutes I felt the sensation of my hair being tugged. Michael Hussey had sidled up to say, 'Come have a drink with us. It's your first tour.' They were not all there – McGrath, Hayden, Damien Martyn and Michael Clarke were among the absentees – but I found the company enjoyable. Hussey was warm and enthusiastic, Shane Watson and Brett Lee amiably musical as they took turns strumming a guitar, and Simon Katich notably thoughtful as he pondered his ever-precarious place in the One Day International (ODI) team. Ponting was friendly enough, though he quickly became animated when I took issue with his view that Nathan Bassett, the Adelaide Crows' half-back, should never have made the 2006 Australian Football League's All Australian selection. Later, I earnestly told him I was going to do my best to be fair and honest in writing about his team if ever fortunate enough to tour again; he very patiently accepted the kid journo's words.

That tournament and its closing night were my first peek behind the facade of the Australian team, at men who were more flawed than public relations staff would have it but also more human than the headlines suggested. By the end of the summer that group had begun to break up, and the years since then have given a similar insight to many watchers of the game in Australia. Before this, stories about the Australian team largely concerned which record they would break next, but the retirements, defeats and squabbles of the past decade have given us glimpses of a more vulnerable team wrestling often with its limitations.

We have also seen Cricket Australia (CA), the nation's cricket governing body, fumbling around in the dark as board and management tried to cope with the loss of a wondrous generation and the realisation that its successes had allowed the system that spawned it to be neglected. This was not true only of cricket but of all Australian sport, for the arc of targeted funding, talent identification, training and success that spanned from the early 1980s to the Sydney Olympics in 2000 did not reach as far as 2007. Cricket's change of fortunes hadn't simply been a matter of Warne retiring.

Often in daily journalism it is possible to miss the wider view, as the need to form a conclusion or deliver a verdict on one day's events for a deadline leads to a picture that is less than complete and even distorted. Australian cricket has had few better chroniclers than Gideon Haigh, partly because he has never restricted himself to writing only about the game. In March 2008 he was speaking alongside author and journalist David Marr at Adelaide Writers' Week following the release of Haigh's *Asbestos House*, an investigation of James Hardie Industries. Towards the end of the session, he outlined why such works had become increasingly valuable: 'Often these days when you're writing at book or extended essay length, what you're trying to do is disabuse people of the mistaken notions they've picked up from daily journalism. People often come to stories with a kind of perception they already think they know what the story is, and your job is to persuade them otherwise. Writing about James Hardie, I thought I knew the story when I arrived at it, because I'd gone on what newspapers had told me, but I knew enough about the way newspapers treat stories for me to realise that probably wasn't all there was to it, and I made a point of trying to forget all I knew about that story when I arrived at it.'

This book attempts a similar approach to chronicling Australian cricket from 2007 to 2014. I have tried to get away from the daily accounts, spending most of my time interviewing many of the central characters from the period, from players Ricky Ponting, Michael Clarke and Shane Watson to coaching and administration staff Tim Nielsen, Mickey Arthur, Pat Howard and James Sutherland. Interviews for this work are attributed in the present 'says', while secondary sources and past conversations in the past 'said' or similar. If these people's roles in the drama were to be judged by newspaper reports alone, the verdicts might not be too inaccurate, but they would lack the details afforded by closer inspection. Cricket and sport in general are often cast in the simplistic terms of heroes and villains. The truer position is that there is a little of both in everyone. These were flawed years for the Australian game, its players and its decision-makers.

Of course, no event takes place without varying views emerging, and there are plenty of contentious episodes covered in these pages. Monkeygate, Clarke's dressing-room fracas with Katich, the Ashes losses of 2009 and 2010–11, Hussey's last night as an Australian Test cricketer, the Mohali suspensions and the sacking of Arthur for Darren Lehmann are all subjects that have generated strong, and strongly divided, opinions. In reference to these events I will return again to Haigh's musings on long-form journalism: 'A story like James Hardie is a very divisive story, where people are extremely entrenched in their opinions. Everyone expects you to tell their particular side of the story, so your job is to leave everyone uniformly dissatisfied and somehow in the course of writing the story to find your own way . . . to navigate your way through the competing versions of narrative that are being put to you.'

It has been a great challenge, but also a great pleasure, to go back over these times and hear the many divergent views of Australian cricket's great and good. I can only hope that when the uniform dissatisfaction subsides, the lessons of the period will remain.

Daniel Brettig, Sydney, December 2014

I

There's
1200 Wickets
Out the Door

JANUARY 2007

England in Australia

Ricky Ponting wept.

As Channel Nine's cameras and thousands of Sydney Cricket Ground (SCG) spectators fixed their gaze upon Shane Warne, Glenn McGrath and Justin Langer, Ponting let himself go. He did so in a way he would not allow himself again until the moment of his retirement from the Australian team, six years later. The tears were for plenty of reasons, not least the joy and relief at having accomplished the return of the Ashes in the most definitive fashion. But the abiding emotion was sadness at the loss of four men who had underscored almost fifteen years of Australian domination. The fourth, Damien Martyn, was soon to join the team in the dressing room. It was 5 January 2007. 'I bawled my bloody eyes out,' Ponting told McGrath's biographer, Daniel Lane. 'I did my best to keep clear of the media so they didn't pick it up. When I ran out on the field, it hit me that would be the last time I'd be out on a ground with McGrath, Warne and Langer . . . it was over.'

Warne was the once-in-a-lifetime spin-bowling maestro without whom Australia's unbroken years of success could never have been contemplated, let alone achieved. McGrath was a proud member of an Australian pace-bowling lineage that stretched back to Fred Spofforth, and the pragmatic counterpoint to Warne's sorcery. Martyn, part of the rich Australian batting vein that also included Ponting and Hayden, had been a top-six contributor to the twin subcontinental triumphs of 2004, considered the peak Test match achievements of the era. And Langer stood as the least gifted but the most determined of them all, custodian of the team's song and of much of its spirit.

Individually, each left a gulf. Warne's skills, in particular, may never be replaced. Departing together, they opened up a breach not seen since Dennis Lillee, Greg Chappell and Rod Marsh also chose the SCG for their final Test, in January 1984. Those departures had combined with the after-effects of World Series Cricket and the South Africa rebel tours to send the national team tumbling to rare depths and led to a pact between Allan Border and David Boon as survivors, then selectors, to 'make every endeavour for that situation not to happen to Australian cricket ever again'. Warne himself had written in 2006 that he hoped gradual change to the team would be managed by the panel of selectors. 'We can't afford to lose four or five experienced players inside a year, but if we are not careful we could have the likes of Hayden, Langer, Martyn, [Adam] Gilchrist, McGrath, [Stuart] MacGill, [Jason] Gillespie and myself all leaving at roughly the same time. One or two of us might get a tap on the shoulder when we are not quite ready, simply to smooth the transition.'

Such taps had arrived regularly during most of Trevor Hohns' decade as chairman of selectors, from 1996, fracturing relationships with the likes of Ian Healy and Mark Waugh but maintaining a relatively seamless transition of players. But the balance of power between the selectors and the dressing room had changed with Steve Waugh's bloody-minded challenge to Hohns' suggestion that he should give up at the end of 2002–03. An unforgettable Sydney century in a dead

Test match had bought Waugh another year and a farewell lap of the country the following summer. And when a weary Hohns had resigned in 2006, his successor, Andrew Hilditch, was far less trenchant about guiding great players to the finish line, feeling that they had earned the right to retire largely on their own terms.

At a management and board level within CA, there was an awareness of what was likely to happen, though it could not be said that every effort had been made to prepare for it. A paper penned by Rod Marsh as early as his 2001 departure from the Australian Cricket Academy had warned that the nation's talent conveyor belt was not merely stuttering but stuck. As Waugh and Ponting had gathered victories, it had gathered dust. Much of CA's growth and investment in the early 2000s concentrated on growing participation in the game, driven largely by the chief executive James Sutherland. But the club, state and academy system that had bankrolled the national team was no longer a world leader – England in particular had caught up (even if it did not look like it in January 2007). Paul Marsh, chief executive of the Australian Cricketers' Association from 2005 to 2014, summed up the sense of inertia: 'It wasn't a high-performance culture around the team at that time, more a cost-saving culture. In some respects it was understandable, because we were just about unbeatable for a few years. Many people just thought that would continue.'

By 2004, the business consultant – later CA head of strategy and now Cricket New South Wales chief executive – Andrew Jones had been alarmed by plateaued participation figures and revenues. 'My view in 2004 was that cricket was asleep,' he says. 'The overarching message was, "You've taken your position for granted, you've been a summer monopoly, and you're doing what monopolies do, which is basically be lazy. So wake up: there's a war on and you're losing it. Go out and fight it."' In the words of Michael Brown, then head of cricket operations, 'A business that had lived in the fat land for so long struggled to realise what was coming. We knew the next generation was not of the same standard, and that blokes were not performing to the levels of their predecessors. But when you're caught up in the middle of it, people don't tend to make change.'

Australia lost the Ashes in 2005 with the first team not to contain any survivors from the last defeat, in 1986–87. Similarly, no-one in the CA management had known anything other than employment under the banner of the 'world's best team'. In truth, what should then have been an orderly transition of the Australian team from one era to the next was hijacked by the collective will of Ponting, Langer, Hayden, Gilchrist, Warne and McGrath to retrieve the Ashes before considering the end. By pursuing this dream, many of them ignored an old maxim: if you're thinking about retirement, you're already there.

Gilchrist pondered the question seriously during the summer, before a thrilling Perth century snapped him out of it. Hayden tried to dissuade his confidant Langer from retiring with the idea of 'one more year, mate, and we'll retire together next summer'. Warne, who played the 2005 series as though it was his last, chose to defer his exit until 2006–07. Martyn, dropped before earning a recall for the tours of South Africa and Bangladesh in early 2006, abandoned his own thoughts of quitting in the aftermath of a century and victory in Johannesburg due to pestering from senior players. 'Ideally, yes, I would've liked to get back in, made a hundred and said, "That's it,"' Martyn recalled in 2009. 'But then you spend five months at home doing nothing and then you get talked back into it.'

Langer was ill for some weeks after he was struck on the helmet by a ball from Makhaya Ntini in the same Test. But he protested vociferously about retirement to his mentor, Neil Holder, upon returning to Perth. 'Noddy basically told me it was time to retire. I'd always made him promise me when it was time to retire he'd let me know. After being hit so badly I was really unwell for a couple of weeks and it was like the old trainer throwing the towel in and saying, "Time to retire, mate." I kept saying to him, "No, I promised." We'd made a pact on the plane home we were going to win the Ashes back.'

So the team pushed on, through the short-lived ICC Super Series against a less than motivated World XI, Test series victories over West Indies and South Africa (twice), then a pair of exhausted Test matches in Bangladesh. Reservations about coach John Buchanan's elaborate boot camp in pre-season were subjugated beneath a desire to unite for the Ashes, and ODI tournament successes in Malaysia and India suggested the team were humming towards a final peak at home against Andrew Flintoff's Englishmen. They were helped by the fact that Flintoff and his coach, Duncan Fletcher, had grown tired of each other, while England's planning seemed redolent of a common army curse: preparing for the last war.

Brisbane duly went the way of almost every Gabba Test since 1988: an Australian victory by a vast margin. But it was the Adelaide magic conjured by Ponting, Warne, McGrath, Brett Lee, Michael Hussey and Michael Clarke that effectively sealed the series. The finality of the result can be quantified not so much by the rapturous celebrations that followed it, nor by the utterly downcast reactions of England's players – tempered by Flintoff's almost unreasonable keenness to drink with the team that had just rogered his – but by how it set off the chain reaction of retirements that Ponting was crying over a month later.

McGrath was the first to conclude it was time for the exit, having talked the matter over with his wife, Jane, and manager, Warren Craig, in between Brisbane and Adelaide. A badly bruised and blood-blistered heel had left him a questionable starter for the second Test until match eve, when the team physio, Alex Kountouris, tried an old taping method handed down from his predecessor, Errol Alcott, that alleviated McGrath's pain. Although it was enough for the selector Jamie Cox to have McGrath insist that he'd 'never felt better' after passing an afternoon fitness test on Adelaide Oval No. 2, the strata-gem did not help him dominate on the pristine surface prepared by curator Les Burdett. His first-innings figures of 0–107 from 30 overs tell a story as stark as the impudent way in which Kevin Pietersen treated him on the way to 158.

On day five, as Warne orchestrated most of the mayhem, McGrath hobbled around the outfield, waiting until the midpoint of the day for Ponting to grant him the ball. That he claimed the final two wickets soon afterwards said everything about McGrath's value, but Ponting's earlier preference for Lee and Stuart Clark gave a less glowing indicator. A dressing-room conversation with Buchanan that night and with the chairman of selectors, Andrew Hilditch, the following day confirmed that McGrath would be finishing in Sydney. He was not happy about the advice but chose not to reveal his intent until the urn was won. 'I didn't want John or Andrew to think they had put the seed in my head,' McGrath told Daniel Lane, 'because it was my decision.'

Martyn's subsequent confession that he was part of the team only as a result of matey coercion provided an explanation for his few skittish contributions to the series. Innings of 29, 11 and five were returns that depreciated not only in volume but also in cohesion. His final four-ball stay as Australia strode towards their winning target is best summarised as a block, a sweep, a slog and a surrender, backing away to slice a catch to gully. Martyn's unhappy air remained into the evening, as all around him was delirious celebration followed by inebriation. Late in the night Hayden became entangled in a lengthy argument with his fellow 1993 Ashes tourist.

By the time Martyn returned to the Australians' hotel on Hindley Street, passing a happy and somewhat oblivious Gilchrist in the front bar, he had made up his mind to quit and to do so in a manner that left no room for doubt. Before he closed his door, Martyn's last act was to hand Warne's music player to a staff member, who wondered why he'd bothered to do so when they were all going to Perth the following day. The next morning, the players assumed that a missing Martyn was still asleep, but he had caught the first flight to Sydney for some time to collect his thoughts at the compound of the broadcaster Alan

Jones. Soon an email landed in the inbox of the CA chief executive, James Sutherland. No-one in the Australian team saw Martyn again until the final day at the SCG in January.

'I just kept trying to do the right thing and play and by the end I'd had enough, wanted to get out and get on with the rest of my life,' Martyn said. 'They might've liked a fairytale phone call that morning saying "I'm retiring," but I knew I couldn't do that in a sense because I'd get talked back into playing . . . Everybody in the group, if you walked around a team and told fifteen blokes what you were thinking of doing, of retiring or doing this or that, you'd have fifteen different answers. Some will be your mates who just don't want your mates to go, some probably want you to go . . . so it's something you just have to do yourself.'

Martyn's decision might have been irksome, to Ponting in particular, but it set Warne thinking about getting his own retirement over with. In the throes of the Adelaide victory, he commented, 'I'm going to miss this,' and by the time the team settled into their Perth hotel he had begun to consider announcing the conclusion of his Test match career even before the Ashes were formally regained. Tellingly, his discussions were not with Ponting but with the young and ambitious Clarke, who had in 2005 filled the vacuum left by several curdled relationships with fellow senior players to become Warne's best friend. Clarke felt Warne had the right to retire whenever he wanted, but eventually the announcement was postponed until Melbourne, with plans for a major press conference orchestrated under the guise of a sponsorship announcement at the MCG.

Warne's intentions were a million miles from those of the selectors. Aware that McGrath was set to depart and fairly sure Langer was also thinking about it, Hilditch, Boon, Cox and Merv Hughes recoiled in collective shock when informed at the end of the Perth Test that Warne too was about to quit. Martyn's flight from the team had also surprised them, though the panel's intent to plan for the future was illustrated by the inclusion of a wide-eyed Adam Voges in the squad for the Perth Test alongside Andrew Symonds. Cox recalls: 'There was a good understanding that McGrath and Langer were going to go, but Warne and Martyn were a shock. I remember Digger [Hilditch] ringing and saying, "I've got some very interesting news." I was thinking, "What?" There was just no indication Shane was going. Maybe to people around him, but not to Digger. I don't think many people in the team knew – maybe Pup [Clarke] or Ricky. But that was a shock, and it did make it look like, "Oh, the great Warne has gone as well as the great McGrath . . . There's 1200 wickets out the door."'

As befits a master of playing cricket between the ears, Warne maintained an even and confident visage in the lead-up to Perth. Voges chuckles at the memory of his first Australian team meeting and Warne's part in it. 'John Buchanan talked to the boys about how they were trying to get better,' he says. 'Warnie made a bit of a smart-arse comment: "We're going pretty good, mate. We'll just keep doing what we're doing and we'll win this Test match and the Ashes," and that was the end of the meeting.' After the Ashes were won, on the fifth day, Warne repeated his nostalgic line. 'Like I said in Adelaide, I'll miss this. I'm closer to the end than the bloody beginning.' The end duly took in his 700th wicket amid a five-for at the MCG on Boxing Day, a final tilt at an elusive Test hundred in Sydney and a fitting last wicket: Flintoff lured down and stumped.

Langer was the last of the quartet to conclude that Sydney had to be his final gig. While he had wrestled with the issue ever since Ntini's stunning blow, he mirrored Allan Border in his reluctance to make the final call. That changed over the course of the last day of the Melbourne Test. First Boon, who had been at the other end when Langer walked to the middle for the first time in a Test, at Adelaide in 1993, sidled up to his former teammate in the change rooms. 'In New Zealand in 1993 I was actually with Boonie when his father died. We were rooming together. So I always felt he was a really good sounding board for me. I said, "What about retirement?" and he said, "Oh, is it on your mind?" and I replied, "Yeah, I guess it is," and he said, "I'll give you a bit of advice, mate. If it's on your mind, you're a lot closer than you think you are."'

A second sign arrived later that evening when Langer sat with Hayden and realised that, for once, their motivation was not at comparable levels. 'I was sitting there and knew I'd put everything into that Ashes series and winning them back, whereas Haydos had that "eye of the tiger" look. The desperation to get back into the one-day team was a real driver. My driver was to win the Ashes back. And I kept thinking, "What's going to drive me now?" That night I had to get up and sing the team song. But after Boonie had spoken to me and that moment with Haydos, I was thinking, "I've got to sing the team song here and get pumped up for the boys. We've just won 4–0 and it's all great, but I'd rather be with Sue and the kids." I left my dad a message that night and we caught up the next morning. I told him I was retiring and he said, "I was going to tell you the same thing."'

Looking past the innings and ten-wicket victories that completed the 5–0, some signs of decay were evident even then. Australia's first-innings batting was bailed out in each match, first by Hayden and Symonds from the depths of 5–84 at the MCG and then by Symonds, Gilchrist and a freewheeling, free-sledging Warne from 5–190 in Sydney. It may be argued that England were neither good enough nor functional enough to take advantage, particularly as the relationship of Flintoff and Fletcher wilted. But for well over a decade, Warne, McGrath and a succession of assertive, gifted batsmen had enabled Australia to compensate for the odd poor start or session by delivering lethal, counterattacking salvos. Not only were Ponting and company used to winning Test matches; they were used to doing so without needing to put it all together in every session against opponents who were mentally beaten down, if not outright beaten, before a match began.

Still, few were in any mood for sober reflection about what lay ahead as the on-field farewells at the SCG migrated into the members' stand. Langer and Ponting indulged in a final dressing-room wrestle, after the fashion of Rod Marsh and Bruce Laird decades before. In the evening, James Packer's boat hosted a team celebration on Sydney Harbour that saw Langer hand the team song over to Michael Hussey and players' partners included in a rousing rendition. A verse was sung for each of the five Test match wins. Jane McGrath, to be lost to breast cancer in 2008, spoke to Langer. 'It was the last time I saw Jane. She came up to me with a big smile on her face and said, "I never really understood the team song, but thanks so much for including us – now I understand why you guys love it so much."' For many, the night on the harbour felt like the pinnacle of success, but also the end of it. Ponting, Langer, Hayden, Gilchrist and their wives lunched together at Bondi Icebergs the following day, marking the break-up of a merry band within the team.

Twenty-four hours earlier, Ponting had composed himself in time for the regular round of post-match media duties and had stated his desire to keep pushing the team to maintain a dominant perch in cricket's official and psychological rankings. 'Hopefully, we can find some young blokes who can come in, step up and slot into a fantastic cricket team,' he said. 'The next challenge is to try and maintain the status as best in the world. I grabbed Michael Clarke on the way around the ground and had a word about the next era. For the next few years, hopefully it's he and I and Michael Hussey being able to be the leaders and win games for our country.'

Among the least certain that success would simply continue to roll on was Hussey, who watched the farewells and congratulations with some misgivings. Pessimism is a quality Hussey has always retained, even in that moment when he boasted a batting average of 79.85 from sixteen Tests, none of which had ended in defeat. 'I remember sitting there having a beer with the boys and thinking, "Right, things are going to get a lot tougher from now on." And sure enough, they did. You lose those two bowlers in particular and you can't replace them. The other thing about that team was it didn't really change much for almost ten years, so they got to know each other extremely well, like brothers.' Stability fosters trust, but the first of these was about to disappear. Of those in the dressing room in 2007, only Ponting, Clarke, Hussey, Stuart Clark and a visiting Shane Watson made it to the 2009 Ashes tour.

John Howard, no stranger to Australian sporting celebrations during his prime ministership, was a guest in the dressing room that afternoon. The late political writer Matt Price once outlined a never-hatched plot through which Howard might have been outed as a confected 'cricket tragic'. The plan involved a Middle Eastern colleague of Price's and the story of an invented uncle, 'Punjab Singh', who he would claim had bowled finger spin for India in the late 1960s. Had Howard gone along with it, Price would have known him to be bluffing. At this point, however, it was Clarke who tested the prime minister's knowledge, with an invented an Ashes ritual. The Waterford Crystal trophy modelled on the Ashes urn had been added to the winners' celebrations only in 1998–99. But it was filled with champagne this day, and Clarke told Howard that a cherished tradition was to drink from it. To much laughter, Howard duly did so, adding a touch of humour to the pathos of the occasion. As he wandered back out into Sydney's late-afternoon sunshine, Howard could not have known that before the year was out he would lose both his government and his seat in parliament. Australian cricket's rude shock arrived even sooner, in an embryonic format for which no-one that day spared a moment's thought – Twenty20.

2

The
Revolution
Televised

JANUARY – SEPTEMBER 2007

ICC World Cup in the West Indies
ICC World Twenty20 in South Africa

No-one ever accused Jimmy Maher of not saying what he thought. Among the fringe players during Australian cricket's era of riches, Maher was highly regarded for his honesty and ability to provide a robust sense of team spirit in any dressing room, most notably at the 2003 World Cup. His views were not always the most enlightened, but they often reflected the thoughts of other cricketers. With one statement in January 2005, Maher summed up Australian cricket's initial attitude to Twenty20 (T20), an addition to the sporting landscape that few mistook for anything other than a marketing tool: 'We can't let the message slip that it's not real cricket.'

Two years on, the fast-food format had proven its ability to attract vast crowds to fixtures that otherwise would have drawn handfuls, and had gained credibility by the scheduling of the first ICC World T20 event, in South Africa in September. Yet in Australia the game was still regarded with scepticism. Its seriousness was a matter for debate, and ideas on developing its appeal oscillated wildly, despite a two-week Big Bash state tournament having been minted in 2005–06 following a trio of exhibition matches in 2004–05 that had attracted huge audiences.

Two days after Australia's Ashes sweep, 10 652 spectators at Newcastle Sportsground witnessed the bizarre sight of New South Wales' Simon Katich declining singles from the bowling of South Australia's Shaun Tait as the home side sought 13 runs from the final over. Katich felt compelled to protect the former rugby league great and number 11 Andrew Johns, who had been parachuted into the team by the New South Wales chief executive, David Gilbert, as a way of drumming up public interest. The Blues players had cautiously approved of Johns' inclusion, but by day's end many were angry to see their chance of victory reduced by the use of a celebrity ring-in.

South Australia's captain at the time was Darren Lehmann, nearing the end of his long and eventful first-class career. His view post-match echoed Maher's two years previously: 'I just don't want it to stand too much away from domestic cricket. It's fantastic for the state associations. I think as long as we don't get too greedy and over-pack the games and not play too many, and take it to regional centres like New South Wales has done, then I think you will always have great content. As soon as they get too many games and play too many, maybe it will lose its edge.'

Internationally, T20 remained a novelty. Australia took part in the first of the form's national contest, at Eden Park in Auckland, at the start of their 2005 tour of New Zealand. In a retro-fest memorable for New Zealander Hamish Marshall's afro frizz, Glenn McGrath feigned an underarm for the final ball as the tourists won easily. Later that year, Australia's squad trained for four hours prior to a T20 game at Hampshire's Rose Bowl and put in a fatigued display against an England side eager to use the fixture to set down a psychological marker. But there was no question of Duncan Fletcher thinking this was the main game. When Ricky Ponting's men set off for South

Africa in the spring of 2007, they had played a measly five T20 internationals in three years. India, meanwhile, had played one.

Australia went through a brief post-Ashes lull before roaring back to
life for the World Cup in the West Indies. England regained some
measure of self-respect by winning the triangular ODI series that also
included New Zealand, who then barrelled to a 3–0 series sweep in
the Chappell-Hadlee Trophy. Ponting, Michael Clarke and Adam
Gilchrist all opted out of that tour, while Brett Lee tore ankle liga-
ments at the first training session in Wellington and flew home. But
the captain, vice-captain and their successor were all on the flight to
the Caribbean. Tait, who proved a more than adequate substitute in a
remarkably straightforward title defence, replaced Lee.

Aura carried Ponting's men over most opponents, most notably a
keyed-up South Africa in the semifinal. Their coach, Mickey Arthur,
later voiced his regret over not addressing the team's fears on match
eve, and their captain, Graeme Smith, described the psychological
effect of facing Australia at the time. 'At that stage all of us felt like we
had to play out of our skins to beat them,' he says. 'That came through
in the way we played. Bat first on a wicket where maybe you think
you need 350 but you only need 240, you try to hit every ball for four
and you all nick off behind. You end up thinking you need to do more
than you do, instead of backing your skills and being smart.' McGrath
retired as a three-time World Cup winner, and James Packer supplied
another of his boats for more celebratory hijinx, this time off the coast
of Barbados.

An absentee from those heady days was Tim Nielsen, who suc-
ceeded John Buchanan as coach following the World Cup. Formerly
a neat wicketkeeper for South Australia, Nielsen had found his post-
playing niche as an assistant coach whose commonsense had balanced
with the more high-minded theories of Greg Chappell in South
Australia and then Buchanan with the national team. Recognised by

CA as a potential replacement for Buchanan in 2004, Nielsen had served two years as head coach at the Australian Cricket Academy (by then renamed the Centre of Excellence and relocated to Brisbane) in order to build relationships with the coming generation. He had been given the option of rejoining the team in the Caribbean ahead of taking the senior role but preferred to wait until the winter to establish himself.

Assignment number one was the World T20. The chosen squad was a strong one, very similar in composition to the group that had carried all before them in the 50-over event. Yet there was a feeling of uncertainty, as none of Australia's players or coaches knew quite what to make of the T20 tournament. Nielsen recalls, 'In some regards a T20 international was a bit of a pest for us, because it was blocked into the middle of an international summer where we had no time to prepare for it, really. There wasn't enough cricket at home and Joey [Andrew Johns] playing meant we weren't taking it seriously enough from a selection point of view, so we were still picking players out of one-day cricket.'

Also, following the refreshment of a four-month break after the Caribbean, Australia's build-up in South Africa was disjointed by a combination of personal tragedy and injury. Ponting missed the warm-up matches to stay at home with his wife, Rianna, after she miscarried, though CA understandably referred only to 'illness' at the time. Shane Watson and Stuart Clark were also late to arrive, while Michael Clarke and Matthew Hayden wrestled with ailments during the warm-ups. Tait was missing altogether due to an elbow problem.

Nevertheless, Australia's opening fixture, against Zimbabwe in Cape Town, did not appear likely to be anything more than a chance for the world's most feared team to ease into some rhythm. The African nation's cricket had long slipped into a cycle of administrative waste and on-field despair, summed up by the fact that their only previous T20 match had resulted in a 43-run defeat at the hands of Bangladesh. And a proposed Australian tour of Zimbabwe preceding the World T20 had been called off. Whatever the vagaries of the new format that no-one quite took seriously, Australia would brush them off easily enough. Wouldn't they?

After being part of a slide to 1–7, 2–12, 3–19 and 4–48, Gilchrist was interviewed at the boundary's edge. 'We'll see at the end of this tournament just how serious it is and how everyone's taking it.' What everyone present could already see was that Zimbabwe were well ahead on that score, bowling and fielding diligently against opponents seemingly out for an early-evening stroll around the wintry Newlands Cricket Ground. Hayden, Gilchrist and Ponting fell thanks to indiscriminate strokes, the captain's sliced slog to third man one of the most unsightly he ever played. The top scorer in the final tally of 138 was Brad Hodge, one of the few squad members to have developed some sort of T20 game in English county competition.

Guided by Brendan Taylor, Zimbabwe scampered to victory with a ball to spare. In the space of a couple of hours, Australia's veneer of invincibility had been significantly cracked, and Ponting was fuming. 'I can't remember walking off a cricket field feeling that way in quite a while, and the rest of the team felt similarly aggrieved,' he wrote in his diary. 'I told the boys straight after the game that it was as bad a loss as I've been involved in with the Australian team. We didn't respect the game or our opponents as much as we needed to. The thought was, "We'll go out and smack these blokes all over the place, make 250 and that'll be it." All of a sudden, we were 4–48. Cricket can bite you if you go into it with an attitude like that . . . we didn't perform as true professionals.'

Nielsen, coaching his first official fixture after Buchanan's eight years of more or less unbroken success, was mortified. 'It was as much of a kick in the guts as anything, losing the first game I ever coached to Zimbabwe. I'll never forget that. Sitting in the rooms after finishing off the day, I cracked a beer and Gilly said, "Bet you're glad you took this on." So we had a bit of a giggle about it. But I went back to the hotel that night and sat on my balcony by myself, had three or four beers and thought, "We can't even beat Zimbabwe. What have I done wrong?"'

Roused to a state of more heightened awareness, the chastened team won through to the semifinals, though lost also to Pakistan. Pakistan's coach at the time was Geoff Lawson, who had stressed to his players that for the first time in some years there was not quite so much to fear from facing Ponting and company. 'My exact expression was, "If we get to play Australia they're vulnerable,"' he says. 'The reputation of the Australian players among the Pakistan players was such that they almost idolised them, really felt they were great players. I was surprised at the degree to which they revered them.'

A little of that reverence was stripped away in the aftermath of Pakistan's victory, in Johannesburg, when it became apparent that the Australians were not gracious losers. Says Lawson, 'Some of the players' behaviour was extraordinarily rude and disrespectful because they lost. Not shaking hands and things like that. A couple of them were very good, a couple not so good. It's good to be pissed off when you're beaten, but the behaviour that went with it was not what you'd expect of a national sporting team. They didn't handle it very well.'

Yet by the day of the semifinal against India, in Durban, most still considered Australia warm favourites. India's mere presence at the tournament was a shock to many, since the Board of Control for Cricket in India (BCCI) had opposed the introduction of T20 internationals. Niranjan Shah, at the time the board secretary, had argued fervently against the scheduling of the tournament in 2006. Eventually, its conception was approved, but only narrowly, by the ICC executive board, and with the condition that a nation's attendance at the first event would be optional. Following a first provincial T20 tournament that was not even televised, India did send a team – minus key players Sachin Tendulkar, Sourav Ganguly, Anil Kumble, V V S Laxman and Rahul Dravid. M S Dhoni's young side had done well to get this far.

India were propelled to 5–188 by the laconic talents of Yuvraj Singh, who carved up Clark, Nathan Bracken and Andrew Symonds on the way to 70 from a mere 30 balls. Yuvraj had form in terms of destruction, having already clouted England's Stuart Broad for the mythical six sixes in an over. Australia's pursuit began decently enough, and at 3–143 in the 14th over they had the target in sight. However, in setting off for a second run, Hussey felt his hamstring go. The resultant interruption sapped precious momentum from the innings, and the final five-run Australian defeat was the cue for Indian paroxysms of delight. The outcome, notable in and of itself, was also memorable for India's abrasive (and, it proved, highly portentous) response to Australia's aggression. Gilchrist noticed the cheek of S Sreesanth, along with how Robin Uthappa took it upon himself to sledge Hayden. The manner in which the game was played reversed that of the past seven years, during which Hayden had dished it out more than anyone.

It is not quite true to say that without this result, and without India's subsequent win in the final over against Pakistan, the Indian Premier League (IPL) would never have happened. Lalit Modi's plan for a city-based limited-overs competition had existed since the 1990s, and soon after his ascension to the post of BCCI vice-president under Sharad Pawar in 2004 he sought to recast it as a 20-over vehicle; the league was formally launched two days after the 2007 World T20 began. But the tournament's progress into an Indian victory narrative ensured that the IPL's growth was as rapid as that of any event ever conceived within the slow and unwieldy BCCI.

The other factor in the IPL's rapid turnaround from bright idea to brassy reality was the emergence of the rival, unsanctioned Indian Cricket League. During an Australia A tour of Pakistan that followed the World T20, several players were approached to join the league, including Stuart MacGill, who was then poised on 198 Test wickets and finally out of Warne's shadow. 'The idea of money up front appealed to me, but people were getting banned from Test cricket if they'd signed up,' he says. 'I spoke to my wife, my family, people on the ground in India [and] a couple of people in Australian cricket I respected, about what it would mean to me to get 200 wickets. While playing the second game in Pakistan it transpired that I needed a knee operation. So I decided I wasn't going to be able to fulfil the ICL contract, came back home, had surgery and missed the first Shield game instead.'

New contracts, of both the Indian Cricket League and the IPL varieties, began to muddy what had to that point been quite a simple career equation for Australian cricketers. The best played for Australia and were paid handsomely for the privilege, while the rest fought gamely to reach that pedestal. Now, the prospect of sizeable cash rewards for less apparent effort caused the vision of numerous players to be diverted from the 'baggy green dream'.

Modi's initial meeting with Australian players in Mumbai was equal parts carrot and stick, reminding members of the world's number-one team that they would be a major asset to what was going to be a cash-rich competition but also that it would be able to go ahead without them. Impressed by Modi and reassured that international cricket would always take precedence over the IPL, Ponting, Bracken, Hussey, Symonds, Clarke, Hayden, Gilchrist, Mitchell Johnson, Brad Haddin and Brett Lee, alongside Warne and McGrath, agreed in principle to take part in the IPL.

The meeting had taken place away from the Australian Cricketers' Association, leaving chief executive Paul Marsh with plenty of concerns when he saw the contracts. 'There were documents signed that players hadn't consulted with anyone on, and funnily enough the reserve amounts they agreed to were ridiculously low compared to where it's got to,' he says. 'The BCCI wouldn't deal with us, but we started pointing out the issues with the contracts. The players started getting cold feet, and a number said they didn't want to play. Funnily enough, and this is one reason why I'm so confident the BCCI wouldn't have followed through with a lot of their threats, when they got wind the players weren't going to come they started dealing with us. I dealt personally with an intermediary to Lalit Modi and we got the contracts changed.'

Jason Gillespie, Michael Kasprowicz, Michael Bevan, Matthew Elliott, Ryan Campbell, Ian Harvey and even Jimmy Maher departed the Sheffield Shield en masse, in pursuit of Indian Cricket League pay cheques that turned out to be phantom. Alongside the international retirements of the preceding summer, these absentees widened the holes that had already begun to open up in the domestic game. But any CA foreboding about the drain of experience was minimal. Apart from reminding all who participated in the Indian Cricket League that their involvement would mean a ban from approved cricket, administrators were preoccupied by dealings with India around the IPL and other events proposed and realised.

In 2005, CA had pushed for the establishment of a 'Southern Premier League' involving teams from Australia, South Africa and New Zealand and modelled on the concept of Super Rugby. Talks regarding the project were substantial enough to have the global sports management firm IMG set up a temporary office within CA's headquarters, in Jolimont, Melbourne, to work on it, before it was overtaken by events in India. The development of a Champions League for T20 domestic teams from around the world was more successful. Dreamed up in Australia, it was first discussed with numerous boards in mid-2006 but rejected by a still-sceptical India. When retabled, once the IPL idea caught fire, the league found a far more interested audience with boards and broadcasters and was announced at a glitzy launch in New Delhi in September 2007, during the World T20.

The two new tournaments created their own market pressure, resulting in a pair of television deals without precedent in domestic cricket. Sony signed on to cover the IPL for ten years at the price of $1 billion. Suddenly panicked by the prospect of missing out on the new new thing, ESPN Star Sports coughed up $900 million for the Champions League T20, also over ten years. In the case of the IPL, the money was to go to the BCCI, the franchises and the players. The Champions League windfall was divided up between the boards of India, Australia and South Africa, after the England and Wales Cricket

Board argued itself out of the equation. England's resulting fear of T20 exclusion led ultimately to an ill-advised tryst with the former Texas billionaire, cricket entrepreneur and now convict Allen Stanford.

At a board and an administrative level, the sudden rush of money was welcomed, for reasons articulated by the ESPNcricinfo editor Sambit Bal: 'In no other team sport in the world has there existed such a disparity between the highest levels and all forms below. It has been cricket's greatest weakness that no layer below international cricket has been financially viable. Domestic cricket has merely served the purpose of being the supply line to the national level, and has subsisted on the charity of national boards . . . That the proposed league could help create a vibrant and viable second tier is a welcome prospect.'

Frequent visitors to India, whether for IPL or international duties, Australia's cricketers crossed paths with some members of the disapproved Indian Cricket League troupe on either side of a 2008 tour match in Hyderabad, including Jimmy Maher and the former New South Wales coach Steve Rixon. During one catch-up at the Taj Krishna hotel, Maher broke dramatically from his earlier position on T20, declaring how serious the tournament was for everyone involved. Nielsen good-naturedly put him down with the words 'It's not that important, Mahbo. It's just a vehicle for has-beens; you know that.' But for players, coaches, umpires and the rest, the Indian Cricket League, the IPL and the Champions League T20 were attractive for much the same reason: the new stream of money flooding into the minds – if not always the bank accounts – of the participants.

By the time of the second Indian Cricket League, in 2009, held in South Africa due to India's general election, attitudes to international cricket were being shaken. Upon his return from the tournament, for example, a senior Australian player was heard to proclaim, 'There's got to be something done about this. It's a disgrace that countries don't stop all the other tours and allow the IPL to flourish.'

But as the state of international cricket became a secondary concern, so too did security, and in 2010 another issue underlined how much the players had been swayed by the IPL's effect on their incomes. That year brought a specific al-Qaeda threat against the tournament, of the kind that had stopped international tours in the past. Marsh witnessed the change in attitude after informing the players that the security adviser Reg Dickason could not guarantee their safety. 'There was a really mixed view in the room,' he says. 'The players had started to see how big this money was, and for many of them the IPL was their primary employer in terms of income. The players at that point, I think, made a big mistake in deciding to go to that IPL, and in doing so sent a message that they could be bought, just like the boards have been. The IPL knows the players aren't pulling out, so any leverage we had as a players' association worldwide was given away by the players at that time.'

And in the words of one former CA official, 'They treated it for what it was: a vehicle to make a massive amount of money in a very short period of time. I can't blame the players for going to the IPL, but I don't think any, hand on heart, could say it was important in cricket terms. It was important in monetary terms.' Such a conclusion may sound cynical, but by the end of the summer of 2007–08 more than a few Australian cricketers found themselves in a disenchanted frame of mind. The reasons for their rancour began to develop on the same India tour during which they had signed up for the IPL, and it surrounded the singular talent and personality of Andrew Symonds.

3

Monkeygate I

OCTOBER 2007 – JANUARY 2008

Australia in India

Sri Lanka in Australia

India in Australia

A brooding Andrew Symonds watched India's players dance around the Durban pitch in the minutes following their World T20 defeat of Australia. How dare this young Indian collective carry on so in front of the world's greatest team? How dare they celebrate victory in a minor tournament mere months after Symonds' side had lifted the only global cricket trophy that mattered? Did they have no respect? Symonds carried his sense of indignation to the subcontinent as part of Australia's squad for seven ODIs and one T20 and fed on it with the bat and in the field. 'Watching members of Team India in open-topped buses going around the cities, being worshipped by thousands of people, rankled me more than I realised,' he wrote later of the nation's response to the tournament. 'So I got on my high horse a bit and probably didn't endear myself to anyone in the Indian playing group by bluntly expressing a view they had carried on a little too much. I might have suggested that they needed to be a little more humble, which didn't go over terribly well either.'

That was no surprise, since fondness for Symonds was not always easy to find among opponents. Alongside Matthew Hayden, he had emerged as Australia's chief antagonist, customarily using his physical presence and blunt language to ensure that his advantage in skill and experience was more than matched by verbal intimidation and general nastiness. Symonds and Hayden took their cues from the Queensland dressing room of the mid-1990s, a tough and uncomplicated environment with a well-defined sense of hierarchy and a rich grasp of abusive vocabulary. Many past players, former captain Mark Taylor included, have remarked that Sheffield Shield and club cricket played host to far more brutal exchanges than anything at Test level. Symonds and Hayden got closest to replicating the behaviour in international matches, becoming archetypes of the saying 'He's a great bloke if he's on your side.'

In 2010, his international career long gone, Symonds conceded this in conversation with Harsha Bhogle: 'I played with a lot of the old-fashioned cricketers, and that rubbed off on me. The way they played in the middle was uncompromising. Some of them [opponents] would be hurt, and that was a weakness in the opposition and that was when you went in, both feet. That was one of my roles in the Australian side. Myself and Matty Hayden would gang up on someone, we might see something and go for it. Sometimes it's to get yourself going as well. You might have a day where you're carrying an injury or you're a bit sick or tired or sore. Just to get you up for the battle you might pick a fight with someone. That used to work for me.' It worked in India in 2007, carrying Symonds to the man of the series trophy in a 4–2 victory for the tourists.

After one of the 50-over encounters, Indian bowler Harbhajan Singh made known his views about the Australians' behaviour. 'They think they are superior and can do and say whatever they like, but that is not the case,' he said. 'They are very bad losers. They were beaten in the [T20] World Cup and they clearly did not like that. They say they play the game in the right spirit, but they don't in reality. There is nothing gentlemanly about the way they play . . . They think you cannot fight back, and they do not like it when you do.'

At the same time Symonds was picking fights with India's play-ers, subcontinental crowds picked a fight with him. The first 'monkey' chants came from the stands in Vadodara, during Australia's comfort-able eclipse of India in the fifth ODI, though there was some dispute over their intent. Adam Gilchrist thought the crowd had been refer-ring to how the players were trapped inside the caged stadium like monkeys at the zoo. Local authorities denied the chants had occurred at all, police claiming they had been exhortations for Lord Ganesha to save India's floundering batsmen. Symonds had noticed the chants, and discussed the issue with the team, but did not wish to take it fur-ther. He was annoyed, however, to hear both the BCCI president, Sharad Pawar, and the secretary, Niranjan Shah, refer to the episode as 'a misunderstanding'. Symonds knew what he had heard.

All were aware of recently instituted ICC regulations about racially motivated chanting from crowds, following complaints by South Africa of racist Afrikaans abuse hurled their way during the 2005–06 tour of Australia. Theoretical penalties for such abuse included heavy fines, life bans for spectators and the stripping of a ground's international status. Having been accused of a lax response to the South African abuse, CA pushed the line of zero tolerance with its players during a pre-season camp and with its spectators through public awareness campaigns featuring Merv Hughes. Indian reticence to acknowledge the chanting left CA's public affairs manager and anti-racism officer, Peter Young, needing to be very delicate in his commentary about the episode on radio and televi-sion in Australia.

Despite Symonds' hope that it would all blow over, the chants were heard again in Nagpur, this time by an Australian filmmaker, Gus Worland. They escaped the attention of Symonds, as he crashed an 88-ball 107 that sealed the series for Australia, but kept the issue burning for the teams' arrival in Mumbai. India's largest and most commercial centre is known for its brashness and crassness, and at Wankhede Stadium all semblance of doubt about the chanting was removed. Choruses of 'Symonds is a monkey' were clearly audible to those present at the ground, while the Getty Images photographer Hamish Blair captured the image of the series: two men mimicking monkeys.

Whatever his desire to keep the issue away from official recourse, Symonds was affected, becoming increasingly withdrawn around the team and distracted from his on-field tasks. The stadium and the story spooked him when he went out to bat. Finding himself back in the dressing room after clouting his first ball straight to short cover and departing for a golden duck, he exclaimed, 'Well, what the fuck happened there?'

Brandishing a copy of Blair's photograph, Australia's team manager, Steve Bernard, visited Niranjan Shah in the BCCI's office, which happened to be at Wankhede. As the afternoon drifted into night, the stadium's big screen flashed a warning about racist chanting in belated acknowledgement that these were not chants of worship towards any sort of god but racially themed attempts to disrupt the game and distract a key Australian player. After the match, Ponting said Symonds had been hurt by it all.

Running parallel to the crowd issues were battles between the Australians and several members of the Indian team, most notably S Sreesanth and Harbhajan. In Kochi, Sreesanth and Symonds had clashed twice when Australia was batting, and Harbhajan responded to his dismissal by Michael Clarke with the words 'Do you want a fight? Do you? Do you?' Sreesanth had been 12th man in Mohali but still offered numerous choice words to Ponting during one drinks break. By the time of the second innings in Mumbai, something was bound to snap. It did, and in a way that took the racial issue from the boundary to the middle, when Symonds heard Harbhajan call him a monkey in the 35th over of India's chase. Harbhajan was soon dismissed, and Symonds kept it to himself while the hosts scrambled to a two-wicket win.

Away from prying eyes and cameras, Symonds told Ponting,

Gilchrist and Bernard what Harbhajan had said. They reacted with considerable anger, and immediately the question of reporting the matter to the match referee, Chris Broad, was raised. After Symonds baulked at that possibility, Bernard advised him to speak with Harbhajan, state his dissatisfaction and seek an assurance that it would not happen again.

The dressing rooms at Wankhede were at the time separated by a small outdoor area near the boundary, and it was there that the two antagonists met. Bernard kept Australia's door ajar to watch the discussion, which he estimated to last about a minute. Harbhajan kept his head bowed, listening, while Symonds spoke.

Symonds later gave his account of the encounter: 'I basically told him, "Look, the name-calling is fine with me, it doesn't particularly worry me what you call me, but you know what is going to happen. One thing will lead to another and you blokes will end up going to an umpire and it will get out of hand." I said that the word he used was offensive and hurtful and he apologised and said it wouldn't happen again. We shook hands and I said, "That's the end of it."'

Ponting gave a slightly different version in his diary: 'When Symmo returned to our room, he told us that after he explained how much the insult had affected him, while Harbhajan had not admitted that he said it, he did acknowledge that it was unacceptable, had apologised for any offence, and assured Symmo there'd be no repeat.'

Before the team left Wankhede Stadium that night, Ponting and Gilchrist told Symonds that if Harbhajan was ever to utter the word to him again, the matter would be taken further, whether he liked it or not. Both remained exceptionally angry about Harbhajan's act, more so even than Symonds himself. But Ponting and Gilchrist knew Symonds and how he had been affected by the episode, having witnessed his increasingly withdrawn and moody responses to the crowd abuse. No-one wanted a reprise.

*

The Australian summer ahead was meant to be a showcase for Symonds. In the wake of Warne and McGrath, he was perceived by many to have become the most popular member of the national team, and the one to whom most fans could relate. Symonds' manager, Matt Fearon, had urged him to make his fortune now, saying the previous season's Ashes century at the MCG had raised his value enormously. Ford and Schweppes, among others, featured him prominently in their advertising, on the premise that his 'outdoors everyman' appeal would win over the public. The publishing house Hardie Grant commissioned one successful book, *Roy: Going for Broke*, then lined up another, *Roy on the Rise*. Together with his sponsors, they sold the idea that 'Roy' Symonds would happily have a conversation with anyone: the ideal guest at a barbecue.

This was marketing spin well removed from the reality. Away from his on-field bluster Symonds was shy, private and wary of outsiders. His charismatic presence in the middle was possible because he had grown to know his fellow players, but this did not necessarily translate to instant warmth for unknown members of the public. Loyal yet slow to trust would be an accurate description of Symonds the man, but no-one around him saw fit to call out the advertisers on their loose depiction of his character – too much money was being made. When the summer began to unravel, images of a haunted Symonds in matches and at training contrasted sharply with the commercials that were interspersed with them.

Tossing the coin at the Gabba on 8 November, Ponting looked upon his changing team with plenty of brio. 'All the guys who have come into the side have worked really hard for the opportunity,' he said, before sitting down to watch as a combination of old and new worked their way diligently through a Sri Lankan side missing Kumar Sangakkara due to a hamstring strain. Hayden's new partner Phil Jaques compiled an admirable, patient debut century after Australia

were sent in, before Michaels Hussey and Clarke showed their affinity
for batting with each other by adding 245 surefooted runs. Brett Lee,
Stuart Clark and Symonds shared the wickets with Stuart MacGill,
who spun through Michael Vandort for his 200th Test wicket, and
another stripling, the fast left-armer Mitchell Johnson.

Ostensibly Warne's successor, MacGill was now the oldest man in
the team and felt the strain of bowling again when Ponting enforced
the follow-on. 'Physically, I'd been under the hammer for a couple
of years, and that was the big thing for me,' he says. 'People may say,
"We fully expected Stuey to be a big part of things for the next couple of years," but it was never communicated to me. I bowled a lot in
Brisbane, and when I got the 200th wicket I remember very vividly
just about not being able to go on. It was just, "I've got there now; it is
done." Little did I know at the time that was almost it.'

Barbs slung between Shane Warne and Muttiah Muralitharan,
even as the trophy bearing their name was about to be unveiled,
marred the lead-up to the Hobart Test. Ahead of the launch, Warne
suggested in his News Limited column that Muralitharan and others should have their bowling actions tested under match conditions,
causing his Sri Lankan rival to state that Warne 'must be a miserable
man' to keep stirring the pot. However, Warne's thoughts, and those
of other Australian players past and present who had wondered about
Muralitharan's unorthodox action, were left to one side as they smiled
and chatted before the cameras at Bellerive Oval.

Warne's presence proved an ill omen for MacGill, who experienced
a dramatic loss of feeling in his bowling hand after landing on his elbow
in the field. Though Jaques totted up another 150 and Hussey a second
century as the hosts again crested 500, the lack of sensation sabotaged
MacGill's bowling. 'It's like your fingers are made of plasticine. I felt
like sticking pins in them. I tried hot water, cold water . . . and then I
was bowling head-high full tosses.' MacGill's second-innings figures of
1–102 from 20 overs caused Ponting's brow to furrow almost as much
as did being forced to witness a sublime 192 from Sangakkara, who

helped guide his side to within 100 runs of an implausible victory.

Only a risible decision by the umpire Rudi Koertzen, ruling Sangakkara caught off his shoulder and helmet, spared Ponting further despair. MacGill resolved to have hand surgery, leaving Australia's spin berth in the eager but uncultured hands of Brad Hogg. Themes of poor umpiring and a spin-bowling deficit grew in the following weeks but soon had to compete with other, more pressing concerns. India were coming, and Ponting gave an intimidatory warning of what lay ahead to their captain, Anil Kumble. 'A lot of very, very good players in the past haven't been able to cope with captaining India,' he said. 'Sachin Tendulkar probably didn't ever really want to do it. Rahul Dravid did it for a short period of time. When he resigned he said he just wasn't enjoying the role.' Within months, Ponting himself would feel similarly harried.

Scheduling series for India offers a unique headache. Well aware of the team's value, boards must often wrestle with the fact that the BCCI's suggested dates do not always fit. When Michael Brown, head of Australia's cricket operations, spoke to Niranjan Shah ahead of the 2007–08 season, he was initially told that Kumble's team would arrive on 2 January. Subsequent negotiations preserved the Boxing Day and New Year's Tests but left India with only the desultory preparation of a single three-day match, in Melbourne. When that was ruined by rain, the visitors were ill prepared and were summarily clattered by Hayden and the pacemen in the MCG Test. Somewhere in the blur, Kumble had accepted Ponting's request that batsmen take the word of fielders for low catches. The tourists resolved to fight more boldly in Sydney.

They were doing rather better than that by mid-afternoon on the first day, having pushed Ponting's men to 6–134. Erroneous umpiring decisions had fallen equally to both sides, as a Ponting feather down the leg side not heard by umpire Mark Benson was squared up by his l.b.w. dismissal to Harbhajan, despite a sizeable inside edge. But when Symonds, on 30, edged Ishant Sharma behind and umpire Steve Bucknor declined an appeal first vehement then desperate, India took on a wounded air that endured throughout the match and its aftermath. A pair of debatable stumping reprieves contributed further to their annoyance as Symonds and Hogg lifted Australia to an improbable 463. Walking off with an undefeated 162 next to his name, albeit having admitted he 'smashed' the delivery from Sharma on the first evening, Symonds' stocks had never seemed higher.

Psychologically, Australia might have expected to surge through on the wave created by their earlier good fortune, but India were well served by their sense of persecution and by two avowed lovers of the SCG. Tendulkar and V V S Laxman crafted contrasting centuries; the latter's as silky as the former's was sturdy. Feisty partnerships down the order caused Australian tempers to fray. 'So this is life without Warnie,' Ponting mused to Hayden. Without Warne's genius or tactical brainstorms to winkle out the tail, Symonds resorted to the familiar alternative of picking a fight. He found one when Harbhajan gently tapped Brett Lee on the backside in acknowledgement of a yorker he had squeezed down to fine leg. 'You've got no fucking friends out here.'

Those words began an exchange that fell somewhere between banter and abuse. It continued between overs, until Hayden walked past. What Harbhajan said at that moment was not audible on any audio recording, but the tenor of the conversation clearly changed abruptly. Symonds asked, 'Did you call me a monkey again?' and Hayden instantly turned on his heels as though doing a double take. Tendulkar was by that point also in the frame. Hayden's terse 'Trouble is, you've got a witness now, champ . . . That's the last time' caused Tendulkar to motion for calm. Harbhajan's protest of 'No, listen, he started it' brought a further admonishment from Hayden: 'It doesn't matter, mate. It's racial vilification, mate. It's a shit word and you know it.' Clarke also professed to hearing the offending word and reported its use to Ponting, who notified Benson of his intent to press a charge.

Covering his mouth, in apt anticipation of the fury to come, Benson informed Harbhajan before Ponting left the field to tell Bernard, the lone witness to the Mumbai 'accord'. After play, Harbhajan denied using the word, while Tendulkar passed it off as 'a couple of lines exchanged here and there'.

Two events that day gave Ponting an impression that this was not going to be a typical code-of-conduct affair. First, James Sutherland met him in the dressing room and asked what he wanted out of the process. And later that evening, Ponting took a call from Kumble, who warned him of the political implications of pursuing the charge. 'He said, "Don't do this; you've got no idea; this could be bigger than you imagine,"' Ponting recalls. 'I said, "Mate, put yourself in the same situation. What are you going to do? It's not the first time it's happened."'

Aided by some more umpiring errors – declined appeals for l.b.w. and a caught behind against Hussey on his way to a third century of the summer – Ponting was able to set India 333 to win from a minimum of 72 overs. Clarke had enraged India's players by declining to walk when cutting to slip first ball. For most of the final afternoon, criticism of the declaration as too conservative filtered from television and radio commentary boxes to the dressing room as Australia's appeals became more insistent. After tea, Dravid was wrongly given caught behind by Bucknor when an off break from Symonds brushed pad not bat, before a low edge from Sourav Ganguly was claimed by Clarke. Despite inevitable ambiguous replays, the catch appeared clean in real time. But Ponting's insistence that Benson raise his finger, due to the pre-series catches agreement, caused Sunil Gavaskar to deliver a warlike broadcast tirade against Ponting and Clarke, highlighting the younger man's earlier refusal to walk. Similar objections were raised in India's rooms.

With a little more than ten minutes left and three wickets required, Ponting handed the ball to Clarke. In a trice, the match was won by his left-arm darts, which found enough purchase to confound

Harbhajan, R P Singh and Sharma. Raucously and unapologeti-
cally, the Australians celebrated their 16th consecutive Test win – or,
more accurately, their fourth victory in a row since losing Warne and
McGrath. In that moment, Ponting pumped his fists in the direction of the broadcast booths and press box, where the columnist
Peter Roebuck took iconoclastic note. Still flushed with pride at the
result, Ponting spoke happily enough to the media, though he took
issue with one Indian correspondent over a contention that he had
grounded a ball before appealing for a catch off M S Dhoni.

Cracking their first beers in the team rooms, Ponting, Symonds
and the rest did not hear Kumble's angry words to the press that
'I think only one team was playing within the spirit of the game.' Nor
did they hear the applause and cheers of the visiting media in response.

The hearing to determine Harbhajan's fate was presided over by the
match referee, Mike Procter, the former South Africa all-rounder and
coach who had to that point officiated in forty-five Tests. Reluctant to
take the case himself, and as a gesture of legal backing from the ICC
management, Procter was accompanied by QC Nigel Peters. Over six
hours, Procter and Peters heard Symonds, Hayden and Clarke repeat
their allegation, Harbhajan's denial and Tendulkar's admission that he
had not heard the remark. 'I note that Sachin Tendulkar only became
involved when he realised that something was happening and was ges-
tured over,' Procter wrote in his judgement. 'He tried to calm things
down because something had happened that he did not hear.' With
the SCG members stand clock ticking past 2 a.m., Procter found
Harbhajan guilty of racial abuse and suspended him for three Tests.
He concluded, 'I am satisfied that the words were said and that the
complaint to the umpires, which forms this charge, would not have
been put forward falsely. I dismiss any suggestion of motive or malice.'

4

Monkeygate II

JANUARY – MARCH 2008

India in Australia

As Andrew Symonds hung around the SCG for the end of Mike Procter's hearing, his girlfriend at the time, Katie Johnson, waited for his arrival at the Quay West hotel in The Rocks. She was dressed up for her birthday and hoping for a night out. At midnight she informed Symonds she was growing tired of waiting and drifted off to sleep. When Symonds did finally arrive, around 2.45 a.m., he found Johnson dozing in her outfit. The best the couple could manage was a nightcap in the hotel bar.

Delays aside, Symonds, Ricky Ponting, Adam Gilchrist, Michael Clarke and Matthew Hayden slept that night content that Harbhajan Singh had been punished and that at 2–0 up in the series Australia had retained the Border-Gavaskar Trophy while reaching the cusp of a new world record for consecutive Test match wins. A sweet 17th on what promised to be an uncontrollably fast WACA Ground pitch seemed near enough to a formality.

In their cosiness, however, they were mistaken. The world they woke up to on 7 January was exceptionally fraught. The whole of India seemed irate, and numerous influential Australians were also unhappy. A horde of media was gathered at the front of the hotel that morning, leading Symonds and Johnson to escape to lunch by a back door.

In the hours that followed, the issues of Harbhajan's ban, umpiring standards and the Australians' on-field conduct were whipped
up together into a mighty and confusing storm. Indian indignation
about the way the Test had unfolded and the decision-making of Steve
Bucknor and Mark Benson fused with outrage that any citizen of the
nation of Gandhi could be accused of racial abuse. Australia's senior
cricketing administrators tried to grasp the seriousness of the situation
during the day and were left in no doubt by the evening that the tour
itself was at risk of collapsing. India's squad had remained in Sydney
rather than travelling to Canberra as scheduled, at one point sitting for
an hour on the stationary team bus before returning to their rooms.

Tendulkar was central to India's protest, relaying to Sharad Pawar
his belief that the BCCI must stand by Harbhajan. They did so unre-
servedly. The board's rebuttal statement, which was accompanied
by a countercharge against Brad Hogg for telling Anil Kumble and
M S Dhoni, 'I can't wait to go through you bastards' on the fifth day,
resembled the Australian Board of Control's infamous cable to the
Marylebone Cricket Club at the height of bodyline, which damned
the actions of the tourists as 'unsportsmanlike'. The BCCI communiqué read in part: 'The Indian Board does not accept the findings of the
match referee and has decided to challenge the unfair decision to suspend Harbhajan Singh as it deems it patently unfair. The Board will
appeal to the International Cricket Council to review the decision of
the Match Referee and suspend its operation till the appeal is disposed
of. The Indian Board realises the game of cricket is paramount but so
too is the honour of the Indian team and for that matter every Indian.
To vindicate its position, the Board will fight the blatantly false and
unfair slur on an Indian player.

'The Board, in particular, is unhappy with the charge of racial slur
against India's off-spinner Harbhajan Singh. Here it may be mentioned that it is an avowed policy of the Indian government to fight
racial discrimination at every level and the Indian Board has been at
the forefront to eradicate it from the game of cricket. For the Indian

Board anti-racial stance is an article of faith as it is for the entire nation which fought the apartheid policies.'

Malcolm Speed, the ICC chief executive, was soon aware of the gravity of the situation. Its discussion at the highest levels of government in India and Australia was confirmed when he took a call in Dubai from the Australian prime minister, Kevin Rudd, seeking a progress report ahead of his next contact from India. The BCCI vice-presidents, Rajiv Shukla and Lalit Modi, wielded the threat of their team withdrawing from the tour in the event of Harbhajan not being exonerated on appeal, though the former president Inderjit Bindra contributed a more conciliatory presence after his arrival in Australia.

Nonetheless, Bindra called on Speed to suggest the withdrawal of Bucknor from his scheduled appearance in the Perth Test. Sympathetic to CA's concerns about the tour, as a former chief executive of the board himself, Speed duly replaced Bucknor with Billy Bowden, James Sutherland having stated he would not be fussed either way. Speed also decided the appeal hearing would be held at the conclusion of the Test series, allowing Harbhajan to play on and reducing the risk of an immediate Indian departure. Kumble's tour party travelled to Canberra a day later than previously scheduled but were back playing cricket rather than volleyball, which they had indulged in at Bondi while awaiting further instructions. The boards reached a temporary truce, pending the outcome of the appeal. To hear it, in the stilted atmosphere of Adelaide's Federal Court, Speed selected the New Zealand Justice John Hansen.

India's tour manager, the former opening batsman Chetan Chauhan, acknowledged the occurrence of Harbhajan's Mumbai meeting with Symonds. But he told Indian television that Harbhajan had walked away from it thinking the agreement was less to do with the use of the word monkey than it was an understanding that neither man would sledge the other. 'In Mumbai they had a friendly pact, an oral pact,' Chauhan said. 'I would say the first person to have broken that pact was the person who has complained. [Symonds] has said it everywhere that it was he who started it.'

As all this went on, Symonds and the team weathered a hail of criticism, emanating principally from columnist Peter Roebuck but also coming from the widely respected Gideon Haigh and the touring Indian contingent. Roebuck's column for the *Sydney Morning Herald* on 8 January matched the BCCI's statement for anger, asserting that Ponting must be sacked and Hayden and Gilchrist packed off to an early retirement – causing Ponting's wife to tearfully ask him if he was going to lose his job. (Gilchrist later called Roebuck to state his case, without success.) Harbhajan was described as a 'Sikh warrior', the Australians a 'pack of wild dogs'. Haigh denounced Australia's behaviour on the ABC's *7.30* program though stopped short of Roebuck's extreme demands. Meanwhile, at *The Australian*, Malcolm Conn and Peter Lalor wrote staunchly in defence of Ponting – their fellow columnist – while revealing details of Symonds' meeting with Harbhajan in India.

Upon reassembling in the west, the Australians found themselves in a meeting that seemed to be aimed at changing the way they played the game, much as Roebuck and others had demanded. Ray McLean, a leadership expert, had developed a system of peer empowerment and shared values that was proving fruitful in the Australian Football League with Sydney, Geelong and Adelaide. Sutherland and Tim Nielsen were familiar with him as supporters of two of the clubs, and CA had worked with him to find a time that he could make an introductory address the Australian team. A long-term relationship was mooted.

The venue they had settled on was Perth, but in the aftermath of the SCG match all talk of behaviour and public perception was viewed dimly by the players as evidence of the board taking Roebuck's side in the argument. Soon after the meeting with McLean, Paul Marsh, chief executive of the Australian Cricketers' Association, was taking calls from players wondering what they had done wrong. 'The players thought this was about CA saying the Australian cricket team was in crisis after Roebuck's article,' he says. 'Talking to a few of the senior players, they felt, "If this is the team you want us to be, then I don't know if I want to be part of it any more." I don't think anyone in that team thought they did anything wrong in that Sydney Test.' Years later, Ponting wrote in *At the Close of Play* that the memory of the McLean meeting still 'pisses me off now'. 'We were advised not to give the media opportunities to bag us, but when someone asked for examples of where we'd gone wrong they couldn't help us.'

Whether McLean would have made a difference to the team's future is a question left unanswered, but some clues may be found in his work elsewhere. An earlier foray into cricket with South Australia had been greeted by an unpleasant mix of wary senior players and ambitious younger players who excelled at saying the right things in meetings. One of the older heads was Jason Gillespie. 'What I noticed was that in those workshops there was a definite shift in some players within our squad. They got wind that SA was looking for leaders so they almost adapted their personality to fit the model.'

Gillespie and Darren Lehmann both left South Australia during McLean's involvement, while the state captaincy was thrust disastrously at Nathan Adcock, an impressive speaker but no-one's idea of a sturdy first-class batsman. Not surprisingly, McLean subsequently devoted his time to corporate and football clients, with whom he has remained broadly successful. As his website boasts, 'Contracted clients of ours have played in seven of the past nine Grand Finals.'

Hamstring trouble for Hayden and the promise of a fast WACA Ground surface caused Ponting and the selectors to make two changes. Opener Chris Rogers made his debut, while Shaun Tait played his first Test since the 2005 Ashes tour in place of Hogg, whose abusive-language charge had been dropped by India in a gesture of reconciliation.

Tait's inclusion was driven largely by his terrifying display at the WACA during a T20 against New Zealand, when Gilchrist commonly took the ball above his head and still rising. Rogers, best known for collaring 209 against the 2005 Ashes tourists for Leicestershire, was rewarded for consistent run-making with Western Australia. Neither he nor Tait enjoyed the match, as a distracted and hesitant Australian side was set upon by India.

Worried about the prospect of a three-day Test, the WACA switched the surface from one of the recently relaid and fast wickets, as used against New Zealand, to a more benign strip similar to that used for the drawn 2005 Test against South Africa. No-one saw fit to tell Ponting this. Tait was not entirely upfront either, concealing a hamstring niggle during net sessions out of his desire for a first Test appearance in more than two years. He struggled mightily with his action and run-up throughout the match and soon announced he would be taking an indefinite break from the game. An uncomplicated soul from country South Australia, Tait battled with the hermetically sealed world of international cricket.

For Rogers, the Test was also problematic. Aware of his status as a stand-in, he stayed at his Perth home during the match rather than joining the team, and on match eve dined not with his teammates but with his parents. Rogers sensed a strong residue from events in Sydney. 'Walking into that Australian change room, I wasn't really sure what to make of it,' he wrote in 2012. 'On the one hand, my life had just taken off dramatically, and on the other all the talk was about how we had to be on our best behaviour. There was an unmistakable current of tension running through the side. The fallout from Monkeygate, and Cricket Australia's reticence to pursue it, were playing havoc. It seemed as though the cricket was a sideshow.'

Harbhajan did not play in Perth. Replaced by Irfan Pathan, he instead ran drinks and watched as Kumble expertly marshalled his pacemen. Ishant Sharma gained a measure of recompense for Symonds' Sydney escape by delivering a wondrous second-innings spell to Ponting that ended with an edge to slip. Australia's chase of 413 was determined but doomed, the failure of each batsman to go on from a start hinting at mental fatigue. When last man Tait was yorked by R P Singh, Harbhajan raced onto the field waving the Indian flag. Symonds and Ponting didn't quite know where to look, their resolve to head off India's appeal hardening by the second.

The Adelaide Test may have been billed as a chance for India to square the series at the last, but its true function was to provide a venue for preparations ahead of the Harbhajan appeal hearing. Symonds, Ponting, CA chairman Creagh O'Connor, team manager Bernard and the acting chief executive, Michael Brown, spent hours in meetings alongside CA's choice of independent legal council, Brian Ward, discussing how the hearing would be tackled. Dean Kino, the board's head of legal affairs, was sidelined because Sutherland felt it better the players were not represented by a CA employee, lest the BCCI develop an enmity for him that might disrupt talks in the future. Having been present for Sydney and its aftermath, Sutherland was on compassionate leave following the death of his father-in-law on Australia Day. He knew Ward, who had worked extensively in Australian Football League circles and was also firm friends with Speed, but others did not. Symonds was particularly uneasy about the unfamiliar face.

Holding court in the oval's committee room, O'Connor and his fellow South Australian board members Jack Clarke and Ian McLachlan were primarily concerned about saving the tour. For them, the word of Symonds and the other players was a secondary concern next to the prospect of CA and the states losing $60 million in revenue, which would be sought by broadcasters if India's squad flew home and their rights contracts were breached. The board's wish was for the Harbhajan charge to be downgraded from the level-three racial charge to a less serious level-two transgression for abusive language. They hoped that excising allegations of racial vilification would appease India enough to ensure the forthcoming limited-overs series went ahead. Little thought was given to the welfare of the players, whom numerous board members considered precious and overpaid. As might be expected, Ponting, Gilchrist and Symonds were adamant the charge should not be downgraded.

Meetings regarding this dispute reached near-comical extremes. On the night before the Test, Bernard's hotel suite hosted a gathering that did not wrap up until after 2 a.m. On day two of the Test, Brown entered the dressing room to say he had to provide Ponting with an update on the situation, asking that he be summoned in from the field. Bernard counselled Brown to wait until tea, and when he did ultimately speak to Ponting, the captain exclaimed, 'Whatever. If you guys are going to get to this level where I can't play cricket, what's the point?' On the fourth evening, Ponting had to put off treatment on a sore back for another late-night meeting, this time a final confirmation that the players wanted to push ahead with a level-three charge. He heard from O'Connor that the board would support him, despite their preference for a compromise, only at lunch on day five.

The next morning, around the same time as the Australian players departed their hotel for the Federal Court, Tendulkar was standing on his own in front of the Hyatt hotel on North Terrace. O'Connor, departing the hotel on his way to other business in town, offered India's star defence witness a lift to the hearing. Chivalrous but also guileless, O'Connor's gesture took on greater significance when he dropped off Tendulkar and saw him into the court through the front door, in full view of the assembled media. Innocent as O'Connor's intention may have been, the image of CA's chairman waiting on Tendulkar heightened the Australian players' sense that their board was kowtowing to India. Though pictures of the pair went around the world, Ponting was unaware of this detail until 2013. Upon hearing it, his expression hardened. 'Unbelievable.'

Inside the court building, Australia's delegation quickly appeared disorganised, despite all their meetings. Sitting behind Ward, Ponting was wearing his team polo shirt, and Michael Clarke and Symonds casual shirtsleeves, while Hayden's T-shirt and sunglasses seemed in preparation for a day's fishing. Their testimony was similarly spotty, as accounts varied on almost every detail other than the fact that Harbhajan had uttered the word 'monkey'. For his part, Ward had not previously viewed the footage and audio that showed Tendulkar's proximity to the events, despite repeated requests from the players that they do so together.

By contrast, Harbhajan, Tendulkar and the team manager, Chauhan, had coordinated both their dress and their story in concert with their legal counsel, V R Manohar, who appeared via video link. Tendulkar's was the most significant change of tack. Whereas Procter's account at the first hearing suggested Tendulkar had not heard the exchange, now Tendulkar stated that Harbhajan had said '*Teri maa ki*', Punjabi for 'motherfucker', in reply to Symonds. Under cross-examination, Symonds accepted this scenario was 'a possibility'.

Hansen did his best to sift for facts, placing little trust in either the notes from the Procter hearing or the agreed statement of facts presented to him jointly by the BCCI and CA at the outset of the meeting, which served mainly to remove any reference to racial abuse in the matter. In contrast to O'Connor's earlier assurance that CA would maintain the original charge, Ward submitted that Symonds 'did not consider it fell under the requirements of level three'. Hansen considered Tendulkar and Hayden to be compelling witnesses but was less impressed by others, calling out Symonds on his assertion that 'a cricket field is no place to be friendly with the opposition'.

Watching from the gallery, Kino, Brown and Bernard agreed the hearing was headed towards a compromise verdict that would still satisfy their players. Pleading guilty to a level-two charge, Harbhajan would have his three-Test ban rescinded but still be suspended for one Test or two ODIs, due to the weight of four prior offences under the ICC code, including a fine and suspended Test match ban incurred in South Africa in 2001. No-one in the courtroom was aware that during the course of the hearing, Modi declared from India that 'if a clean chit is not given to Harbhajan, the Indian board's decision is to call the team home'. Limited-overs players, originally in Melbourne ahead of a one-off T20 fixture, had flown to join the rest of the team in Adelaide, in preparation for a collective departure in the event of Harbhajan's racial abuse charge being upheld.

At Jolimont, however, CA had been monitoring the likelihood of India flying home via their in-house travel agency, which also managed bookings for touring teams. Every day the agency's staff checked not only the bookings, but also cargo loads and passenger load details. CA knew flight schedules, tour bus bookings, international visa clearances and even India's social itinerary. There was little in this paper trail to suggest India were preparing to leave the country, unless they were to do so by a privately chartered plane.

When the time came to assign to Harbhajan a new sentence, Hansen asked for his assistant counsel, the ICC's in-house lawyer, Urvasi Naidoo, to read out a list of the spinner's past transgressions. Having flown from Dubai for this task, Naidoo stood, read out one charge from 2003 and promptly resumed her seat. Speed has noted that the 2001 offence was listed together with those of three other Indian players, with Harbhajan's name not appearing first; but he had no explanation for the other omissions.

Recoiling in shock at this oversight, Kino immediately left his seat and spoke animatedly to Ward, telling him of Harbhajan's other offences. At this point Hansen, unaware of the reason for the commotion, instructed Kino to return to his seat and stop interfering in proceedings. In this, the overly formal setting for the hearing was significant. Ward did not feel it was appropriate to interrupt Hansen, by then about to announce that Harbhajan would be handed the revised sentence of a 50 per cent match-fee fine. Yet there is nothing written in the ICC's code about such formal protocols being followed at a hearing. From his judge's perch high above the court, Hansen could not hear Kino's words to Ward. After handing down the sentence, Hansen retired to his chambers.

As Harbhajan's escape from virtually any meaningful penalty began to dawn on the Australian players, Kino confronted Naidoo and informed her of Harbhajan's record. An argument ensued, in which Kino stressed the point that the ICC code required all past offences to be read out. Ward then went to tell Hansen about the mistake, causing the appeals commissioner to fly into a quite understandable rage. Overnight, while writing his full judgement, Hansen wondered why Ward had not said anything and mulled over whether he could reopen the sentencing process. But by then the world had been informed of his verdict. Harbhajan was free to play, and the lucrative triangular series was free to be held.

While the CA board exhaled and the BCCI rejoiced, Symonds and Ponting felt prize fools. As one courtroom observer remembers, 'Andrew was ropeable and didn't understand what was going on and was just getting angrier and angrier and angrier. There was a lot of disillusionment, a lot of anger and a complete lack of comprehension.' The players vented these feelings at a meeting with O'Connor, Brown and Sutherland in April, before a tour of the West Indies. O'Connor was taken aback by the depth of anger he encountered, while the players concluded they had been naive to simply assume the board would take their side against the BCCI. Players and officials were split into shared discussion groups to identify the most important issues, and all reconvened with a common word in mind – trust. As an attempt to restore relationships it was not truly successful: what had been broken that summer did not mend, leaving distance between the players and the organisation at a time when the Australian team's former strength was ebbing away.

Symonds told Harsha Bhogle, 'It wasn't handled very well. I think CA were intimidated by the BCCI. The thing that was grinding on me the most was the lying. I had four of my good mates in there with me and we were made to look like idiots because this hadn't happened, when it had. The captain was made to look like a fool, and the other players and I was too, and that should never have happened. If the truth and honesty and commonsense had prevailed, there would have been a punishment for a player, it would have been dealt with and it would have set a precedent for the future. But I don't think it's done that.'

Tellingly, Roebuck's critical views of the Australians changed markedly over the course of the affair. His distaste for India's brinkmanship was made plain in the *Sydney Morning Herald* the day after the hearing: 'It is high time the elders of the game in that proud country stopped playing to the gallery and considered the game's wider interests. India is not some tinpot dictatorship but an international powerhouse, and ought to think and act accordingly. Brinkmanship or not, threatening to take their bat and ball home in the event of a resented verdict being allowed to stand was an abomination. It sets a dreadful precedent. What price justice now?'

Hansen's written judgement was delivered to the world in the courtroom in which Symonds had sat stupefied twenty-four hours before. In it he asserted his independence and ascribed the lenient final penalty largely to the error committed by Naidoo. But in subsequent correspondence with Speed, Hansen admitted his frustration at how the BCCI and CA had behaved behind the scenes. 'Their actions undermined the independence of the Code of Conduct Commissioner, were unbecoming, and in my view, contrary to the spirit of cricket.' Among the claims and counterclaims that surrounded the two teams, this was the most apt admonishment of all.

Adam Gilchrist was absent from the hearing that morning, citing illness. On the second night of the Adelaide Test he had informed Ponting of his decision to retire at the end of the home international summer and conveyed his intentions to the world the following day. Unlike Warne, McGrath, Martyn and Langer, Gilchrist was rapidly overtaken by the decision, as he had entered the match thinking of retiring only from limited-overs matches. A dropped catch off V V S Laxman, however, reminded Gilchrist of Ian Healy's turfing of Brian Lara in 1999, one tour before he retired. On the night he told his wife, Mel, of the decision, Gilchrist watched the young French tennis player Jo-Wilfried Tsonga on television, playing utterly without fear at the Australian Open. For years, Gilchrist had been that player, turning matches as swiftly with the bat as Warne could with the ball.

No-one felt the loss of Gilchrist more deeply than Ponting. As his vice-captain for four years, Gilchrist had been most things a leader desired, acting as a capable stand-in, a link to other players and a source of reasoned counsel in difficult times. They were never more vexing than during what had become known as Monkeygate. Tim Nielsen, for one, was certain the issues surrounding the affair had been a factor in draining Gilchrist of his desire to go on. 'I'm sure it sucked the life out of a couple of them, no doubt, it really did,' he says. 'Punter suffered when Gilly left. That changed the dynamic of the side tremendously, as he was left alone a lot more at the top of the tree and therefore less approachable. Gilly was always tremendous at involving the younger players and acting as a conduit to Ricky.'

With increasingly sunken eyes and sullen faces, the Australians slipped to defeat against India in the finals of an ODI tournament that might not have taken place had CA backed them fully in defending Symonds. A streaker during the second final in Brisbane was on the receiving end of a Symonds bump that at least gave the batsman the chance to relieve some frustration – he had been denied another avenue when CA discontinued his ghosted column for News Limited after several pieces had not been to their liking. Hayden was fined for calling Harbhajan an 'obnoxious weed' in a radio interview, further reducing his standing as Australia's enforcer.

Clarke, noticing after one match that Tendulkar was becoming increasingly elusive when the time came to shake hands, marched into the Indian dressing room to find him. Tendulkar told Clarke that he had forgotten. There is no better way to sum up how unimportant Australia's players now felt. Many took years to recover; Symonds never did. Ponting said, 'I hope I never have to go through another summer like it before my career is through.'

Filed away somewhere on a CA hard drive are plans for alternatives to the triangular limited-overs series of 2007–08. Contingency scheduling drawn up by the cricket operations department offered several scenarios by which the board's television commitments could be partly fulfilled, to help alleviate the potential loss of at least $60 million. One had Australia and Sri Lanka joined by Australia A. Another called for the assembly of a World XI styled on that convened for the tsunami charity match at the MCG in 2005. A third mentioned the outlandish idea of North versus South or East versus West 'All Star' matches. CA was that convinced of the BCCI's intention to go home in retaliation for Harbhajan Singh's racial abuse ban.

What did not exist, however, was a plan to deal with the actual fallout from the events of that summer. There was no thought given to how the Australian team might cope with the disillusionment and eventual self-destruction of Andrew Symonds, at that point a pivotal and powerful member of the side, or to how Symonds' fate would cause wider ructions, leaving plenty of players questioning whether they even wanted to play for Australia any more, or to how the team would fare if Ricky Ponting and others felt they did not have the backing of their board to play in the aggressive, abrasive manner they had successfully used for well over a decade. And there was no extrapolation of what backing down to the BCCI's whims would mean in the future.

Towards the end of the season Brett Lee, Stuart Clark, Michael Hussey, Brad Hogg and Brad Haddin agreed to play minor roles in *Victory*, a Bollywood melodrama that chronicled the unlikely rise of a young Indian batsman to dominate the game. Laughing their way through the shoot at the SCG, none of the players appeared to pick up the irony of their roles as hapless extras in an Indian-domination fantasy masquerading as a cricket contest. *Victory* proved an expensive flop. It may not have been art, but it imitated life that summer.

5

The Crown Slips

APRIL – DECEMBER 2008

Australia in the West Indies

Australia in India

New Zealand in Australia

South Africa in Australia

Late in the night at a Barbadian bar, Andrew Symonds spotted Michael Clarke drinking and talking energetically with Brian Lara. Australia's players had been granted time off between the second Test, in Antigua, and the third, in Bridgetown, which they won, to claim the series 2–0. It had been a day full of socialising for Symonds, as a long lunch merged into dinner and more drinks. He was not feeling particularly talkative when he joined Clarke and Lara, who had been imbibing at a somewhat less extravagant pace.

Clarke and Symonds had been close friends for a while, replicating the younger man's tightness with Shane Warne. Clarke referred to Symonds as his 'big brother', and Symonds appreciated Clarke's ability to extricate him from trouble. On the 2005 Ashes tour, Clarke declared to the team that if Symonds was sent home for binging ahead of an ODI against Bangladesh, he would also leave the tour. During the summer of 2007–08, Clarke had acted as one of Symonds' most zealous witnesses for the prosecution against Harbhajan Singh, testifying that he had heard the Indian spinner call Symonds a 'big monkey' without any provocation.

But in the West Indies, the two had been moving in opposite directions. Clarke had become Ricky Ponting's deputy, promoted ahead of numerous more senior men as the heir to the Australian captaincy. He missed the start of the tour to be with his fiancée, Lara Bingle, as she grieved over the death of her father, and then returned to craft a century in Antigua. Symonds, by contrast, had become increasingly disillusioned with the political manoeuvring of CA, the unwanted attention created by his fame and the increasingly regimented life of a celebrity international cricketer. He had always indulged in alcohol but since 2005 had been known among his Queensland teammates for his capacity to straighten up in the weeks and months before Australian duty. Not any more. It didn't quite seem worth it.

Clarke and Lara had first met in 2003, sharing an affinity for batting against spin and acquiring the spoils of fame, whether they were cars, houses or a lucrative brand. No-one can remember what they were discussing that night in the bar or indeed whether Symonds himself was the topic. What is not in doubt is that in the midst of the chatter, Symonds got up, poured his drink over Clarke's head and left.

The transgression went unpunished. For the rest of the tour, Clarke and Symonds did not speak to each other. After Ponting flew home with a wrist injury, for the final two ODIs Clarke led the side nimbly and Symonds topscored in a pair of victories that completed a 5–0 sweep. But their relationship was fractured, and the team noticed.

Entering the Australian dressing room from 2006 to 2008 was no easy thing. An assortment of cliques dominated the scene, each guarding its territory jealously when it was not distracted by a building tide of retirements or a sense of injustice at the fate that had befallen

Symonds against Harbhajan. To crave admission to the group was to feel an invitation might never arrive, but to thrive independently of it, as Clarke did, was also viewed as a faux pas. One player who debuted around that time sweated out three days of anxious training before being offered even a 'well done' or an invitation to dinner. Another called a CA official in Sydney one day with the words 'I don't know what to do. I don't know the town and I'm lonely.' Unable to contact any senior players, the official took the player to Taronga Zoo.

The most public indicator of the problems experienced by newcomers was Shaun Tait's decision to take an indefinite break from the game in early 2008. Tait was a popular figure but grew morose and troubled as he was repeatedly left to his own devices. Teammates professed to having had no idea of Tait's worries until he admitted he did not want to play any more, but then precious few were available to spend time with him in the weeks before his breakdown. All simply assumed that Tait, known as 'Sloon', was doing fine.

Others flitted in and out of the team during this period, including Phil Jaques, Dan Cullen, Chris Rogers, Cameron White, Adam Voges and Mark Cosgrove. Most of them expected senior players to take them under their wing and were left floundering when they did not.

In the West Indies, Ponting was aware of the mounting generation gap between young and old, but his solution was unusual when compared to most Australian sides. In his diary he wrote, 'One thing I always say to the new guys is don't sit in your room expecting that a senior player will call you and ask you down to the bar or out for a beer. Be proactive and do the asking, otherwise – because we've all got so much on – it could be a couple of weeks before we spend any decent time together.' A few years before, in New South Wales, coach Trevor Bayliss had instituted an unwritten rule that team members should assemble in the hotel bar for a nightly catch-up at seven o'clock, irrespective of whether they had other plans later. No such arrangement existed in the national team.

*

Jamaica, Antigua and Barbados witnessed numerous memorable events during Australia's tour, some of them more poignant on reflection than they seemed at the time. This was to be the last Test series in which Symonds, Jaques, Stuart MacGill, Stuart Clark and Brett Lee were glimpsed playing somewhere near their best, or at all. It also featured the only match in which the young wrist spinner Beau Casson was afforded a chance to exhibit his wares for Australia. All these players were good enough to help carry Ponting's team through to several more years of strong results, but circumstances, injuries, personal problems and blue-sky selections conspired against them as the number-one ranking slipped from Australia's grasp.

MacGill was first to go, abruptly announcing his retirement midway through the second Test despite having worked assiduously for months, since his struggles in Hobart against Sri Lanka, to regain fitness and feeling in his fingers. His behaviour on the tour was erratic and irritable at times, compounded by the realisation, as early as the lone pre-series tour match, that his wonky right knee was again starting to fail him. 'I felt like my run-up wasn't right, my technique's not right, everything's not right,' he says. 'In the first Test I couldn't push off my knee; I had a lot of fluid on it and wasn't getting through the crease. The last wicket of the Test was me getting Shivnarine Chanderpaul and it would have hit him on the sternum had he not hit it back to me.'

Further efforts to push on in Antigua were similarly unsuccessful, not helped by the absence of the team physio Alex Kountouris, who had been waylaid by deep vein thrombosis and reduced to instructing the strength and conditioning coach, Stuart Karppinen, from his hospital bed on how to strap an ankle. At the same time, MacGill seemed to be wearing out his welcome. Dissatisfaction with the team hotel forced separate apartments to be booked for the players, and MacGill's was situated some distance from the rest. When he slept in on day two of the Test and did not make it onto the team bus, there were numerous grumbles among the team leaders.

MacGill, however, had already decided to quit, having felt a sickeningly familiar sensation in his fingers. 'Everyone said, "No, you're just going through a bad patch. You'll be fine." But I knew this was a physical problem and I'd already had surgery to try to fix it and it had come back. My right knee wasn't functioning properly, and that's where the run-up troubles and other things were happening. I started getting pins and needles again in my left hand, and the next day in my right hand. And there I knew I was retiring. I knew I couldn't do what I needed to do for the other guys in the team, and you don't want to burn the ten other guys. I didn't retire of my own accord; I wanted to play for the next three years, go to India, South Africa and England . . . No doubt, I wanted to keep playing.'

The national selectors also wanted MacGill to stay in the team, as they had chosen Casson as a short-term understudy rather than a long-term replacement. Merv Hughes, who was on the selection panel from 2005 to 2010, summed up the expectation of the chairman, Andrew Hilditch, and company: 'A lot of the contingency plans we had went askew because of injury. When Shane Warne retired we thought we were going to have MacGill for two or three years, then we went to the West Indies and he retired halfway through the series. You think, "Okay, we've got some good young blokes," but they didn't have time to develop.'

Nevertheless, Casson bowled decently at Kensington Oval in the third Test, his second-innings figures of 3–86 from 25 overs including the top-order wickets of Xavier Marshall and Dwayne Bravo. Casson also fielded well and bounced happily around the dressing room and outfield. But even then the selectors were not sure about taking him to India. 'We saw Casson as an option against a team full of left-handers, which the West Indies had,' Jamie Cox recalls. 'I always thought playing against that left-arm wrist-spin stuff as a right-hand batsman wasn't difficult because they were always bowling into the fresh part of the pitch. There was a bit of worry about taking a young wrist spinner to India, too.'

Instead of Casson, the selectors opted for Jason Krejza and Bryce McGain. When McGain withdrew from the tour due to a shoulder problem that he had picked up on the Australia A tour that preceded the Tests, Cameron White was chosen as his replacement. As Victoria's captain, White had bowled only 84 overs for the 2007–08 season, against Casson's 311. It was thought by the selectors that White would offer value as a lower-order batsman and a capable fielder, but his reluctance to bowl was soon apparent. When the Australians travelled to Delhi for the third Test, Bernard called in Bishan Bedi to work with White and Krejza. While Krejza was all ears, seeking to push his way into the team, White gave Bedi a curt reply when asked about his progress: 'I'm a batsman.'

Krejza's spell in the team was anything but dull. During a warm-up fixture in Hyderabad, Krejza admitted to *Sydney Morning Herald* correspondent Alex Brown that he had tested positive for cocaine some years before after having his drink spiked. Yuvraj Singh, Virat Kohli and Rohit Sharma spiked Krejza's chances of starting the Tests with a calculated mauling, causing Hilditch to report to his panel, 'We can't pick him: they have absolutely slaughtered him in the tour game.' After the Bedi tutorial, Krejza was thrown in for the final Test and mixed the unplayable with the unwatchable while collecting 12–358. 'Everyone was going, "Was that good or not?"' says Cox, 'and then, "Yeah, I think it was good; let's see it as good."' Krejza's best, like the off break and a half that snapped through V V S Laxman's gate to knock out leg stump, was compelling. But his next Test, in Perth, reaped only one such delivery, to Hashim Amla, amid 49 overs that cost 227 runs. Still miffed about some of the field placings given to him by Ponting, Krejza was discarded.

Casson, meanwhile, was affected significantly by his omission and never again bowled as well as he had on the final day in Bridgetown. A pre-existing heart condition worsened thereafter, leaving him to fight for his health instead of his place in the Australian and New South Wales teams. He turned to teaching and coaching, though he had to be careful about bowling too much lest his heart rate rise uncontrollably. 'It was a very unfortunate end,' Cox says. 'There was definitely a feeling that finger spin was more dangerous, and also, if you're going to win in India it's not going to be our spinners that win it but our quicks.'

Those quicks were Lee, Clark and Mitchell Johnson, but by the time of the fourth Test, in Nagpur, only the left-armer, Johnson, was still functioning at a passable level. Clark was afflicted by an elbow problem that flared when he threw returns from the outfield in Bangalore during the first Test. That ailment not only was painful but also robbed Clark of a critical few kilometres of pace and several inches of bounce, reducing his effectiveness in all but the most helpful of conditions. His departure from the attack was never mourned in quite the same way as that of Warne or McGrath, but in the low moments that followed Ponting pined most often for Clark's combination of reliability and incisiveness. Without him, Ponting's tendency to rotate bowlers methodically became increasingly ingrained, as other pacemen and spinners were not always able to follow through on the preconceived plan.

It was a surprise to almost everyone that one such struggler turned out to be Lee. Operating largely in tandem with Clark, Lee looked very much the finest fast bowler in the world in the year after McGrath retired, allying his ferocious speed with accuracy, stamina and enough swing of both conventional and reverse varieties. A shuddering bouncer to fell Chanderpaul in Jamaica had served as a reminder of the dangers Lee could pose, and a series tally of 18 West Indian wickets lifted him to 58 in nine Tests since the start of the home summer. Nothing appeared likely to stop him from pushing on as Ponting's spearhead for years to come.

As it turned out, family rather than cricket caused Lee's slide from his best to his worst. An acrimonious break-up from his wife, Liz Kemp, dominated Lee's off-season, and the funk he fell into kept him well away from any thoughts of training or preparation for the India tour in October and November. Before the tour, Lee told journalists he could not wait to play again, but as he related in his autobiography, 'that was a lie. I wasn't ready for it at all. The last thing I wanted to do was bowl a cricket ball; the closest I came to cricket training before the tour was catching flatheads and kingfish on Sydney Harbour.' Still, Ponting, Nielsen and Hilditch trusted that he would be ready, picking him despite not seeing him bowl a single ball between the end of the West Indies sojourn, in July, and his arrival in Jaipur, the first stop on Australia's eight-week tour.

What followed was disastrous. Lacking conditioning and down on pace, Lee was a minimal threat to India's batsmen, and even to their bowlers. In the first Test, Harbhajan and Zaheer Khan slapped him with impunity around the M Chinnaswamy Stadium, in Bangalore, during a partnership that prevented the tourists from making the most of strong hundreds by Ponting and Michael Hussey in the first innings. Lee also bickered with Ponting, who at times did not bowl him due to mounting problems with over rates. That issue bloomed farcically in the final Test, in Nagpur, when Ponting used White and Hussey in order to avoid a suspension when India offered a narrow opening for Australian victory with a fourth-day collapse. Most damagingly, Lee's personal problems left him in no state to lead the bowlers in thinking about how to bowl effectively in India.

Reverse swing, not spin, was the critical difference between the teams. Zaheer and Ishant Sharma bowled cross-seam with a gear in reserve to rough up the SG ball used in India, before clicking up to their top speeds at the moment they began to see signs of reverse movement. Aided by fielders polishing the ball rigorously whenever they weren't throwing it back to M S Dhoni on the bounce, Zaheer and Sharma achieved venomous bend in Mohali, routing the visiting batsmen twice on a pitch that looked brimful of runs whenever India took strike. Australia's bowlers spent much of the series debating what to do, some favouring traditional use of the new ball and others wanting to adopt India's tactics. Only Shane Watson, playing as a number six batsman and change bowler, seemed able to get the ball swinging. The bowling coach, Troy Cooley, had been hired by CA largely due to England's use of the old ball in 2005 but seemed unable to bring about consensus.

Mentally and tactically, India were a step ahead. Dhoni was emerging as the team's leader, first gaining the captaincy when Anil Kumble was injured then taking it up full time when Kumble retired, at the end of the Delhi Test. In Nagpur, Dhoni showed little care for appearances but plenty for results when he strangled Australian momentum by using an ugly but very effective 8–1 off-side field. After scolding the NDTV correspondent Anjali Doshi for asking why Australia had not tried to counter the tactic with more lateral choices of strokes, Katich observed, 'If you don't get it right, you can pay a price, but they executed it well. That is the bottom line.'

That episode was watched by handfuls of spectators in a sparsely populated stadium, cited by many as an example of the IPL's rapid impact on the tastes of Indian cricket followers. Less reported was the fact that the new ground, built in the home state of the BCCI president, Shashank Manohar, was almost 20 kilometres out of central Nagpur and was selling only expensive five-day passes – hardly the ideal manner in which to greet a Test match crowd. Among the few spectators was Gautam Gambhir, suspended for elbowing Watson while running between the wickets during his double century in the third match, in Delhi. As with Harbhajan, the BCCI had appealed the verdict, but this time the new ICC chief executive, Haroon Lorgat, and the appeals commissioner, Justice Albie Sachs, rejected their entreaties. Gambhir did not play in Nagpur, but the board secretary, N Srinivasan, did not forget Lorgat's stance.

In the West Indies, Australia had won 2–0. In India, they were defeated by the same margin. It was the first time an Australian Test team had failed to win a match in a series since 1999. South Africa, no longer spooked by Australia in the way they had been during the 2007 World Cup and soon to be arriving in Perth, took note of the result. Under Graeme Smith and Mickey Arthur they had put a team together in which every man knew his place, and for every opponent there was a plan.

Between the West Indies and India tours, CA and the Australian Cricketers' Association had begun discussions about their next player payments agreement. Paul Marsh, the Australian Cricketers' Association chief executive, remembers expressing his worries about the way the team was tailing off. The response floored him: 'We were told, "It's not the be-all and end-all to be number one, and as long as we're around the mark we'll still get the money from the broadcasters." That shocked me, because I thought the priorities were all wrong. That may well have been a negotiation tactic, but it was put to me that the performance of the Australian team was not the most important aspect of the business. I think it should be the top priority because almost everything flows out of it. I was somewhat disillusioned when I heard that.'

Others within CA knew of this opinion and were uncomfortable to hear it said numerous times within the Jolimont headquarters. 'There was certainly a view in some quarters that it didn't really matter if the Australian team slipped to third or fourth in the rankings because it wouldn't have a significant effect on the business,' says one former member of management. 'That was a view expressed by more than one person on a couple of occasions. People who only really knew number one didn't understand the cycles of the game. It was a funny time to be there, because it was such a period of sustained success it was almost automatic. You don't really see too many ups and downs in regard to how team performance goes, so your idea of business success cycles with the commercial aspects and not so much the team performance aspects. So I don't think at the top level there was any acknowledgement there was a bottoming-out period coming. It was, "We'll be able to manage this; we might drop a couple of spots."'

*

Symonds did not go to India, as CA deemed him ineligible for selection due to disciplinary issues that had begun in the West Indies. In August he had been sent home from a brief series against Bangladesh in Darwin after going fishing instead of attending a team meeting. Much had been made of the fact that Clarke was stand-in captain at the time the decision was made, but he had been careful to include Ponting in deliberations over Symonds' punishment, calling his leader on speakerphone for the meeting with Bernard and Nielsen that concluded their wayward all-rounder needed to be punished.

Some board members were strongly in favour of tearing up Symonds' contract, but Sutherland and Brown argued for another chance, and he was duly prescribed counselling sessions with the noted psychologist Deidre Anderson, who was also known for working with Ian Thorpe. Soon afterwards, Hayden and Symonds spoke in Brisbane about the direction of the team. It took some prompting from Hayden to elicit an indication that Symonds still wanted to be an Australian cricketer.

He returned to the team in Brisbane and Adelaide but had little to do as New Zealand were swatted aside in the first of two home Test series for the summer. Lee was closer to full health after spending time on a drip in Nagpur and bowled sturdily, while his fellow convalescent from the India tour, Clarke, underpinned each first innings, with 98 at the Gabba and 110 in Adelaide. Simon Katich and Brad Haddin also contributed, the latter's brazen 169 in the second Test shoring up his place – carrying a broken finger through his first series, in the West Indies, had been followed by some indifferent displays on the subcontinent. A 2–0 margin was pleasing, but South Africa would be the main event.

Among Ponting's strengths as captain was an ability to answer media questions earnestly, no matter how trite they were. But when a television journalist asked him, after Adelaide, 'Where does this rate in your career?' he offered only a gentle smirk.

Despite the scoreline against New Zealand, numerous cogs in

the team had been malfunctioning, clouding the heads of Ponting, Nielsen and Clarke. Hussey's usual flood of runs had slowed to a trickle, the start of a sequence in which he failed to average 40 in five series out of six. The moody Symonds was now only contributing sporadically, his body creaking, and Lee's supposed rejuvenation in Brisbane and Adelaide ultimately said more about the paucity of New Zealand batsmanship than about his own form. While those two bowlers muddled through to Perth, Clark succumbed to pain at training and was booked in for elbow surgery. In rehabilitation he crossed paths with Phil Jaques, who in India had fought back problems and a debilitating cycle of cortisone injections and digestive side effects until barely able to move.

Most telling of all was the decline of Hayden, his mind no longer clear and his bearing less than intimidating. He was missing Justin Langer and maudlin about the way Symonds was deteriorating, and his batting slipped back into the uncertain zone of his earliest days in the team. Langer spoke with him numerous times during the summer and felt the previously unshakable confidence and focus draining out of Hayden's body. Home Test scores of 8, 0, 24, 12, 4, 8, 23, 31 and 39 were no way to end a career that corresponded neatly with the most domineering years of Australia's ascendancy.

'When Mark Taylor went through that really tough period, one of the comments he made back then was, "It's just not the same without Michael Slater,"' Langer says. 'At the time because I was one of the guys trying to get into the team I said, "What a load of rubbish. Seriously, you can't be using that as an excuse." But I caught up with Haydos a few times after I retired and he'd say, "It's just not the same, mate." I was getting really disappointed for him because he was missing out, he had retirement on his mind, and he was getting smashed by the press. It wasn't his technique; it was that his mind's not switched on like I know it has been, his mind's in the future and in the past.'

Hayden slogged through a succession of hounding headlines, something Hilditch also found increasingly to be his lot. The two media campaigns crossed during Hayden's final Test, in Sydney, when News Limited snapped Hilditch walking his dog along the beach in Adelaide because David Boon was the selector on duty at the SCG. Players who previously enjoyed mutually beneficial media relationships found themselves feeling as insular and as suspicious of journalists as Symonds had become. A black-humoured guessing game of 'Who's next to get the bullet from the press?' began to circulate the dressing room.

Nielsen struggled to contain it. 'One of the biggest challenges of the job in that transitional couple of years was coping with the media coverage that seemed to love it when we lost. The guys who'd been playing quite a while and weren't necessarily used to that felt they were being turned over by the media. A couple of times I told blokes, "Listen, you've had it pretty good. Very few times they've questioned you. I don't agree with what they're saying either – they're going for the jugular very early – but we can't control that." The only way to change it was to win.'

These worries overtook Ponting in the first two Tests against South Africa, which the visitors won to become the first team to claim a series victory in Australia since the West Indies in 1993. In both Perth and Melbourne the hosts surrendered sizeable advantages, as Ponting was unable to break out of the stolid tactical thinking in which Warne and McGrath had immured him.

Lee and Krejza leaked runs in Perth when Ponting tried to maintain pressure on South Africa's run chase, letting Graeme Smith, A B de Villiers and J P Duminy make remarkably light work of their 414 to win. Afterwards, Ponting showed the strain of it all. He quipped, 'They might have got 600,' criticised the WACA Ground surface as more reminiscent of Adelaide and remarked that 'we had a lot of passengers in the team'. Lee, Ponting said, seemed unable to sustain his pace and was no longer a certain selection.

Away from the microphones, Ponting questioned Hilditch about Lee's inclusion for Melbourne. 'The problem we had in Melbourne was Brett was tired and sore,' he says. 'I actually pleaded for them not to pick him, because we knew he was bowling 130 kilometres per hour, and Brett Lee bowling at that pace is actually the easiest bowler in the world to face. So I pleaded for them to give him a rest that game. A lot of the Test matches we lost were when I knew that we had a guy who was not fully fit or injured going in and we ended up being a bowler down. A lot of them I felt were avoidable.'

Ponting's pleas went unheeded, and Australia were stopped dead on day three of the Boxing Day Test. At 7–184 then 8–251 in reply to 394, Smith's side were set to concede a first-innings lead. But when Duminy and Dale Steyn refused to give their wickets away, Ponting and his bowlers froze again. A ninth-wicket stand of 180 sapped Australian spirits, a state of affairs best exemplified by an out-of-sorts Hussey hovering under a skier before failing even to get a hand to it. Having entered the match carrying injuries, neither Lee nor Symonds could offer anything with the ball. Neither played another Test. Trying to reel in an unexpected deficit, Ponting felt the pressure of the situation closing in on him as he approached a second century of the match and spooned a catch to short cover on 99.

Smith was dismissed before South Africa crested the summit last scaled by Richie Richardson's Caribbean team fifteen years before, but his was the only wicket. Never considered the most agile tactician himself, Smith was the beneficiary of Australia's struggle to adjust to more meagre resources. 'Ricky was truly one of the most competitive guys I've ever played against, but I felt that if tactically you put them on the back foot he didn't have a lot to fall back on,' he says. 'Once we were able to put the pressure on Australia, suddenly they were in a place they hadn't been before and we were asking questions about them. Our plan with Ricky was often just to try to knock him over in that first Test match and then allow the external pressures to work for us.'

Ponting knew how well it had worked. In the hours after defeat at the MCG, he outlined in his diary the weakness of his captaincy – its inflexibility – and how that weakness had been fostered – relying on Warne and McGrath. 'I should have been more adaptable, more pro-active, have recognised sooner that the mood was changing. I feared that switching too quickly to the unorthodox might have been self-defeating, because I was determined to show faith in guys new to the team, but instead I went the other way and let the game get away from me. In the past, when the flow of the game turned against us, champions like Warne and McGrath usually made the right adjustments quickly, to regain the momentum. That is a rare skill that takes time to learn. We have to learn it quickly, because I don't want any more days like day three of the 2008 Boxing Day Test.' The old ways, and the old cliques, were on the way out.

6

Clarke/Katich

JANUARY 2009
South Africa in Australia

In any week other than the first in January each year, the home dressing room at the SCG is not the territory of Australia, but of New South Wales. No trace can be seen on the walls, doors or sixteen lockers that this is the place where more Australian Test teams have assembled, showered, dressed, prepared, recovered, argued, fought, celebrated and commiserated than any other room at any other ground. The only memorabilia present is from New South Wales, and ranges from a note by Sir Donald Bradman on the occasion of his first-class debut at the ground to outlines of several Sheffield Shield victories, with signatures, nicknames or numbers of the Blues players who participated. The stories of the Australian team in these rooms are not recorded on the walls, but are instead kept in the collective memory of the players and staff who set up camp there for a week or so each season.

For those who took part in the final-day victory over South Africa in January 2009, the most vivid recollections are not so much of the game itself or the resultant celebration but of the confrontation between Michael Clarke and Simon Katich that erupted in the midst of the usual alcohol-fuelled revelry. The tale has been recounted many times, but it generally has a subtext attached: that of Clarke the selfish upstart eager to get away and of Katich the old-school defender of traditional dressing-room etiquette. As ever, the truth is a little more complicated.

Most agree that the backstory begins not in Sydney but in Adelaide, a month earlier, following the Australians' comfortable victory over New Zealand. The match finished in mid-afternoon on the fourth day, allowing plenty of time for drinks and celebrations. But it also offered the possibility of an evening flight to home ports and a precious extra day of rest at home. Around these two possibilities a discussion developed, in which as vice-captain Clarke stated the team should spend the evening enjoying each other's company at a restaurant and bar in Adelaide. However, the captain, Ricky Ponting, and senior players including Katich, Matthew Hayden, Brett Lee and Michael Hussey all preferred to get home. Clarke was overruled, a quick rendition of 'Under the Southern Cross' was delivered and the players packed for the airport.

Two years before, in the same dressing room and in the aftermath of the Australians' dramatic and decisive victory over England, Clarke had mentioned there should be more to post-match activities than simply sitting for hours in the locker room, still dressed in the team uniform and drenched in beer. He wanted wins to be celebrated but preferred the idea of freshening up and heading out to another venue, whether it be a bar in Adelaide or a boat on Sydney Harbour. Several teammates did not take kindly to the suggestion.

So in Sydney in 2009, Clarke was eager for a change of scene at the end of the match. Australia's victory in the dead third Test had been hard fought, with Clarke's first-innings century a major factor in its delivery. Soon after the game's conclusion, he discussed with several teammates the option of organising a VIP bar area in the city. As the drinks began to flow in the dressing room, Clarke was on the phone making a booking. At that point, about half the team indicated a willingness to move on from the dressing room at 11 p.m.

But this was not Adelaide, and the opposing team was not New Zealand. Doug Bollinger and Andrew McDonald had made their debuts, and Peter Siddle had experienced his first Test win. Unspoken but understood was the strong possibility that Matthew Hayden would soon retire. This last Test match of the summer also gave impetus to the attraction of hanging around the rooms. As songmaster and unofficial event manager, Michael Hussey was not particularly keen to go anywhere. Nor were Hayden, Ponting or Katich. Slushie machines used by the strength and conditioning coach, Stuart Karppinen, had been filled with vodka and Red Bull in anticipation of a long shift. Within an hour or two, Clarke's plans faded from drink-dulled minds.

Increasingly edgy about his earlier booking, Clarke was showing the odd sign of irritability and ran his proposed timeline past the team manager, Steve Bernard. Singing the team song signifies the point at which players can go their separate ways, and, with the logistics of equipment and transport in mind, Bernard was not against the idea of the song being sung at a reasonable hour. So he asked Hussey how far away it might be. Holding court on the couch to the left of the dressing-room door with Hayden and Katich, Hussey replied that it was still some time away, cheekily adding that every time Bernard asked him, he would add another fifteen minutes to the deadline. Unimpressed, Clarke delivered further, testier reminders to Bernard.

At this point, a little history is useful. Katich and Hussey were old friends from Perth, and Katich had been best man at Hussey's wedding. Katich's move to New South Wales and appointment as the Blues' captain in 2002 had usurped the burgeoning leadership skills of wicketkeeper Brad Haddin, a mentor to Clarke. That issue had bubbled in New South Wales for some years, complicated by Haddin's close relationship with the state coach, Trevor Bayliss, though never badly enough to affect the state's strong performances. Clarke and Katich thus had differences of opinion in several areas and worked together professionally without any great mutual warmth.

These factors added to the building sense of enmity in the dressing room as the clock ticked towards eleven. Clarke kept looking at the clock above the door; Hussey and Katich kept chattering happily, and

Bernard relayed the vice-captain's preference twice more. Eventually, Clarke's indignation and Katich's mirth became obvious enough to spark an exchange. Angered by what he thought to be sniggering in the corner by Katich, Clarke spoke up. He was standing by the physio bench near the middle of the room, as an assortment of players and staff milled around.

'Say it to my face, ****,' Clarke fired at Katich.

'What did you fucking say?' came the reply.

'I called you a ****.'

Katich's capacity to dominate any physical altercation was well known within the team, and in that instant he demonstrated it. Leaping up, he grabbed Clarke in a tangle of shirt, collar and neck. In the next few seconds, his hand slipped up to close around the vice-captain's throat before a momentarily dumbfounded team responded by breaking up the pair. Karppinen managed to drag Katich away, while Clarke retreated hastily into the front viewing room and within minutes had left the ground. Marks on his neck were still visible the next morning.

For a moment, the dressing room paused in stupefied silence. Hayden spoke first. Addressing the upset Hussey, he observed that there had only ever been two players not to hang around for the team song, 'and he's one of them'. Katich apologised to Bollinger and McDonald, who drily broke the ice by quipping, 'Oh, mate, don't worry. This stuff happens all the time in Victoria.' The ensuing laughter returned the room to something like its former bonhomie, but several witnesses remember a sense of unease lingering for some time afterwards. About 11.30 p.m., Hussey finally convened the team to sing the song, less one member. 'I felt responsible because I was the reason the argument started, and also because one of our brothers wasn't there for the team song,' he says. 'It is a black mark against my name.'

In dribs and drabs over the next few hours the team and staff members melted away into the night. The last three there were Hussey, Siddle and Hayden, who at a time approaching 4 a.m. began to wax philosophical about how much he was going to miss the team, and the dressing room. 'I was sort of surprised that Haydos stayed so long because normally he liked to get back to the hotel with his family,' says Hussey. 'But he had stayed late and when it was just the three of us he was saying, "I'm going to miss this when it's all over." Sidds and I were saying, "You've got plenty of time left in you, Haydos. You're fine; you've got ages, plenty of cricket left in you." And Haydos laughed it off, but then we went up to start the one-day series in Brisbane and he announced that he was retiring.'

When the sun rose over Sydney later that morning, Clarke awoke early and tried to contact Katich. His call went unanswered, but a follow-up text message resulted in a more civil conversation than the pair's previous contact. They resolved to move on as quickly as possible. The episode was kept in-house for nearly a month, until Andrew Webster broke the story in the *Daily Telegraph* on 9 February. It has lingered ever since in the public mind, symbolising the angst of a fading team, the generation gap between Clarke and others, and the myth of universal mateship in Australian cricket.

Says Bernard, 'It's not often you see a physical issue happen between the guys, but if you're living together for an extended period it's not unusual to see some snappiness go on, and that's just human nature. Michael and Simon talked about it and made sure there wasn't any issue, because it was important for the sake of the side to get on with things. It really wasn't something that dwelled in everyone's minds, but you can understand the fascination.'

There are no plans for a commemorative plaque.

7

A False Dawn

FEBRUARY – MARCH 2009

Australia in South Africa

Amid the last-minute checks for baggage, personnel and South Africa departure plans, Michael Clarke and Simon Katich shared a quiet coffee at Sydney airport. This was not an orchestrated summit or a conscious show of unity – the pair had merely arrived at the terminal at about the same time and found themselves with half an hour to kill. But the happy accident of their meeting was a serendipitous start to the team's most significant achievement under the shared leadership tenure of Ricky Ponting and Tim Nielsen.

Comfortable history informed Australia's plans for the return series against Graeme Smith's men, with the sleepy university town of Potchefstroom providing an ideal base for training and familiarisation of a kind that had become harder to create as schedules grew increasingly crowded. Ponting, Nielsen and the team manager, Steve Bernard, remembered 'Potch' as the venue for fruitful days at the 2003 World Cup and the 2006 Test tour, and used it to spend time with a squad far younger than either of the earlier conquering ensembles. Located a little less than two hours' drive south-west of Johannesburg, the town's fairly basic facilities helped foster a collegiate spirit that had been elusive in the aftermath of the fractious 2007–08 season. In the sparsely populated car park of the team's hotel, players and staff indulged together in the simple pleasures of piloting remote-controlled cars. They also bonded over the shared discomfort of a stomach bug that ran through the team.

Touring gave Ponting more opportunities to mix with his players than the summer at home, which was often backed up with sponsorship appearances and events, while any time away from cricket was taken up by his wife and their infant baby, Emmy. During these summer interludes, Tim Nielsen, Michael Clarke, Andrew Hilditch and even the chief executive, James Sutherland, often found Ponting fiendishly hard to contact, and they were not shy about leaving voicemails telling him these were not merely social calls. But in South Africa, Ponting was far more accessible, allowing Phillip Hughes in particular, on his first overseas Test tour, to grow comfortable in his company.

Also helping the team to gel was the mix of characters assembled for the trip. Absentees such as Andrew Symonds, Shane Watson and Brett Lee gave the squad a different feel, but also allowed a sense of freshness to emerge. In their stead, Marcus North, Ben Hilfenhaus and Andrew McDonald offered a decent spread of Sheffield Shield experience and equable temperaments to the team room. All three were liked for their good sense and lack of too much front. North had been captain of Western Australia and McDonald a key cog in a highly accomplished if occasionally combustible Victorian side. Hilfenhaus' unaffected air was such that he had once attended a CA contract meeting at ties-mandatory Jolimont in a backwards baseball cap, T-shirt and shorts.

'If you look at some of the characters that come in for that tour – Northy, Hilfy, Siddle; McDonald was a good inclusion; Hadds had been in for a little while – it had some pretty good characters that came in and I think that was a big part of any team,' Ponting says. 'The turnaround in Australian cricket in the 1980s was a lot to do with that, how Simmo [Bob Simpson], A B [Allan Border] and Laurie Sawle identified characters and stuck with them over prettier players at times. In South Africa everything just fell into place for us with that group.'

Equally reassuring was the presence of David Boon as selector on duty. While the other members of Hilditch's panel occasionally struggled to occupy the right space on a tour, in which they were available to consult but not expected to coach, Boon was seldom viewed with suspicion or confusion by the players. His strong relationship with Ponting helped, as did the occasional public utterance, including the one he made in the week before the first Test, at the Wanderers Stadium in Johannesburg: 'I firmly believe we have young players who are going to step up to the mark and do really well, as long as we are patient.'

In contrast to Australia's quiet construction of a new team ethos, South Africa's players were dealing with the flood of adulation and attention merited by their victories down under. Smith and the coach, Mickey Arthur, were concerned by the amount of time the team spent in a mode that was more promotional than preparatory ahead of the Tests, and they found themselves reckoning that Australia's constructive early days on tour had mirrored their own ahead of their victories in Perth and Melbourne. A host of new endorsement deals and contracts were also being waved in the faces of Smith's players, and the uneven distribution of these riches was thought to have caused little fissures, whereas the Australian tour party appeared more united. As Arthur put it in his biography, *Taking the Mickey*, 'While we were battling to maintain our focus as a team spending hours and days as individuals and responding to requests for our attention, Australia were working together as a unit and planning their response to the defeat at home. They were in combat mode, with no distractions. They were hungrier than us.'

That this change and its effects were noticeable so soon after the series in Australia is not altogether surprising, given South Africa's breaking of a fifteen-year drought for touring sides. But it can also be viewed as a marker of the quality Australia once possessed, as over the course of that period only one major series – the 2005 Ashes in England – can be seen to have been lost due to similar problems in Ponting's team. South Africa and Australia were at different stages of discovering how hard it was to maintain success. Whereas Smith's side had hit a peak in December 2008, now it was Ponting's turn.

The world's first sight of Phillip Hughes was not auspicious. Four balls into his Test debut at the Wanderers, in place of the retired Hayden, Hughes offered an apparent wild swish at Dale Steyn with two feet off the ground and snicked to Mark Boucher behind the stumps. South Africa rejoiced in expectation of a quick kill, in the match and the series. Back in Australia, the selector Merv Hughes groaned. 'I was sitting at home watching it on TV thinking, "What have we done here?"' The dismissal proved misleading in two ways. First, it suggested to South Africa that a nervous Hughes would be easy prey. Secondly, it led them to conclude that balls angled across Hughes in the slashing and cutting zone would reap edges and catches. Had they been asked, a long line of Australian domestic pace bowlers could have testified otherwise.

Hughes went on to an important 75 in the second innings, before stunning South Africa by clattering a century in each innings at Kingsmead, in Durban. His almost-instant success was bewitching for Australian watchers after the grim home summer and likewise a tonic for other touring players. But how much was it a result of South African miscalculation based on that first dismissal? Smith remarked later that 'we never coped with his strangeness', while Arthur reckoned he had never misread a batsman more thoroughly. 'We felt he would be vulnerable if we could get him coming forward just outside the off stump, which was a reasonable approach,' Arthur wrote. 'However, we were painfully slow to realise how proficient he was at the square cut and how painfully small the margin for error was in terms of length. He also hit a lot of his cut shots in the air close to gully and backward point, which gave us the impression he was not in control and could be dismissed at any time. Unfortunately for us, the opposite was true.'

By contrast, Hughes was discomforted by the rare deliveries he faced that were short and at his body. Twice in the second innings he gloved balls down the leg side and was reprieved because South Africa did not utilise the newly minted decision review system to overturn the on-field call of not out. This addition to the game was another area in which the Australians landed on their feet, judging its vagaries rather better in this series than they did in several subsequent bouts.

But as much as they loved Hughes' runs and attitude, some team-mates harboured doubts about how sustainable it all was. Michael Hussey, who at the time was struggling badly to recapture his own honeymoon batting form, remembered wondering how long it would last. 'Sometimes you can see people come in; they're just so excited to have the opportunity and they've got no fears and doubts and just go for it,' he says. 'After you get through that initial excitement, the opposition spends more time on you and it becomes harder. I personally thought he had some technical deficiencies and as an international cricketer they're generally going to get found out. But whenever he went back to New South Wales or South Australia he plundered runs. They weren't speculating on him; he'd performed and dominated the level below and deserved his chance.'

Another man enjoying a tour without doubts or anxiety was Mitchell Johnson, who was delighted to find that Johannesburg's thinner air and humidity offered him the perfect environment to swing the new ball. When setting out to defend a first innings of 466 that he had played a large part in, Ponting at first wanted to open up with Hilfenhaus and Siddle. But he was stopped by the bowling coach, Troy Cooley, who had used much of his time in Potchefstroom and Johannesburg encouraging the swing that Johnson had sought for some years before the tour. 'Troy said, "Mate, Mitch is swinging the ball; he'll get Smith," and he got him first over," Ponting says. 'The next Test Mitch roughed them up big time in Durban, broke Smith's hand, hit Jacques Kallis in the throat, and ripped Mark Boucher's pegs out with a yorker.'

Smith was familiar with Johnson's speed and sporadic venom, having already suffered a badly broken thumb at the SCG. At the Wanderers he was still thinking about how to better avoid short balls at his ribs when the ball slung down at him began to bend away treacherously late. 'The best I've ever seen him bowl was after we beat Australia and they came back to South Africa and beat us,' Smith says. 'He actually swung the ball away from the left-hander, and that made him an absolute nightmare, because with his action, the ball felt like it was swinging from middle and leg stump.'

If Hughes and Johnson were the headliners in the most unexpected victory, then North and McDonald offered solid support in roles that were as important as they were understated. North's first-innings hundred at the Wanderers won the admiration of Smith, who felt he was watching a player with forty Tests in his pocket, rather than one. His off spin was also useful enough to have confounded more domestic batsmen over the preceding two summers than any full-time tweaker. McDonald offered the sort of consistency with the ball that Ponting had craved from his spin bowlers during the home summer, bowling stump-to-stump seam and swing with persistence and guile.

At this point the selectors had more or less given up on a specialist spinner, even though both Nathan Hauritz and Bryce McGain went to South Africa. 'Everyone said, "Why are you playing Andrew?" and basically we played him as a spinner because we knew he could bowl 20 to 30 overs and not go for many runs, so we could attack with our fast bowlers,' Merv Hughes says. 'We saw our fast-bowling stocks as our weapon, and our spin bowler needed to be able to come on and bowl 20 to 30 overs for 50 to 60 runs. When they were going for 80 to 100 runs in the same amount of time you couldn't afford to bowl them. There was that view that we needed a defensive spinner to chock up an end.'

In Durban, it was Katich who applied the coup de grâce with his left-arm wrist spin, tailing a match he had topped with a first-day century in the company of Phillip Hughes. That victory, on a surface that offered plenty of life on the second day in particular, was even more stirring than the one in Johannesburg. Johnson bowled with rare intimidation; Siddle showed little regard for either stumps or skulls, and Hilfenhaus' new-ball swing looked increasingly likely to be useful in England later in the year.

Little wonder Ponting was haughty at the conclusion of the match. 'World Cups are great, Ashes 2006–07 was an amazing achievement to win that 5–0,' he said. 'I'm not putting it above any of those but if you look at our group of players . . . there'll be a lot of people around the world who didn't think that this was achievable. So for us to have achieved what we have done over this week would make this win as special as any.' In a nod to his young team, Ponting made a rare trip out to a Durban club that night, and all enjoyed a subsequent week of rest in Cape Town.

It seemed that Australia had stumbled upon a formula that would work and a balance of players who could function together not only on the field but off it. Apart from Hughes and Johnson their methods were regimented and methodical but had been demonstrably successful. So why did it not carry on?

McDonald, notably, did not play another Test after South Africa, and his absence spoke volumes about the selectors' misjudgement after that tour. As Nielsen said of McDonald's short-lived Test career in 2011, 'He filled a role but it was in some regards conditional: the conditions in South Africa allowed us to not play a spinner, and we had Marcus North in the side. We were still desperate to play with three quicks and a spinner as a legitimate frontline attack, and to be honest we felt if there was going to be an all-rounder playing in our side it was going to be Shane Watson. So it wasn't about chopping Andrew McDonald off but asking, "Is this the sort of formula that will get us back to being the best team?" It won us a series in conditions that suited, but I don't know if it would've had lasting impact.'

As the result allowed Ponting to lift the ICC's Test Championship mace after twelve largely barren months, this seemed a conclusion that was hasty if not outright flawed. Beggars can't be choosers, but Australia's hierarchy was still thinking in terms more familiar to the wealthy.

In the dead third Test, at Newlands, in Cape Town, South Africa regrouped with an innings victory, to some degree vindicating the view of Arthur and Smith that their charges had been underdone at the start of the series. For Australia the match provided a sobering few days, not least due to the hiding dished out to McGain, a curio of a leg spinner whose displays for Victoria had been characterised by flight, accuracy and decent if not outrageous turn, while his largely self-taught methods had been honed not along any elite pathway but in more than a decade in Melbourne club competition. He made both of his two Test tours while afflicted by a muscle tear in his right armpit. Chosen to go to India in late 2008 with Australia A, he had sustained a muscle strain that had then progressed to a tear when he was training with the Test team ahead of their warm-up match in Hyderabad. Surgery to repair the damage had kept him out for half the summer. Seemingly heedless of how long it had taken Shane Warne to recover from shoulder surgery in 1998–99, Hilditch's panel chose McGain for South Africa on the strength of a fortuitous 5–104 against South Australia late in the season. 'It just took a long time,' he says. 'I didn't have pain but I didn't have my full range of pace, which meant I didn't have drop, which is pretty critical.'

At thirty-six, McGain was an IT worker and a single parent, worlds away from the sorts of career cricketers and support staff that had been booked to fly to Johannesburg in mid-February. The gap between them grew appreciably when he missed the flight. 'I'd separated from Liam's mum about two years earlier but we were going through a settlement. That's a challenge for anyone day to day, let alone doing a job that is pretty public. I wanted to take Liam over and it didn't work out. We were trying to arrange shared care. Liam's mum was asking, "Can you hold up your end of the bargain, when you're in another country for a month?" It had happened in a hurry. And that contributed to the build-up, the lack of rest before I went, and missing the plane.'

That event had alienated McGain from some members of the tour party, and the unflattering label 'clubbie' was uttered once or twice out of his earshot. However, a sense of missing professionalism ran both ways. McGain discovered there was even less knowledge of spin bowling in the national side than he had enjoyed at Prahran. Two years after Warne's retirement, few seemed conversant in the art, leaving McGain and Hauritz to fend for themselves. 'Michael Clarke was great. He said, "You're here because you're good enough. You're the best performed spinner; I've spoken to Warnie and he's seen them all." He spoke about fields in a way that made sense,' McGain says. 'But the difficulty was, it wasn't cohesive. I had Troy Cooley telling me another thing. It was all well meaning. I'd sit down in a break where I'd bowled six overs for maybe 40 runs and someone would come over and say, "Have you thought about this?" The coach would come over and say, "Mate, you've got to do this," and the captain had another view. What I learned out of that is you need to own a plan.

'Before the South African tour Nathan Hauritz and I had video of South African players batting, predominantly against fast bowling, and we had to work out plans to get them out. My mouth just dropped. Surely you know the percentages of how often they score on this side of the wicket and what they do against different spinners around the world? Surely you've got that body of work and from that we can extract the right statistics? But it was just, "You're the spinners – you work out what you're going to do and we'll see how that fits." I understand why that was the case: because they weren't going to play any spin anyway, just go with the four quicks.'

The spin-free strategy worked in Tests one and two, but on the eve of the Cape Town match, North fell ill enough to be sent to hospital. Still lacking power in his bowling shoulder, McGain had been outdone by North in his only tour match, but in a dead rubber, the selectors preferred to try the unknown quantity rather than pick Hauritz. This made Ponting uneasy. 'Bryce wasn't right to play,' he says. 'I always said, "Let me face them in the nets and I'll know straightaway if they're right." In Cape Town he couldn't get the ball down the other end with the same energy and work on it that he was used to. Northy was in hospital, the series was over, all these things. They wanted to have a look at him. And that shouldn't happen in Test cricket.'

Given his one chance at a time when he knew he could not bowl at his best, McGain hoped for favourable circumstances, scoreboard pressure, footmarks. Australia's first-day demise for 209 denied him all three. Having been brutalised by Johnson in Durban, South Africa's batsmen vented their spleens against a leg spinner who could not frighten them as Warne and MacGill had done. Yet McGain's enduring memory is not that his second ball went for 6, or that seven others also disappeared onto the Newlands banks, or his wince-inducing statistics of 149–0 off 18 overs. Instead, it is the cap presentation on day one, a surprise that no-one had hinted at, even though McGain later learned that the rest of the team had known the line-up the night before. 'It was like a little surprise party. Brute [Bernard] snuck the baggy green out from the back of his jumper and there it was,' he says. 'I can't believe it; I was just an average Mornington junior cricketer. This is pretty cool. I thought about my family, because Dad had died when I was six and Mum had been there the whole time. Wouldn't it be cool if she was here? Then I thought about my son. It would have been nice to get some of those emotions out of the way the night before.'

By the start of the 2009–10 summer, McGain's shoulder had recovered. Six scalps in the Sheffield Shield final capped a first-class return of 26 wickets at 32.10, as Victoria ran through Queensland. But his chance had gone. 'Once I understood what I had to do, then I could go and do it,' he says. 'What it does allow me to do now is share those experiences with kids, tell them, "You've got to have a plan; you've got to have everyone on the same page; work with your captain and coach." That's why they kept going through spinners. We didn't know what we needed. "We want a matchwinner but we can't replace Warne." When I was told I wasn't going on the Ashes tour, I asked Andrew Hilditch, "What were your expectations of a spinner?" He said, "Don't go for any runs and take heaps of wickets." I spoke to other spinners after Shield games during that time and they had no idea what was expected either. There were twelve of us and I feel for all of them.'

Unburdened by much expectation following the loss of the home series to South Africa, the Australians had found themselves revelling in the unfamiliar freedom of their unfancied status. They had also been a happier, more cohesive and united squad, helped along by a handful of shrewd selections – among the best made by Andrew Hilditch's panel. Phillip Hughes, Marcus North, Andrew McDonald and Ben Hilfenhaus all made major contributions in their first overseas Test assignment, while Mitchell Johnson conjured pace bowling of a spiteful, swinging standard that the hosts regarded more highly than anything else he subsequently produced. Johnson also played a pair of innings that had many using the term all-rounder to describe him.

For Ponting, the victories procured in Johannesburg and Durban were the proudest of his career – no small boast for a man who went on to play in well over a hundred Test match wins. They briefly returned Australia to the top of the Test match rankings and suggested that perhaps the holes opened up by Warne, McGrath et al. could be filled in a timely fashion. But it was also a tour during which problems in the team were obscured by circumstances and conditions, from the conspicuous absence of a full-time spin bowler to the advantage of surprise enjoyed by the likes of Hughes, Hilfenhaus and North. Though Australian cricket shone briefly in that South Africa series, the new-found sense of vitality did not last. Ultimately, it proved more a statistical outlier than the herald of a new dynasty.

8

Losing the Ashes

MAY – AUGUST 2009

ICC World Twenty20 in England

Australia in England

Sitting down together between commentary stints during Australia's 2003 Top End matches against Bangladesh, Mark Taylor and Ian Healy pondered the future. Australia were then untouchable, having just retained the Ashes and the World Cup in the same summer. But the warm Darwin air and serene times had them musing on when they could see Ashes trouble ahead. 'We actually said 2009,' Taylor recalls. 'We thought that Ashes series was the one we could lose based on what we could see coming through. Two thousand and five was the aberration, I think, that surprised us all. Could we have done any different for us not to lose in 2009? I don't know.'

In the tale of Australian cricket between 2007 and 2014, no tour stirs up quite so many imponderables as that of 2009. Following the apparent new dawn in South Africa, Ricky Ponting's team entered England with a confident strut. They had the players, the spirit and the plans to topple England, who under captain Andrew Strauss and coach Andy Flower were battling to mount a cohesive Ashes challenge following Peter Moores' departure as coach and Kevin Pietersen's resignation as captain. A few months earlier, in the West Indies, they had been bowled out for 51. Most assumed that Flower, the caretaker coach, would not last.

But strangely, the tours of the West Indies and South Africa were misleading. Flower and Strauss responded admirably to the pressure they were placed under, putting together a team that stuttered and spluttered but ultimately held it together at the most critical times in the series. And while Australia turned in some fine days and strong matches, they also let slip a trio of disastrous sessions that left the urn in England's possession. Whether it was the result of suffocating anxiety, the weight of history or the occasional moment of poor judgement, the Australians in 2009 were not good enough.

Preceding the Ashes, the second World T20 tournament largely passed Australia by, memorable only for the sad conclusion to Andrew Symonds' saga of disillusionment and poor behaviour. Having signed a CA contract featuring a clause that precluded him from drinking in public, Symonds broke it with an extended binge following the first State of Origin match, which numerous members of the T20 squad watched in a London bar. The scale of Symonds' drinking that day is remembered by many who saw him during the game, which finished at around 10 a.m., and then at a 3 p.m. fitness testing session. In the words of one teammate, 'He was that drunk it was insane – I don't know how you can be that drunk in the afternoon.' Combined with a handful of other missteps, it convinced Ponting that Symonds no longer wanted to be there. His Australian career was over at the age of thirty-three.

As a teammate for both Queensland and Australia, James Hopes watched Symonds unravel: 'He used to be very switched on, but from early 2008 he started to get a little bit different, a lot more wary of everything and disillusioned. He rightfully got sent home from Darwin, and he did the wrong thing at the World T20, but that wasn't him. He was one of the guys who enjoyed a beer and a drink with mates, but he could flick a switch a month or two out from a series and all of a sudden his training would be two or three times a day and his intensity would go through the roof. It just never happened after that summer. He drank in the West Indies, he drank in Darwin, he drank in England, and he was disruptive. It was a shame.'

For Symonds, an idealistic vision of playing for the Australian team surrounded by his best mates and backed by loyal support off the field had mutated into something far more sterile, uncertain and blurred by legal clauses. His abiding regret was signing the contract that forbade him from public drinking. 'I did give an inch in some areas but not in others,' he told Harsha Bhogle. 'I signed a contract no-one else signed and I was held to ransom, if I didn't sign it I couldn't play for Australia. That's the only regret I really have – I should never have signed that. In the end the bearings were starting to wear in the wheels, there was a wheel going to fly off at some point, and it did. Then I was ousted from the side with the choice that if I wanted to work my way back I could. But it got to the point where I didn't want to.'

After the enjoyment, time and space afforded them in South Africa, Australia's players felt rather more constricted by the attention and expectation of the Ashes tour, something only Ponting, Simon Katich, Michael Clarke, Michael Hussey, Brad Haddin, Stuart Clark and Brett Lee had experienced before. In the words of one player, 'You go from playing in South Africa with no crowds, so all you have is just you and the bowler and hardly any media exposure, to going to England and it just being hectic with the public, the crowds, the media, so many different dynamics. If you've never been there before, or even if you have, it can get full-on.'

Not all of this hype arose organically. Having exploded to life in South Africa, Phillip Hughes had gone from South Africa to Middlesex, where in the second division of county cricket he ran up such good numbers that his name was placed a little hastily alongside that of Sir Donald Bradman. Three matches reaped 574 runs, and on a brief trip home between assignments Hughes was even pictured at the Bradman Museum in Bowral, brandishing a blade used by the knight in 1934. Small of stature, bush of technique and lofty of ambition, Hughes was no Bradman, and he later admitted to Tim Nielsen that the Middlesex stint had not prepared him for the Ashes as he had hoped.

Unlike South Africa, Flower's England were far better drilled in their plans for Hughes and helped by the way Steve Harmison twice bounced the twenty-year-old out for the England Lions in a warm-up fixture. Andrew Flintoff followed up with high pace and a suffocating line at Cardiff and Lord's, and with the help of a disputed catch by Strauss in the second Test, Hughes was dropped after four underwhelming innings. Nielsen, Ponting and the selector on duty, Jamie Cox, all felt Flintoff had intimidated Hughes. They replaced him with Shane Watson's greater bulk in the hope of a more counterpunching new-ball approach. Feeling Hughes was being worried out, Australia were worried out of picking him.

'England had worked out how they were going to attack him; they bowled at him so much more,' Nielsen says, 'and we had Watson waiting in the wings, who we thought could play off both front and back. The other thing that pushed the barrow was Flintoff's spell on the last morning at Lord's when he bowled ten overs on the bounce and destroyed us. We couldn't afford to be intimidated out of it, so we changed the team to change the feel of the group and put someone up front who would take them on a little bit more and put some pressure back on them.'

Similarly, Mitchell Johnson found himself coping with unwanted attention, and crowd heckling, which he had never faced before. Early tour headlines offering comparisons with Flintoff were flung back at Johnson by the Barmy Army, while a combination of injury and poor form among more senior bowlers left Johnson as Australia's spearhead entering the series. Lee had suffered a side strain in a tour match while searching for the extra pace that would guarantee his return to the Test team, and Ben Hilfenhaus and Peter Siddle were outshining Clark. As much as he enjoyed South Africa, Johnson had not expected to be carrying the burden of bowling leadership in the Ashes.

England, meanwhile, had made every effort to develop cohesion and spirit in their team. Early meetings encouraged honesty but also shared responsibility, and they had adopted the phrase 'The team is not a lease car', meaning they should leave it in the same healthy condition in which they had found it. Flower borrowed an earlier Australian gambit by taking the team to Flanders, where a stone cricket ball was placed at the grave of Colin Blythe, the England spin bowler killed at Passchendaele during World War I. This exercise encouraged closeness among the players, a spirit Strauss felt would make them more difficult to break down.

More crumbly was the Cardiff pitch, as Flower believed that home Test match surfaces should be used to gain an advantage over visiting teams. Australia's success in South Africa and earlier struggles in India led to the word being put about that dry, straw-coloured pitches were England's preference. Many who decried the strip prepared for the fifth Test, at the Oval, were unaware that Cardiff, Lord's, Edgbaston and Headingley groundsmen had been under similar instructions. Though pace did play a significant role across the series, this was generally due to overhead conditions rather than those under foot.

As yet unaware of this, Ponting's men focused on an exercise in which all the players told each other what the Ashes meant to them. Two players a day for a little over a week, the squad ran through childhood memories from the 1989 victory lap around England and Michael Slater's 1993 Lord's debut to matches that Ponting himself had played in. It had an impact on Graham Manou, on tour as the reserve wicketkeeper. 'The passion that came through made me think, "This is the real thing,"' he says. 'I can remember just seeing it in Punter's face, what it meant to him. Huss was similar, and Pup's was a really well done presentation he put a lot of work into. The reality of it was a lot of passion and a lot of hurt after that first Test.'

Test matches in England have a habit of becoming known instantly by the venue and the year. Australians will react enthusiastically to any mention of Headingley 1989, the Oval 1972, Old Trafford 1993 and Trent Bridge 1997. Similarly, Edgbaston 2005 and Headingley 1981 evoke instant memories of triumph for Englishmen. Among Australia's 2009 tourists, mention of Cardiff 2009 causes brows to furrow, eyes to darken and mouths to dry. But for the final wicket, Ponting called it a perfect Test match. Manou had never seen a dressing room so devastated about falling short. Nathan Hauritz remembered it with the vividness of a recurring nightmare. For five days, in conditions made to English order, Australia's cricketers battered the hosts. They have never quite forgiven themselves for fluffing their lines in the final act.

Responding to a first-innings tally of 435 scored at better than four runs an over, Australia's batsmen mined the richest vein of the era. Katich, Ponting, Haddin and Marcus North all crunched centuries, while Clarke's 83 lost little by comparison. A tally of 6–674 declared over three rain-affected days was Australia's sixth highest of all time, leaving the England spin duo of Graeme Swann and Monty Panesar with combined figures of 1–246 on a pitch taking some turn. When Johnson and Hilfenhaus pinned Alastair Cook and Ravi Bopara before the close on day four, England appeared out on their feet.

Entering the final day, Hauritz felt the responsibilities of wrapping up the match more keenly than most. He had bowled neatly in the first innings, notably outfoxing Kevin Pietersen. But as Gideon Haigh wrote in the *Business Spectator*, Hauritz was referred to so often as 'not Shane Warne' that 'he must sometimes feel like issuing a pre-emptive public apology'. Says Hauritz: 'It was tough for any spinner following in the footsteps of Warnie. Media beats up on it, crowd beats up on it, but in the end it's the six inches between your ears that beats you. That probably separates the good players from the great.'

At 5–70 before lunch on the final day, Hauritz stood a chance of becoming great. He had winkled out Strauss and Matt Prior, wheeling away at the opposite end to the fast bowlers, among whom Hilfenhaus had flummoxed Pietersen with subtle variations in line. England were sustained by Paul Collingwood, who carried self-recriminating thoughts about Adelaide in 2006. Despite the brilliant start, Ponting too harboured thoughts of a draw, reasoning that the pitch was still good and his bowlers inexperienced. Wickets became harder to come by, the Australians tensing up with each passing over.

Despite Collingwood, Flintoff and Swann, Ponting's men should still have won. When Siddle's short ball looped off the shoulder of Collingwood's bat and was held by a juggling Michael Hussey, at least ten overs remained with England still in deficit. In those remaining overs, a few images stand out: Siddle getting within millimetres of coaxing an edge from Panesar first ball; Hauritz beating the bat again, and again; Ponting chewing his fingernails while not trusting himself to call on Johnson, who had been wayward for much of the day; England sending out copious batting gloves, and their (Australian) physio; Ponting resorting to North's spin in the hope of squeezing in an extra over. Finish.

Through his exhaustion and creeping sense of impending dejection, Hauritz wondered to himself why Ponting did not swing him around to the other end. Clarke wondered why he did not get to bowl. Everyone wondered why neither Johnson nor Hilfenhaus was afforded even a single over at England's last pair. In his diary, Ponting contended that Johnson had wasted the second new ball and reasoned that using North meant one extra over at England's last pair. Whatever the merits of his argument, what was not in dispute was the effect the match had on the psyche of the Australian team. They had put in everything and gained nothing; the wounds were deep.

Manou had never seen such hollowed-out souls. 'It was a very, very different environment to what I was used to. Because a lot of them had had success, and it wasn't something I was used to in South Australia. That was something I took from that tour, that there is a difference when you do lose – different to "Oh, we've lost again, tried our hardest but just not good enough" to "How did we lose that? There's no way we should be losing cricket matches, because we are number one." Had we got over the line the tour would have been a completely different thing. It was pretty devastating for everyone.'

Ponting recalls: 'One more wicket and that would have been the perfect game. Lost the toss on that pitch, they batted a day, we got 700: that was nearly a perfect start. We did nearly everything perfectly for five days and couldn't get across the line. They took a lot more out of a draw in that first game than we took out of not winning, and then I lost the toss at Lord's again and we were all over the place with the bowling early on and momentum just went. Cardiff was as down as I'd seen the team.'

As they walked from the field, Ponting and Hauritz were snapped together by Hamish Blair. Ponting, his head bowed, looks every inch a thwarted general. Hauritz, exhausted, has turned to wipe his face with his left shirtsleeve. From the boundary, he would have appeared to be wiping away sweat. By the time he made his way up the pavilion steps, another set of stairs and down a long corridor to the dressing room, something else had welled up inside. 'Cardiff is one of the greatest disappointments of my life,' Hauritz says. 'I remember going in after that Test and just bawling my eyes out in the toilets straight after, because I knew what the repercussions were going to be for me – I couldn't spin Australia to victory. All that pressure was on me and the opportunity was there to take that last wicket, bowling to two left-handers on a turning deck – it can't be scripted any better. It will be etched in my memory for the rest of my days.'

Ponting saw those tears, saw that disappointment. As much as he tried to remind Hauritz and others that this young team had just put on a clinic for five days, he also made quiet note of the wounds inflicted by that last hour.

Four days later at Lord's, Strauss and Cook galloped to a stand of 196 in fewer than 48 overs. Australia's unchanged team seemed bruised in body and mind. Johnson was the most affected. His composure had frayed on the final day in Wales but was lost entirely in St John's Wood as stories about his personal life broke in the Australian media. His mother, Vikki Harber, had been quoted complaining that Johnson's fiancée, Jessica Bratich, had 'stolen' him. This pressure, combined with a chanting, mocking crowd and unwanted attention as Australia's anointed number-one bowler, rendered Johnson powerless to prevent a succession of balls whirring invitingly into the pulling and cutting zones of England's openers.

'My confidence had gone, I had stuff going on personally that I didn't know how to handle, and so I just didn't handle it through the whole series,' Johnson told Andrew Ramsey in 2014. 'To make it worse, I was thinking about my bowling technique when I was out there playing because the ball was going all over the place. I was trying to self-correct, which you just can't do during the course of a Test match. Then there was Lord's with the slope (of the playing surface), and I was thinking, "How do I deal with this, do I have to change something to get it on the right part of the wicket?" On top of that there was the crowd . . . and the media, I was starting to think about what they were writing and starting to believe everything I was hearing. I just had no focus at all.'

Nevertheless, Australia's batsmen still began their first innings in pursuit of an England total ten runs slimmer than they had faced at Cardiff. What developed was the second ruinous passage of the series. Though at least one Australian journalist in the Lord's press box wrote feverishly of reverse swing, it was conventional swerve that confounded the touring batsmen, accompanied by a trio of umpiring decisions that could have been reversed. Hughes edged to slip and Strauss claimed a decidedly low catch, Ponting was given out caught off a ball that hit pad rather than bat – albeit close to l.b.w. – and Hussey was given out caught when a Swann off break turned directly out of a footmark to slip. A total of 215 meant the Test was all but lost, though Clarke and Haddin staged a debonair rearguard attempt.

Australia's first Test match defeat at Lord's since 1938 changed the mood of the series and of the touring party. A sense of insularity crept in: relations between the team and the travelling press were seldom worse than after Lord's and during the drawn third Test, in Birmingham. At tour's end, the Australian cricket press corps would send a letter of protest to Cricket Australia.

It was England's turn to be unsettled at Headingley, by the dual distractions of an early match-morning fire alarm at their hotel and then doubt over the fitness of their wicketkeeper. Matt Prior played but was unable to stem a tide of wickets when Strauss chose to bat on the sort of ambiguous pitch and under the kinds of weather conditions with which Leeds can often tease a captain. At the forefront of Australia's rollicking start was Stuart Clark, recalled in place of Hauritz due to the likelihood of swing.

Looking on was an angry Brett Lee, left out despite his insistence that he was fit. Though recovered from the side strain, Lee had no first-class cricket behind him to prove it. Given the events of India, Perth and Melbourne in the preceding twelve months, selector Jamie Cox, coach Tim Nielsen, bowling coach Troy Cooley and strength and conditioning coach Stuart Karppinen would not heed Lee's word. The debate culminated in a bowling session on the eve of the fourth Test, which took place only because Lee demanded that he show the team hierarchy what he could do. 'We basically made the call on that alone, that he hadn't played a game. And that's what he was filthy about,' Cox says. 'It was as angry a dressing room as I've been in, myself, Tim,

Troy and Brett. We tried to call the session off because it was wet and ultimately went into the indoor nets, where he bowled off 18 yards. It was almost like he wanted to say, "But I'm Brett Lee."'

That session, followed by Lee's omission from the team for the Oval, was the moment he gave up on Test cricket. 'I don't believe I got much support from the hierarchy throughout that period,' he wrote in his autobiography. 'If they'd said to me, "Look, Brett, at this particular point of your career we don't believe you're up to the standard that we need you to be at," I would have disagreed with them but I would have accepted it. But they didn't say that; they simply told me I wasn't fit. How would they know? . . . At the time of doing this book, I honestly believe I could play Test cricket for another two years, but I don't want to, and why bother?'

Lee's discontent did not affect the result. England were distracted at Leeds by back spasms to their wicketkeeper Matt Prior during warm-ups, which caused Andrew Strauss to bat first on a day that proved ideal for the swing and seam of Clark, Siddle and Hilfenhaus. Even Johnson found his range in the second innings. A vast victory meant that in spite of Cardiff, in spite of Lord's, in spite of the team's youth and in spite of England's pitch advantage, only a draw was required at the Oval for Australia to retain the Ashes. Australian dressing-room celebrations at Leeds were haughty and prolonged, with Matthew Hayden invited for a team song more throaty and less regretful than the Sydney rendition that had followed the fracas between Clarke and Katich. Anticipation of the urn hung thick in the air. One solid Test match. That's all it would take.

As in South Africa, Leeds was a victory achieved by aggressive pace bowling, methodical planning and forthright batting, but little or no trace of spin. Even without playing, Hauritz still had more wickets for the series at a superior average to Swann, and most assumed he would come in for the Oval, especially once its colour and texture were revealed. Hauritz assumed so, too. 'I took things for granted,' he says. 'I turned up to the wicket and said, "This is going to spin heaps. Can't wait to play this," and then it all unravelled from there.'

Never reluctant to express his feelings, whether good or ill, Hauritz had been managing a pair of niggling injuries to his foot and groin. At a Canterbury tour match before the Oval, he nabbed 2–43 from 16 overs but also spent time off the field. In London, he worked with Pakistani off spinner Saqlain Mushtaq, even honing a form of doosra that he had not yet unveiled in a Test. On match eve, Hauritz began to walk laps with the physio, Alex Kountouris, thinking he was letting his body rest ahead of the workload he would face over the next five days. Hauritz believed Kountouris had exempted him from fielding practice but had not told the coach, Tim Nielsen. Kountouris was surprised when Hauritz joined the lap walkers. Then Nielsen called Hauritz into a fielding drill. Stooping down to fetch a ball, Hauritz winced, and the ball scurried away.

'Mate, how are you going to play a Test match for five days?' Nielsen asked.

Replied Hauritz, 'I don't know, mate. I'm just trying to get through this.'

'Can you bowl?'

'Yes.'

'Can you get through five days?'

'Mate, I have no idea.'

With that brief dialogue, Hauritz scuppered his chances of playing. In an Australian team trying to preserve a sense of toughness, a player offering that sort of equivocal response to questions about his fitness was looked upon dimly. Ponting was particularly worried and cast his mind back to those tears in Cardiff. Treating spinners with the occasional reassuring cuddle had never been Ponting's way. Clarke, his deputy, was not in on the dialogue. None knew the tale of how Mark Taylor once ushered Shane Warne through two days of training for the historic Test at Jamaica in 1995 when the leg spinner was worried by a battered right thumb and complaining loudly about it.

'A lot of the stuff I was worried about with Haury and the reason I felt he probably couldn't give us an answer on his fitness might have been other stuff: maybe he was doubting himself,' Ponting says. 'I spent most of the training session with him trying to see if he could get up and be right, because it was a pretty big Test match. I wasn't willing to take the risk on him going into that game if he couldn't bowl properly.

'I look blokes in the eye and ask them if they can play, and I don't know too many people who wouldn't look me straight back in the eye and say, "I'm right to play." When I could sense that from somebody, I don't want those blokes going on the field – as simple as that. And I don't care who it was. Damien Martyn in the 2003 World Cup final, finger smashed to bits, I went to him the day before the game and said, "Are you going to be right to play?" He looked me in the eye and said, "I guarantee you I'm right to go." He got 88 in the game. That's the way I was brought up.'

Kountouris, used to players insisting they were fit when it was clear to all that they were not, was certain by the end of the session that Hauritz would not be playing, simply for reasons of body language. In conversation with Kountouris, Stuart Clark remarked, 'I'm not sure why Haury said he's not sure; he's just given away a Test match. I want to play, but I'm not sure I should be playing ahead of him.'

The final call rested with Cox, the selector on duty: 'We spoke to him quite often as a group. Maybe that overwhelmed him a bit; I don't know. But all we got ultimately was a bit underwhelmed by how keen he was to play. Maybe that's just Haury's personality, and Troy Cooley was saying, "Play him. We have to push him over the line for every game." But we didn't want him to rip the door down to get out there. We were just saying, "Mate, are you right to go?" And all we wanted to hear was, "I'll be fine," not "I don't know. I think so."

'When you're talking to people like Tim and Punter, "I think so" isn't going to cut it. Are you in or out, mate? So ultimately we made the call for it: unchanged team. I'm sure he wanted to play, and it may well have been the fact that he wasn't convinced he wouldn't let someone down. I honestly don't know the total motivation in his mind, but all we saw was somebody who in the biggest Test match he would ever play just wasn't bursting out of his skin to get over the line.'

The realisation that they would be playing an unchanged team dawned on Hauritz last of all. That night, too late, at the Royal Garden Hotel in Kensington he made a final pitch. 'I spoke to Punter before they were picking the side and I said, "Mate, look, I'm 100 per cent ready to go. If you want me to play, I'll play," but I didn't say that to Tim and Jamie, and in the end it cost me, and cost everyone. There definitely was regret afterwards; it was a really tough time. I knew deep down in my heart that I said the wrong thing to Tim Nielsen about it all.'

Exchanging teams with Ponting at the toss, Strauss was 'absolutely staggered' not to see Hauritz playing. Ponting was equally staggered to see the ball taking chunks out of the pitch on day one. 'The way that pitch turned out halfway through the first day – no-one could see that coming,' he says. 'That pitch looked like it might have turned, but it didn't look like it was going to break up so fast – the ball just went straight through the top. Luckily for England they won the toss.'

England duly forged an Ashes victory, first via the pace bowling of Stuart Broad and then by the surprise middle-order stolidness of Jonathan Trott, which defied most statistical measures of the series. Hauritz watched from the boundary as a haunted drinks waiter. Manou remembers him staring out onto the field and uttering the words, 'I could be out there winning a game for Australia right now. How many times do you get that opportunity?' Urban legends about Hauritz suffering a breakdown have circulated ever since. 'Everyone was asking, "Why aren't you playing?" and I said, "Well, I don't know,"' he says. 'If I explain that situation to them, most people would understand both sides of the story. They'd understand the selector and coach aren't willing to take that risk, and they could understand my worries about not getting through . . . but they might also say, "Why would you say that, Nathan?"'

Australia did not lose the Ashes because they failed to pick Nathan Hauritz. But Australia did not pick Hauritz because he was perceived as a point of potential weakness who did not fit the profile of the ideal cricketer. His story is much the same as the stories of his fellow spinners Bryce McGain, Jason Krejza, Beau Casson and even Stuart MacGill. They deserved better.

9

The Summer of Our Kidding Ourselves

SEPTEMBER 2009 – MARCH 2010

ICC Champions Trophy in South Africa

Australia in India

West Indies in Australia

Pakistan in Australia

As Greg Norman so often did in the wake of defeat in one of golf's majors, Australia tried to atone for losing the Ashes by going on a lengthy streak of wins in less pivotal encounters. Six out of seven England ODIs were swept, the Champions Trophy scooped and an India limited-overs series edged despite a surfeit of injuries. The home summer then became a kind of B-grade homage to some of the undefeated seasons turned in by the great teams of the past: a poor West Indies and a panicky Pakistan were bested in Test and limited-overs series, though not without several notable hiccups. A trip to New Zealand reaped similarly strong results, as numerous members of the team built up sturdy records.

Several encouraging themes emerged: Shane Watson's impromptu move up the order to open during the Ashes resulted in a sturdy opening partnership with Simon Katich; Doug Bollinger's considerable

pace, skill and effort were underlined by his dominance over Chris
Gayle; and Nathan Hauritz recovered from the traumas of England
to nab a pair of fourth-innings hauls against an admittedly dysfunc-
tional and flaky Pakistan. Yet perceptive watchers could see through
the victories to underlying weaknesses both in the team and at CA:
West Indies, Pakistan and New Zealand were some distance from
Test cricket's best performed triumvirate of South Africa, India and
England, while the stalling of Ricky Ponting's previously consistent supply of runs at number three raised numerous eyebrows. The
summer's matches were watched by paltry crowds and returned a substantial loss on the balance sheet, leaving CA to stress the importance
of lucrative tours by India to counterbalance the financial shortfall.

Confidence about the return Ashes bout in 2010–11 grew within
Australia's ranks throughout the summer but did so on flimsy foundations. On the website *Back Page Lead*, journalist Malcolm Knox
dubbed it 'the summer of our kidding ourselves', adding, 'The problem for Watson, as it is for the current Australian team, is that they
show signs of believing their own publicity. That is, they seem to
believe that conquering the might of Pakistan and the West Indies in
an Australian summer ranks them higher than fourth or fifth among
cricket nations. Confidence is all well and good, but no substitute for
ability, and at the moment, the ugly truth about world cricket is that
England have better players than Australia.'

Perhaps understandably, Ponting was bullish at the time about his
team's success, writing confidently in his diary about how the players
had matured together and speaking of them in terms of another all-
conquering epoch about to be reached. 'I feel we've grown as a team
since we lost in England in 2009, as so many members of our team
became more used to the demands and stresses of big-time cricket.
The challenge now is for us to keep improving, as the great Australian
teams of previous eras always did.' Four years later, in his next book,
At the Close of Play, Ponting had rather changed his tune. 'You might
assume I'd look back on this extended season with much fondness, as a

time of triumph, but with hindsight I think we were fooled by our success into thinking everything was right with Australian cricket . . . At
the time, as we kept winning games, we convinced ourselves we were
enjoying a revival. In fact, it was a false dawn.'

For all the countless criticisms levelled at the selection decisions of
Andrew Hilditch, no-one ever suggested that he was lazy. Diligent,
studious, attentive, organised, focused and polite, he juggled his
Adelaide legal practice with the job of chairman of selectors as best
he could. At a Kuala Lumpur limited-overs series in 2006, Hilditch
could be found in the gym of the Australian team's hotel, pounding
out a rapid walking pace while listening to music through headphones
and reading four sets of legal documents laid out on the treadmill
before him.

It is reasonable to conclude that Hilditch spent just as many hours
a week picking Australian cricket teams as his full-time successors,
John Inverarity and Rod Marsh, have done. And yet Hilditch's part-
time status grated on many. Players and observers who disagreed with
his panel's decisions presumed their muddled, misplaced or overly
speculative choices were due to the fact that the chairman was not
putting in all of the time he could. CA management battled with the
outmoded link of the selectors to the board, as both highly influential levels of Australian cricket decision-making retained an old-world
amateurism decidedly out of step with the studied and salaried, if
somewhat antiseptic, professionalism of the players and many CA
employees, all of whom, along with CA's public affairs department,
struggled with the recurring problem of Hilditch's work schedule.
Not once did he fail to return a call or message within the organisation, but it often took hours, if not days, to happen. Many a staffer
found themselves staying at the office late into the night or rising with
sparrows to await a pivotal call from Hilditch regarding the composition of a squad or a CA contracts list and the proposed manner of its

announcement. The head of cricket operations, Michael Brown, had for some years assumed the role of calling players to notify them of inclusion in squads, meaning most seldom heard from Hilditch unless they were going to be dropped. Knowing this, many chose to ignore his calls.

In March 2009, Brown had tabled a talent pathway review to the CA board that addressed several issues around selection, among other things. Such an exercise was not uncommon. All Australia's signal defeats of the period were subject to reviews. Most notably, the 2005 Ashes post-mortem had encouraged the poaching of bowling coach Troy Cooley from England and better financing of cricket operations, so that John Buchanan did not have to resort to cost-saving measures like having the fielding coach Mike Young sleep on Buchanan's hotel-room floor. The Argus team performance review, Crawford-Carter governance review and the CA financial model review, which took place in 2011 and 2012, were conducted on a far grander scale and have had the majority of their recommendations followed through. But 2009 was a different time. Brown called for two measures that are now in place – namely, the appointment of a full-time chairman of selectors and the creation of a national talent manager network so that selection was professionalised at the domestic level.

Hilditch had stated, both privately and publicly, that he would not abandon his lucrative legal practice to take up a full-time position. Another complication was Hilditch's relationship with Jack Clarke, CA's chairman. Both Adelaide lawyers in addition to their moonlighting in cricket, Hilditch and Clarke had already served together on the South Australian Cricket Association board for five years before the review was mooted. Clarke's high opinion of Hilditch and the job he was doing crowded out Brown's argument that selection needed to be addressed on a more nine-to-five, Monday-to-Friday basis. That is, it *would* have crowded out Brown's argument, had he made it. When he reached the point of his review that proposed changes to the selection panel, Brown was interrupted at the lectern by Clarke, who didn't support the plan. Hilditch stayed, and selection remained a part-time affair until 2011.

CA management were left to implement a watered-down version of Brown's plan, with the state talent manager positions jointly funded by CA and the states and reporting to a national talent manager based at Jolimont. That job ultimately went to Greg Chappell, who was also added to the selection panel, though not as chairman. This allowed CA a selector of the management's choice, rather than one of the six nominees habitually put up by the board directors of each state – recruitment and appointment of selectors being as antiquated as the panel's charter. Writing in *The Australian* when this decision was announced, in August 2010, Malcolm Conn decried the creation of a 'two-headed monster'.

Most laudable among Australia's results during the summer was the 4–2 ODI success in India that followed the Champions Trophy in South Africa. This was not so much because of the opposition but the sheer volume of injuries the team encountered. Among first-choice players, Michael Clarke, Brad Haddin, Nathan Bracken and Callum Ferguson were missing from the squad, but others soon joined them back in Australia. Brett Lee, James Hopes, the stand-in gloveman Tim Paine and Peter Siddle were added to the casualty list by game three of the series, and the situation reached a farcical level when the injury replacement Moisés Henriques was himself sent home and replaced by Andrew McDonald. Shane Watson, Mitchell Johnson and Ben Hilfenhaus also carried niggles through the series, with Hilfenhaus succumbing to knee tendonitis and missing most of the summer.

For all that, a comfortable victory in the eastern Indian town of Guwahati secured the series before the final match in Mumbai was washed out. Watson was outstanding, having found a way to manage his fragile body through the self-financed use of external physios Victor Popov and John Gloster. Ponting ranked the result alongside his three World Cups, and the series became a career high point for the likes of Adam Voges, Clint McKay and Graham Manou. Voges remembered the injuries, the effort put in by Ponting to spend time with every individual, no matter how callow, and the remoteness of Guwahati, where the lack of mobile network left players having to actually talk to one another. 'It got down to the game in Guwahati, no mobile reception, and it was the funniest thing ever because Shaun Marsh cannot live without his phone. Every five minutes, "Vogesy, got any reception, mate?" and I'd say, "No, I haven't had any for two days, and I don't know why you keep looking!" But I hit the winning runs in that game, off Sachin Tendulkar. There were so many injuries, such a change in personnel, it was remarkable to win that series. We had blokes flying in the day before games, and for them to get up and perform and feel a part of it all was great.'

Laudable though Australia's victory was, part of their trouble was self-inflicted. In India before the ODI series, the inaugural edition of the international club Champions League T20 had proved a fly in the ointment of the Australian team's preparation, not least because CA's 25 per cent stake in the event and authorship of its business plan meant there was no question of international players due to appear for their clubs being saved for the later engagements. The still-formative knowledge about the effect of T20 on a player's body had been unable to prevent a worrying injury toll in Australia's two competing teams, New South Wales and Victoria. Five out of the six fast bowlers playing for them – Brett Lee, Stuart Clark, Burt Cockley, Peter Siddle and James Pattinson – broke down either immediately afterwards in India or once they arrived back home. In the case of the 34-year-old Clark, a back stress fracture left medical experts everywhere scratching their heads, for it was an injury associated with youth, not experience. Clark never played for Australia again. The only paceman to emerge from the tournament unscathed was Doug Bollinger, but his time would come.

*

Greg Chappell's influence at CA had been growing for some time. Having been appointed as head coach of the Centre of Excellence in 2008, he was particularly close to Tim Nielsen, whom he had schooled in the ways of coaching while South Australia's director of cricket. Tall and stentorian, Chappell was able to dominate a room, helped by his enviable playing record and ability to speak crisply and formally on the game. His record of practically applying his ideas on cricket and business had been spotty, evidenced by a string of failed commercial ventures and mixed results with South Australia and then the Indian international team. However, his views on the nurturing of talent and the provision of opportunities for youth were taken in eagerly by Michael Brown and Geoff Allardice. A paper that Chappell prepared on the importance of recognising and fast-tracking outstanding cricket talent at a young age was the starting point for a drastic change to the second XI competition, which sat below the Sheffield Shield. Its conclusions coincided with ideas developed during a fact-finding tour of the country in 2005 by Allardice, Belinda Clark, the Centre of Excellence manager, and Nielsen. A board subcommittee addressing cricket issues had thought along similar lines, with Mark Taylor being almost as outspoken on the topic as Chappell.

'One of the great worries when the first MoU [memorandum of understanding] was struck between the players and the board back in 1997 and Shield players started getting paid was that we'd end up with county cricket,' Taylor says. 'One advantage we've always got is that we've only got six teams, so we do have a certain amount of natural attrition. But I always wanted to make sure that sides had youth. To some degree that comes from retiring when I was thirty-four. Great players like Steve Waugh, Allan Border and Ricky Ponting can play until they're thirty-eight at the top level. But the last thing you want is a heap of 38-year-olds playing state cricket.'

Statistics for the Shield showed the average age of players had been rising steadily since the late 1990s, and in second XI teams the number of players under twenty-three was said to be 'minuscule'. Growing

numbers of young sportsmen were choosing to take up Australian
Rules football rather than cricket, on the basis that the football code
allowed far better odds of being chosen and well paid. These facts,
alongside the downturn in the national team's results in 2008 and
2009, added urgency to the plans for a change to the pathway.

The Futures League and Futures League T20 competitions (nick-
named the 'Baby Bash') were duly announced at the start of 2009–10,
to little media fanfare but to widespread expressions of disbelief from
players and coaches at state, second XI and club levels. Its key regulations included three players over twenty-three years old permitted per
team; two innings and 144 overs maximum per team (with a 96-over
limit in first innings) across three days; overs not used in the first
innings by each team to be carried over to the second innings; no second new ball; bonus points for spin wickets (0.10 points per wicket);
and an increased reward for an outright result (8 points for an outright
result, as opposed to six the previous year).

Each measure had a sound theoretical basis, from increasing
opportunities for young players and encouraging attacking cricket
to affording greater chances for spin bowlers to get into what was
becoming a pace-dominated domestic game. The lack of a second
new ball was designed to foster better skills in slow bowling but also
in reverse swing.

All of the new regulations could be traced back to Chappell's view
that a champion plays between the ages of eighteen and thirty-three,
not twenty-seven and thirty-three. In the Jolimont office and around
the CA board table, the logic appeared sound. As Chappell explained
in 2011, 'We have six state teams, we have a hundred-odd players on
contract, but only sixty-six can play at any given time, and we need to
have a reasonable number of those players as potential matchwinning
players for Australia. If we have only got one or two in each state who
are in that bracket of being young, talented and potentially matchwinning, we've only got about six to pick from. If we have got five per
team we have got thirty to pick from.

'I think a lot of the criticism comes from particularly players who are in the over-23 bracket. While it's understandable that they are going to have that view, it's very important there are people in the organisations and in CA who look at the big picture. We can't afford to have states focused on silverware at the domestic level. It's not about silverware; it's about development and silverware. If the focus is on winning competitions at that level, it's going to impact what happens at the top level.'

But combined with the loss of a generation of Shield hardheads to the Indian Cricket League and IPL in 2008 and the already-prominent drift of mature players away from state and club cricket, the Futures League measures quickly began to have debilitating effects. Senior-grade players, who had previously stayed in the game for the reward of the occasional interstate second XI trip, left in droves. Sheffield Shield players of decent ability elected to retire well ahead of schedule. In the space of the two seasons the Futures League restrictions were fully in place, the standard of both Shield and second XI players dropped considerably, something noticed and noted by Andrew Strauss when he compared his experience of tour games with England in 2006–07 and 2010–11.

James Hopes and George Bailey, captains of Queensland and Tasmania respectively, saw the effects at first hand. In 2011, Bailey described them. 'It's become really difficult to have guys that aren't in your best XI consistently playing good, hard cricket against other teams with that under-23 rule. I've got no doubt that cricket and the way bodies are, your best cricket you play after you're twenty-three, and it's much the same as the Australian team. I think the best Australian players are better for having a really strong first-class system, and the teams at this level playing good, hard cricket, and we're much the same. Domestic cricket is only as good as the depth in squads, and the guys who, when they do enter first-class cricket, are ready to play.'

Hopes' career had taken time to bloom because his early days coincided with Queensland's strongest era of talent – the men who claimed the Shield for the first time in 1995 and carried on winning it. He saw the effects of theories overruling practical knowledge. 'I appreciate how Greg Chappell goes over and visits Boston Red Sox and Texas Longhorns and says, "We go through their training camps and see the way they treat their young players." But anyone who follows baseball knows that, yes, they get their young players to training camps, but then they send them off to play minor leagues for four years. It just staggers me they thought the way to fix things is to pick a bunch of twenty-year-olds and give them experience.'

At the time the Futures League was unveiled, Jason Gillespie was still persona non grata due to his dalliance with the Indian Cricket League. Unable to find cricket work in Australia, he had started pondering overseas pathways that later took him to Zimbabwe and then to a county championship win as coach of Yorkshire. From his Headingley perch he could see what the Futures League attempted, and what it unintentionally achieved. 'As a seventeen-year-old I played a second XI game against Queensland at Adelaide Oval,' he says. 'They had a couple of blokes coming back from a lay-off and their bowling attack was Andy Bichel, Michael Kasprowicz, Greg Rowell and Joe Dawes. Once Futures League came in, would you have that?

'Now I'm in coaching, part of me can understand the mindset, but they didn't get the balance right. You want to keep those more senior guys who perform in grade cricket. Because if the carrot of getting a couple of trips away is there, these thirty-year-old players who perform game in, game out on weekends are probably going to hang around for a couple of years, passing on knowledge. Some will never play first-class cricket, but playing a second XI game for SA or Queensland, that's their Test match.'

In time, the Futures League was rolled back. The playing conditions reverted to four-day matches and dispensed with limited overs for the 2011–12 season, while age restrictions were reduced to six over and six under the age of twenty-three, before being quietly rescinded altogether in 2013. When CA resumed the job of strengthening its talent stocks and maximising its opportunities in 2014 it did so with greater sophistication than it had in 2009, taking in club and school cricket plus the acknowledgement that even the most talented teenagers need to have their skills stretched by competition with older, wiser heads. Balance is the thing.

In Ponting's team, only a vague indication could be traced of the changes at state level causing the foundations of the national side to weaken as the West Indies fell 2–0 and Pakistan 3–0. Australia's batsmen continued to offer up regular collapses, as had happened in England, and the bowlers continued to wrestle with inconsistency. Ponting was struck a fearful blow above the elbow by the young West Indian paceman Kemar Roach in Perth and struggled with timing, fluency and confidence until he regathered with a double century in the dead rubber third Test against Pakistan in Hobart – but even then, he was dropped on 0.

Perhaps coincidentally, this was the only summer of the period in which Australia stuck with one spin bowler across Tests and ODIs for the whole season. That man was Hauritz, who atoned for the Oval by pushing through eight Test matches (33 wickets at 31.55) and thirty-three ODIs (34 wickets at 34.05) for more than adequate returns in a winning team. With the help of Shane Warne, who had agreed with CA to be on hand to advise any Australian spin bowler if he happened to be on commentary duty, Hauritz briefly regained Ponting's confidence and seemed ready for more.

'It was a happy summer after Boxing Day Test day five,' Hauritz says of his first five-wicket haul in Tests. 'There were still question marks on my spot, but I think coming out as a nightwatchman and getting runs and then having a good chat to Warnie the night before helped. It was nothing too tactical; it was just very simple, about putting the ball in the right area and not putting too much pressure on yourself. I remember getting Kamran Akmal stumped by a ball that bounced more, and Punter giving me a massive hug. That relieved the pressure from there, and after that we had the runs on the board; I put the ball in the right spots and got some good wickets. I definitely felt like getting the fifth wicket was a massive weight off my shoulders . . . for a while anyway. It was definitely nice to feel that way, instead of waking up each morning wondering whether you're going to play the next Test.'

Hauritz took another five wickets on the final day of the dramatic Sydney Test, which was Pakistan's for the winning until an unfathomable surrender when pursuing 176. Mohammad Yousuf's men were chasing that many only due to a stand of 123 by Peter Siddle and Michael Hussey, during which Pakistan's captain offered some bizarrely spread fields. Australia's players and a small SCG crowd were elated by events, but it was hard to escape the sense that just about any team other than Pakistan would have held their nerve. Sober analysis of how Australia's batsmen had been filleted on day one by Mohammad Asif and a well-grassed SCG pitch was drowned out by television and tabloid debate over Ponting's decision at the toss.

At the end of the Test, Ponting asked for a show of hands among the press corps from those who had doubted his decision to bat first. After all fourth-estate hands went up, Ponting smiled. 'I feel better now,' he said. 'It comes down to results and we've got a great result here. So I look like a genius where I didn't a couple of days ago.' Genius can be fleeting. By the end of the New Zealand series the following month, Ponting had enjoyed his last Test series win as captain.

10

A House Divided

MARCH – OCTOBER 2010

Australia in New Zealand

ICC World Twenty20 in the West Indies

Pakistan v. Australia in England

Australia in India

In April 2010, Australia's cricketers departed home shores for a major assignment under the captaincy of someone other than Ricky Ponting for the first time in more than seven years. The World T20 the following month, in the West Indies, was the subject of the team's most focused preparation for the truncated format yet, and the squad was being led by Michael Clarke, who had taken up the T20 captaincy the previous October. At the time of his retirement from international T20s, Ponting had discussed the identity of his successor with his selection chairman. As far as Andrew Hilditch was concerned, Clarke was the only choice.

By the time the fifteen-man squad flew out of Sydney for the Caribbean seven months later, Clarke had made one major change to his life and was looking at others. A trip home before the Wellington Test in March had brought a conclusive end to his high-profile, high-maintenance relationship with Lara Bingle, and within the year he had moved out of the Bondi apartment they had shared and returned to Sutherland Shire, near to his family. Both decisions indicated that Clarke was intent on repositioning himself to become the leader CA had expected him to be when the selectors and board endorsed his promotion to vice-captain in 2008.

Granted a first opportunity to lead the team on his terms, Clarke quickly demonstrated his strong opinions. They were illustrated by his fierce conviction that the team physio, Alex Kountouris, long a salve for Clarke's degenerative back trouble, had to go to the tournament as a key member of the support staff. Kountouris had been shaken badly by his potentially life-threatening case of deep vein thrombosis in Antigua on the 2008 West Indies tour and preferred not to make the journey. But Clarke was firm, and Kountouris ultimately did make the trip, reasoning that it was better to face up to his past trauma than to avoid it.

On the field, Clarke's alertness and intelligence were writ large across Australia's advance to the tournament final, even if his limitations as a T20 batsman were also clear. Aided by a Hail Mary of an innings by Michael Hussey in reeling in a steep target in the semifinal against Pakistan, Clarke's campaign remains the most successful by the team at a World T20 event. The young squad performed evenly and creditably, with Steve Smith's fledgling leg breaks particularly arresting. Clarke had previously expressed distaste for the off-field demands inherent in the captaincy – at the end of the T20 segment of the recent New Zealand tour he had remarked, 'Ricky can have this back.' By the time he returned home from the World T20, Clarke was looking and sounding less like a captain in waiting than a captain awaiting his moment.

One element of the tournament was unsatisfactory for Australia. It ended in a comprehensive loss to England in the final, meaning the team led by Paul Collingwood had secured that nation's first ICC trophy thirty-five years since the inaugural limited-overs World Cup. Two months later England won another encounter, this time a five-match ODI series shoehorned into the schedule ahead of Tests at Lord's and Headingley against the stateless Pakistan side.

The loss of successive meetings with England in an Ashes year boded ill for the series to be played down under in the summer, but no-one seemed to pay much attention. Preoccupied with other matters, including a stillborn attempt to usher former prime minister John Howard into the ICC presidency, CA also allowed ructions within the team to fester. The closer the Ashes crept, the further away unity and cohesion seemed to drift.

Australia's preparations for the 2010–11 Ashes were meant to be the most precise yet devised. Much was made of how all the players' schedules were finely tuned down to the last hour for the six months leading up to the first ball at the Gabba in November. Yet on a broader strategic level they could not have been much worse. The Champions League had caused enough problems for the national team's fitness and medical staff in 2009, and in October 2010 the commute of players from South Africa, venue for the next edition, to India for another ODI series promised to add further levels of complication. In addition to this, the home summer was going to have a disjointed beginning in which a limited-overs series against Sri Lanka was scheduled into early November, meaning Australia's players would play fewer first-class matches down under than the England tourists.

So when India proposed a more substantial tour for October, changing the ODI series to two Tests and three 50-over matches, it seemed natural for Australia to respectfully decline. Players customarily need a focused, ten-week preparation for lengthy Test assignments like the Ashes, so to chuck in an extra two Tests against India on distant shores seemed too extravagant a request. But Monkeygate had established the BCCI's intent to have their way in any event, as by this time had the board's opposition to the decision review system. News of the change was announced in late June, while the Australians were playing ODIs in England. Ponting was not overly perturbed, feeling the Tests would bolster the team's preparation more than another glut of ODIs.

But privately, CA's fitness staff were aghast, and Tim Nielsen wasn't much happier. He later cited the episode as evidence of his limited power. 'I was pretty dirty on that whole set-up because they changed the tour from being seven one-dayers to two Tests at late notice. Just as difficult to cop was playing three one-dayers against Sri Lanka [in Australia in November] when we wanted our players preparing for the Brisbane Test. Those are things that made the job as coach of the Australian team bloody difficult at times. My backside and our team's was on the line with our performances, so I debated it and fought as hard as I possibly could to get what we thought was right for the team, but once the decision was made we didn't complain about it.'

Adding to the team's anxiety about the Ashes was an uneven display against Pakistan, who at Leeds enjoyed the sort of victory they should have secured in Sydney. Ponting's men won confidently enough at Lord's but were razed for 88 on the first morning in Yorkshire, after Ponting had again forsaken swinging conditions to bat first. With the ball, Shane Watson showed his development as a swing and seam merchant, with striking figures in both matches, but none of the full-time pacemen had the ball singing, and the only other five-wicket haul was claimed by Marcus North at Lord's.

Following his return home, Simon Katich offered a blunt critique of the team's penchant for spontaneously combusting with the bat. 'Being brutally honest it's still been a problem, because it's happened a couple of times since the Ashes last year. Until we can actually rectify that in a match that's going to be still hanging over our heads, and unfortunately you can't replicate it in the nets. It's got to happen in Test matches when the pressure is on and there's big crowds there, which is no doubt going to happen during the Ashes.' No more prophetic words were spoken by an Australian cricketer that year.

For the first half of 2010, CA's board directors had thought they had secured the ascent of John Howard to the position of ICC president.

A protocol for the rotation of the most senior position in cricket governance had been created by Malcolm Speed when he was ICC chief executive in 2007, which called for the pairing of the ten Full Member nations into groups of two, with each to nominate one presidential candidate between them in coming years. The system had begun when the BCCI expressed its wish to have an Indian president at the time of the 2011 World Cup on the subcontinent. Australia and New Zealand were the next two countries set to choose the man to take over from Pawar in 2012.

Problems with the choice of Howard began even before reaching the ICC boardroom. Jack Clarke, the CA chairman, was unable to persuade enough members of his own board to support him as Australia's candidate. New Zealand had put up Sir John Anderson as a logical candidate of much ICC experience. Determined not to let New Zealand carry the field, Clarke's deputy Wally Edwards ran the idea past Howard on a trip to England. He was enthusiastic, and a joint subcommittee of the two boards was convened to determine who would take the nomination. Howard prevailed, and in March 2010 he was announced as the nominee. A joint statement issued by the two boards appeared to assume Howard was over the line: he had told Edwards he would only be nominating if assured the role.

Around this time, CA made a pair of international decisions that appeared motivated by a desire to smooth any potential opposition to Howard's role. The BCCI's request to change the October series from ODIs to Tests, in deference to India's newly gained status as the number one–ranked Test nation was accepted over the aforementioned objections of the team. And cricket contact with Zimbabwe, in the form of reciprocal 'A' tours with the promise of full internationals to follow, was also resumed, after the visit of the nation's sport minister David Coltart to Australia. Howard and Clarke even visited Zimbabwe in the hope of changing perceptions after the former's staunch opposition to Robert Mugabe while prime minister. A point of critical mass appeared to have been reached when President Pawar said he was supportive of Howard's nomination.

But Clarke miscalculated. Pawar's view was divergent from that of the BCCI's president Shashank Manohar and secretary N Srinivasan. They were sceptical about inviting an 'outsider' into the ICC board-room in a position of such influence, and so resolved to withhold any backing. Even after Howard's visit, Zimbabwe's board representatives remained opposed, and with West Indies, South Africa, Bangladesh, Sri Lanka and Pakistan also falling into a state of opposition, only England, New Zealand and Australia were left arguing his case at the ICC annual conference in Singapore on 1 July. Like Kevin Rudd's ousting as prime minister only days before, Howard's removal from the halls of cricket governance did not even need to come to a vote. 'I don't think embarrassed is strong enough a term,' fumed Clarke.

Snubbed by the nominations committee, Anderson declined to be a reheated meal for the ICC, leaving the NZ Cricket chairman Alan Isaac to take up the role. Speed made one concluding observa-tion about the affair in *Sticky Wicket* that was less about Howard than it was about Clarke. 'I suspect it would not have happened if [former CA chairmen] Malcolm Gray, Denis Rogers, Bob Merriman had been representing Australia or [former NZC president] Sir John Anderson representing New Zealand, but there is no point living in the past.' Arguably the only man to gain anything out of the affair was Clarke's deputy Edwards, who resolved to lobby more subtly when his time as CA chairman rolled around in eighteen months' time.

Justin Langer had walked out of the Somerset dressing room at the end of 2009 and straight back into Australia's. His decision to sign up as a batting coach and team mentor was in response to a request from Ponting and Nielsen that he consider the value he might offer to young players who related to his intense and uncertain younger self. Nielsen was particularly eager to bolster his support staff, having twice sounded out his former South Australian teammate Darren Lehmann about joining in. Lehmann, by that time coach of the Deccan Chargers in the IPL, had demurred. Langer accepted, even if CA could spare only a modest salary.

'There was definitely emotional attachment there,' Langer says. 'Ricky and Tim spoke to me in the change room at Lord's in 2009 when I was still playing. They initiated the conversation with "Why don't you come and do some coaching with us?" The day I retired they both rang me . . . Tim Nielsen I could almost feel was looking for that support, having their boys around them who they knew were going to be loyal.'

Trust, frankness and loyalty were all taking time to foster, and the recruitment of Langer was but one attempt to encourage the process. Less successful was a return to corporate leadership programs, an idea hatched in the months before the India tour.

A science, medicine and coaching conference at the Centre of Excellence in June had been addressed by Martin West, a former pilot with the Royal Australian Air Force and an advocate of regular team meetings aimed at closing what he called the 'execution gap'. West's company was called Afterburner, and he based his ideas upon the concept of debriefs following an airborne mission. The fine margins of aerial combat, in which a small mistake could result in a violent death, called for total clarity over what the pilot's plan would be. If anything went slightly wrong, they were duty bound to be very clear about this at the brief and debrief, which took place either side of every flight.

The concept was introduced to the Australian cricket team at their pre-season training camp in Coolum, Queensland, before West was flown into Chandigarh, home to one of India's largest air-force bases, where, ahead of the first tour match, he took the team through his ideas. West had successfully adapted the concept of 'no recrimination' debriefs to the corporate world, and Ponting and Nielsen felt it could be used to encourage more open conversation among the players. Such 'cricket chats' had once happened naturally but by that point had almost ceased to exist. The first attempt to run a post-play session occurred after day one of the match against a BCCI Board President's XI at Chandigarh's Sector 16 Stadium, which ended with the tourists on a serene 1–319.

Each debrief was to be run by a different member of the team, with Ponting taking the first session. Some members of the team and support staff were lukewarm about the concept, worrying that it would waste time better spent in a less structured fashion. No day of cricket is the same; some encourage a mood for discussion, others quite the opposite. Some players preferred to be concentrating on their physical recovery or simply getting back to the team hotel and felt the idea too inflexible. But all agreed to give it a try . . . with one exception.

'It was all about at the end of a day's play like at the end of a mission, have a 360-degree feedback thing where we talk about what we did well, what we didn't do well, what we can improve on,' Ponting says. 'Michael [Clarke]'s attitude towards it the whole time was he didn't think he needed anybody else to tell him if he was going well or not. But he was vice-captain at the time, so to make it work we needed him to be 100 per cent committed. We told him that, asked him to be a part of it and as involved as anybody else.

'So we were sitting down; I took over to run the first one, being the captain, let everyone else have their input, and then I'd move it on through the guys and let everyone have a chance at running a debrief. I started off, and Pup was over in another part of the room packing his bag up and doing something, getting out of the shower, and just didn't want to be involved in it at all.'

For his part, Clarke felt the team too much in thrall to Ponting and Nielsen for the debriefs to function truthfully and fruitfully, and said as much to West from the outset. Though Clarke had tried to express his opposition privately in leadership meetings, he felt compelled to spell it out in front of the team when the issue was forced. Ponting admits the debriefs argument spoke of a more general disconnection between captain and deputy. 'Once he was named vice-captain,'

Ponting says, 'everything I tried to do with him was trying to shape him and help him get a bigger picture of what a leadership role should be. Other people were seeing it as well, that he wasn't as involved as he should be.'

After the first day of the first Test in Mohali, in which Australia ground their way to 5–224, Clarke did involve himself in the debrief session, offering the view that they had batted too slowly. Unbeaten on 101, the only time he had batted through a full Test match day, Shane Watson took this as a slight on his progress. Says Ponting, 'Watto batted all day for 100 and Michael got 14, but he was the one who came out that night and said to Watto, "Mate, we could have scored a lot quicker today." That's where we wanted to go with the debrief stuff: if there's ways we were to get better that stuff had to come out. But it was more that everyone else felt Watto played really well on the day – in India your scoring rates are generally a bit lower. It was almost a throwaway line – he said it and sort of turned away – and everyone's like, "What?"'

Watson stewed over the comment until Australia's second innings, when he batted in a fury that appeared to be directed at Clarke. Lest any room be left for doubt, Watson sent a message to Clarke via the 12th man, Steve Smith: 'This fast enough for you?' The comment did little to enhance the mood in the team's viewing area. After Watson was dismissed for 56, the tourists slid from 0–87 to 192 all out. Clarke was out twice in two balls, flicking Ishant Sharma to midwicket off a no ball then flinching at a bouncer and gloving behind. That night, Watson visited Clarke's hotel room and the pair engaged in animated debate. They eventually called an uneasy truce.

The debriefs themselves ultimately came to be regarded as clumsy and were stopped after the first Ashes Test in Brisbane. This revealed more about the way the team had chosen to use Martin West's advice than about the concept itself, as Clarke showed later, by utilising West once he became captain. Hussey sums up the mixture of thoughts that had bubbled around the idea. 'There were times when you'd been in the field a long day and you just wanted to do recovery and get back to the hotel, but no, we had to sit down and have this meeting. A positive out of it was it gave an opportunity to hear from everyone. Generally speaking the coach spoke, the captain spoke and a senior player or two would speak, whereas now we were getting input from even the newest players in the team – I remember Peter George piping up after one day in his first Test. There were certain times when I couldn't be bothered doing it, but this is what you've got to do in a team sometimes. We didn't get out of it what some people thought we could have, but at least we tried.'

Whatever the merits of the idea, the abiding memory for most involved with the team was that in the months before the Ashes series, Australia's captain and vice-captain were at odds with one another about how to take the team forward.

Michael Hussey was furious. A morning meeting with Michael Brown over his availability for the preparatory phase of the India tour had degenerated into a shouting match over breakfast in Johannesburg's Sandton Sun Hotel. Hussey was adamant that he and Doug Bollinger were contractually bound to join Australia for the start of the Test tour, while Brown was equally convinced that they would stay in South Africa until the Champions League T20 had run its course. Hussey and Bollinger were playing for Chennai Super Kings, the team owned by the BCCI secretary and soon-to-be president, N Srinivasan.

'You've got to get me out of the Champions League,' Hussey insisted.

'I can't,' Brown replied. 'Your Australian duty under your contract is to be here for this.'

'But I don't want to play in the Champions League. I want to prepare for a Test match.'

'This is a new tournament; we own part of it; we want to support it. You're staying.'

In India, Australia's players were mystified as to why Hussey and Bollinger had not yet joined them, and some disquiet had emerged about their priorities. Ponting and Nielsen tried to calm the situation by telling the players of Hussey's frustration with CA but were blind-sided by Clarke, who said publicly that players had to manage their own priorities. 'You don't have to play IPL; you don't have to play Champions League,' Clarke said in Chandigarh ahead of the first Test. 'For me, personally, right now it is about representing my country, and every game I can play for Australia, I will do that . . . If, as an individual player, you are tired or your body needs some rest, you need to make that commitment outside of international cricket. You need to, maybe, play less in the IPL or play less in the Champions League.'

In isolation, Clarke's words seemed sensible enough. But they did little to endear him to other players who were now earning a major share of their income in the IPL and Champions League T20. Certainly, Hussey was annoyed, and he insisted James Sutherland put out a statement clarifying that the players were remaining with Chennai against their preference. Sutherland's words suggested there was now very little difference in how CA regarded T20 and Test matches. 'Michael Hussey made it clear to CA before and during the CLT20 that his strong preference and preferred intention was to leave earlier than the final to prepare for the Test series in India and it was only because of our requirement and the performance of his franchise that he stayed until the end of the CLT20 final. Michael had nothing but the best intentions of preparing for and playing for his country as his absolute priority, but there was a fine balance between a high-profile, elite club T20 competition and preparing for international cricket.'

When the pair finally arrived at the Taj Hotel in Chandigarh, only two days remained before the Test began. For Hussey, the issue was one of rhythm, both in the change from South African to subcontinental pitches and in the switch in formats. Bollinger's problems were more to do with conditioning. Well as he had bowled the previous summer, he was known for struggling to keep up the required fitness base. In South Africa he had been given a training program in addition to his T20 workload but had struggled to fulfil it. Watching Chennai's victory in the Champions League final, the Australian team's strength and conditioning coach, Stuart Karppinen, had been concerned to see that at high-veldt altitude, in a high-adrenaline atmosphere and required to bowl only four overs, Bollinger's pace never crested 135 kilometres per hour.

On his arrival in Chandigarh, Bollinger looked unready for the task. Karppinen told Ponting and Nielsen that he expected the bowler would be injured – a hamstring or side strain – in the match, essentially because he would try to overcompensate for his lack of fitness. But with a squad heavy on youth and lacking the injured Peter Siddle, among others, Ponting, Nielsen and Andrew Hilditch wanted Bollinger to play ahead of the reserve pacemen, Peter George and James Pattinson. On two days of preparation and still jet-lagged, he was chosen alongside Hussey.

The foot-arch strain that Nathan Hauritz had worried over in 2009 had finally given way after the New Zealand tour early in 2010, forcing surgery that ruled him out of the Tests against Pakistan in July. Ponting had been supportive, stating in August that Hauritz was a 'lock-in' for the Ashes: 'What he's done over the last twelve or eighteen months as our number-one spinner has been of the highest quality.'

In 2001, Shane Warne went to India soon after recovering from a broken finger and struggled in one of the poorest series of his career. By the end of the third Test, Steve Waugh had preferred to use Colin Miller's finger spin when the match was at its tightest. All knew the perils of playing in India soon after completing rehabilitation. 'I had a stress fracture in the top of my foot that came from the plantar fascia,' Hauritz says. 'I pretty much did nothing for about nine weeks.

I went to India having just been bowling a bit in the nets and that was it.' Nevertheless, he was confident enough of bowling well in the India Tests. He had the added benefit of the Centre of Excellence's spin coach, John Davison, making the trip to provide some brotherly spin-bowling counsel. His trusted method of relying on drift, drop and natural variation off the pitch was honed ahead of the Test.

But as the match unfolded, Hauritz was spun off his axis. Ponting had long felt that the most challenging off spinners in the game – Harbhajan Singh and Muttiah Muralitharan – delivered the ball from wide of the crease, angling it towards the bat before spinning it in even further. He had suggested that Hauritz try to bowl from that kind of angle. Not wanting to fail his captain again, the memories of 2009 still nestled somewhere in his subconscious, Hauritz tried his best. The result was an addled bowling rhythm and a damaging lack of consistency. Unable to land the ball as Ponting wished, Hauritz was duly ignored by the captain on the final day, when the match edged to its desperately tight conclusion (Australia lost by a solitary wicket). This proved a major blow to Hauritz's confidence and ultimately the catalyst for his omission from the Ashes.

Trying to adjust his method had 'stuffed me around a little bit with my body and my rhythm,' Hauritz said between Tests. 'I don't think I'll be fiddling around too much in the second Test with that sort of thing. I was really happy with the way the ball came out in the first innings; there were periods when it didn't work, but the majority of it was really good. I guess that's what was so disappointing in the second innings, and I think that came about because I was trying different things which, in hindsight, I should never have tried.' Despite that realisation, Hauritz fared little better in the second Test. 'I spoke to Davo just before going out on the last day of the last Test in Bangalore,' he says. 'He just said, "Do what you feel is right." At that stage I was nowhere. Couldn't bowl, had no confidence in my ability to land it, and even when I did land it the Indian batsmen were just attacking me and all over me.'

In the first Test, Bollinger broke down with the side strain that Karppinen had predicted. Following this, Ponting, disappointed in Hauritz's bowling and still irritated by Clarke's intransigence over the debriefs, did not grant his vice-captain's repeated requests for a bowl at Ishant Sharma in the closing overs. With six runs required, Mitchell Johnson had a very adjacent l.b.w. appeal turned down, and then Steve Smith, as substitute fielder, missed a chance to throw down the stumps. Hauritz, lost in thought at forward square leg, did not get around and back up, gifting India four overthrows.

Publicly, the result was attributed largely to the genius of V V S Laxman, in the last of his many matchwinning turns against Australia. It is interesting to ponder what restorative effect winning that match might have had; given the battles being fought with CA and in the dressing room among the players, it seems remarkable they got that close. In Bangalore, Ponting's men put in another doughty effort but faded at the finish and were beaten comfortably amid Twittersphere criticism by Shane Warne of the tactics used by the rattled Hauritz – something Warne laid at Ponting's feet.

Soon after the Australians returned home, Jamie Pandaram wrote in the *Sydney Morning Herald* about divisions within the team and hesitance over Clarke's potential leadership. Pandaram also suggested that Marcus North might emerge as an alternative candidate, a red herring that allowed Clarke and CA to refute the story. But the following passage, at least, was correct: 'Michael Clarke's popularity within the side continues to wane following a bitter tour of India. The team is not divided to the point of implosion, but a number of senior players remain firmly opposed to the idea that Clarke will succeed Ricky Ponting. Clarke has been able to harness great support among younger members of the team, who realise their backing would be rewarded should Clarke gain the captaincy full-time.'

Quite apart from the fraught state of affairs within the team room, Australia's results were trending downward at exactly the wrong time. The defeats at Headingley, Mohali and Bangalore marked the first time the team had lost three Tests in a row since 1988. Ponting, Hussey and Clarke had each failed to make a century since January. In Clarke's case, a move from number five to number four, ostensibly designed to give the vice-captain more responsibility for building big innings, had seen his run-making dive sharply.

England, meanwhile, bore little trace of their opponents' maladies, either on or off the field.

I I

Turkeys at Christmas

AUGUST 2010

Australian cricket has always held a few truths to be self-evident. Batsmanship is about not merely survival but also scoring, bowling attacks are best assembled as a combination of speed and wrist spin, and the game itself is a pastime to be enjoyed, not a profession to be endured in the fashion of those dullard Poms. For more than a century there were two other tenets in the Australian game, less widely known but equally fundamental: New South Wales, Victoria and South Australia had three votes apiece at the CA board table, Western Australia and Queensland two, and Tasmania one. Board members met as representatives of their states, running the governing body as a members' organisation along lines drawn up in 1905.

That all changed in the space of a few hours at Victoria's Aitken Hill conference centre in August 2010, when the board were confronted with the fact that a handful of their directors were the only people left clinging to the old ideal. A day later, they resolved to change in ways that had been resisted for almost as long as the game had been played in Australia. Cricket would now be governed in the national interest, not administered at the pleasure of the six states. Money would be distributed on a basis of need, not dished out in six equal portions offset by gate receipts to the bigger centres.

Many attempts had been made to shift CA's governance and finance customs over the years, most pointedly in 2002 when the chief executive James Sutherland and general manager of finance Kate Banozic requested a KPMG analysis of the financial model. CA's burgeoning central management departments had begun to cross over with many of the states' traditional functions, particularly game development, and the KPMG recommendations included that of a more centralised method for distributing revenue.

But the suggestion drew concerted opposition from several states, most notably SA and WA through the trenchant views of the directors Wally Edwards and Jack Clarke. As Australia's second-smallest cricket state but most influential through its three votes, the SACA stood to lose most by change. As Sutherland said in *Inside Story*: 'Everyone knows that the distribution model is not perfect, but they say to themselves: "What would we be getting into if we decided to look at it? I'm not sure I want to go there."' There was indignant talk of CA management trying to take over the game by stealth.

As the years went by, others stressed the need for CA to adopt a more forward-thinking system, notably through successive versions of the governing body's strategic plan, titled 'From Backyard to Baggy Green' for most of the 2000s. NSW and Victoria were conscious of the fact that the equal-distribution model for revenue was leaving them further out of pocket each year, as the money attainable from gate receipts had diminished significantly in relation to the television-rights dividends sliced six ways.

Queensland complained of an inability to fund their efforts to develop the game in the nation's most diffusely populated state. 'Tassie ending up with the same distribution as Queensland with about 20 000 participants over a small area, and Queensland five times that over a massive area,' says one board member. 'You could link Tasmania's recent Sheffield Shield success to being the best-resourced state because of those distributions.' It was also felt that board directors who represented their states spent far too much time haggling over money while ignoring strategic issues. Asked to describe the conduct of many board meetings, officials and board members alike acknowledged the phrase 'seagulls arguing over a chip'.

Andrew Jones, who joined CA as its first head of strategy in mid-2010, was a particularly strong advocate of change, and upon his arrival was commissioned to set out a plan for the first Australian Cricket Conference. Damien De Bohun, the head of game development, had dreamed up the idea of bringing all management and board figures together for a week of focused departmental meetings but also wider discussions of the future. In all, more than 180 delegates would attend.

As their starting point, Jones and his offsider Sachin Kumar surveyed invitees on what they viewed as Australian cricket's major issues. They then assembled a discussion paper dealing with ills such as the game's 24 per cent shrink in television audiences over the preceding decade, the imperfections of a revenue model hugely reliant on the visits of India, a drop-off in the interest and participation of children once they reached teenage years, and the age-old problem of low female interest in the game. They set aside two days for functional meetings, followed by a day discussing cricket's aspirations for fans and children. As a consequence of this day, plans for the city-based T20 Big Bash League were to be brought forward by a year, while the running of the junior programs In2Cricket and T20 Blast were nationalised. CA's head of marketing, Mike McKenna, was central to these decisions.

More problematic was the shared conviction of Jones, De Bohun and other CA management figures including Dean Kino, the head of business and legal affairs, that the issue of governance needed to be boldly tackled. While plenty of corporate and sporting examples could be found to show the benefits of change, speaking that truth to the power of the board was going to be a risk. Jones met Sutherland to discuss the agenda, and after running through the items, they paused at governance.

'I think it should be fixed, a lot of other people think it should be fixed, but you're a CEO questioning the board in a public forum – do you want to do that?' Jones asked.

Sutherland could have been forgiven for seeing his job flash past his eyes, but replied bravely in the affirmative. 'Yes, let's do it. If it's an issue, it's an issue.'

At 8 a.m. on 12 August, a panel of CA and state management assembled at the front of Aitken Hill's main hall and tackled the question: how well does Australian cricket work now? Among their number were the NSW commercial operations manager – now WA chief executive – Christina Matthews, Kino and Jones. All the aforementioned issues were discussed, with the board's drawbacks dissected. This was not met with a universally happy response. Clarke, who was by now the chairman, retorted, 'I actually think we've done pretty well.' His fellow SA board member, the former Labor premier John Bannon, was equally staunch in his defence of the status quo, as might be expected of a political historian who wrote the book *Supreme Federalist* on the political life of Sir John Downer. Bannon was adamant that neither the board nor the state associations should be dictated to by management on matters of strategy.

The third member of the SA triumvirate, Ian McLachlan, was to be a key figure in later negotiations. For some years, McLachlan had been adroit at working the numbers in the boardroom – understandable skills given his standing as one of the elders of Australian conservative politics. His eloquent argument that a model of more independent governance would turn the game into an east-coast affair was respected but superseded. 'It was the public embarrassment of the board and the chairman,' says one member of the audience. 'They were confronted by the angry mob for the first time saying exactly what they thought, out of their ivory tower and amongst the people. They didn't all enjoy it, but there was a very strong appetite for change.'

Once the panel had completed its work, the room was broken up into smaller groups for a series of hackneyed but nonetheless effective management camp exercises. One asked delegates to 'rate Australian cricket out of ten versus its potential' and to write down their number on a Post-it note and stick it on the wall. A forest of fives and sixes told a mediocre story. Another instructed them to 'choose three words to describe Australian cricket' and 'three words that describe how you'd like Australian cricket to be'. Column A filled with words like conservative, slow-moving, old, male, traditional and staid, while column B expressed desire for something dynamic, aggressive, innovative and energetic.

Having stretched the horizons of those in attendance, the final push for change was delivered by Colin Carter, the architect of the Victorian Football League's evolution into the Australian Football League and its attendant draft and salary-cap measures. Some years before, Carter had altered the sectarian ways of the CA board table by advocating simply that state representatives should mingle rather than sit in spots according to their association. The tweak of group dynamics soon had directors thinking a little less about their state and a little more about the broader game. This time, his address sought less to hit the directors over the head than to illustrate how growing sports were now organised. Says Jones, 'All those problems he mentioned, it was like *Wheel of Fortune – bing, bing, bing –* they were our issues, and how to address them.' Carter finished at 11 a.m. Now the board game could start.

Carter's words were still fresh in the minds of directors when the following day's board meeting rolled around. Most critical was Clarke's change of heart, concluding as chairman that the old system could not hold. Governance reform had not been on the agenda for that meeting, yet by mid-afternoon he was able to announce a review tackling that exact subject, to be conducted by Carter and his fellow corporate reformer David Crawford. Intriguingly, Carter and Crawford offered their services in a most unusual deal. They would not be paid for the review, in exchange for CA acting on their recommendations. It was a commitment not all were comfortable with, and in the lengthy haggling that followed the delivery of the review in 2011 there were times when the process might have collapsed.

Through the leadership of Geoff Tamblyn, Victoria was the first of
the 'three vote' states to accept the idea, followed by New South Wales.
Kino and Edwards, who as Clarke's successor would usher in the new
board structure in 2012, played critical roles in negotiations. Edwards
advocated a moderate path that contrasted with the hawkish defence
of his state a decade before, while Kino prepared the nifty manoeu-
vre that allowed SA's opposition to be circumvented. According to
Australian company law, the constitutional changes required 75 per
cent approval among all classes of shareholders, and noes from three
of SA's fourteen directors was enough to block reform. To sidestep
this, each state was temporarily upgraded to three votes each, a tweak
that could be achieved by a simple majority of the six states. Once
that was done, the views of McLachlan and Bannon became irrele-
vant, though the SACA threatened legal action until the last possible
moment.

Ultimately the will for change evident at Aitken Hill was strong
enough to allow a new model to be agreed upon, with one other con-
cession to the federalists. Nutted out by Edwards and McLachlan
over a drink at the Hilton on the Park the night before the vote was
the assurance that on the new nine-person board, at least one director would be based in each of the six states. But all would eventually
be appointed by an independent panel, allowing the board to be constructed along the lines of complementary skills and a unified vision,
rather than the disparate interests of six competing bodies. Key to the
states' acquiescence was a guarantee that none would receive less than
its last revenue distribution under the old 'six-ways' model.

Mark Taylor, a member of both versions of the board, describes
the difference. 'It's much more nimble,' he says. 'There are things now
discussed that weren't before. There's so much more time for strategy
now, and so much more of it to me is a learning curve than it was. It
used to be just the finances, how's each state going, how can we make
a deal so everyone gets a bit of a share and keep the business ticking
over. Now we spend a lot more time talking about things like risk

assessment. Those were things we never talked about, that was left to management as "You better go and do that."'

At the end of the review and reform journey, Jones and Kumar indulged in an experience as old as the board itself – a trip to Adelaide for the Test match. Due to his role in setting up the conference agenda and upsetting a few board members along the way, Jones had deferred to Edwards, Sutherland and Kino for the negotiating phase. But here at the end of it all, he raised a glass of wine with McLachlan, the patrician embodiment of SA's former influence. 'I said to him, "I really enjoyed the battles," and he was very good about it,' Jones says. 'We had as difficult a relationship as any pair in the process, and he's still a feisty fighter for what he believes in. But it's fair to say now the general consensus is the board's a lot better, and people are a bit like the question of Ian Healy getting a farewell Test at the Gabba against Pakistan in 1999. Everyone thought he deserved it until they picked Adam Gilchrist and he made 81 on debut then 149 to win the Test in Hobart. All of a sudden everyone's saying, "I can't believe Healy was there for that long."'

12

Ninety-eight
All Out and
All That

NOVEMBER 2010 – JANUARY 2011

England in Australia

England arrived in Australia on 31 October and eased into a schedule of training and tour matches that loosened up the squad for the Ashes series ahead. Andrew Strauss and Andy Flower had settled their first XI but had brought a deep and varied battery of fast men. Chris Tremlett offered bounce and movement in the vein of Stuart Broad, Tim Bresnan had swing and accuracy, and Ajmal Shahzad's skiddy trajectory was deemed ideal for a deteriorating wicket in Adelaide if required. Notably, the fast-bowling coach, David Saker, planned to take Broad, James Anderson and Steve Finn to Brisbane after the team's first two tour fixtures, preparing them specifically for the tropical first Test while their back-ups played Australia A at a crisper Bellerive Oval, in Tasmania.

Strauss cajoled his team into thinking of the warm-up fixtures as their own mini-series, matches to be won rather than centre-wicket net sessions to be flaunted. A victory against Western Australia, a draw against South Australia and an innings defeat of Australia A meant the tourists had secured a 2–0 'win' before reaching the Gabba, emboldening the team's senior pro Paul Collingwood to announce after the Hobart match, 'Lads, we have just thumped Australia's best young players by an innings. We are 100 per cent ready.'

In those early weeks of the tour, Strauss noticed that the standard of the players and the competition his team was encountering bore very little resemblance to those of the 2006–07 tour. Whereas once the visitors had expected a serious fight no matter where they played, now they were surprised to feel unthreatened. What's more, Strauss intuited that the Australian public knew it. 'What had also struck us all by then was just how negative the Australian public were being about their team's chances,' Strauss wrote in *Driving Ambition*. 'The Aussies did not rate their cricket team as they once did.'

In the movie *JFK*, Donald Sutherland's Mr X suggests how an assassination conspiracy may have started at the highest levels of the United States military. 'No-one's guilty, because everyone in the power structure who knows anything has a plausible deniability.' CA's explanations for the announcement of the seventeen-man Ashes squad at Sydney's Circular Quay in November 2010 seemed to be based on a similar outlook. While the event took place, no-one is prepared to admit signing off on it.

The facts are these. CA's marketing department wanted to hold a major announcement to declare the start of the Ashes series. The concept was born of a 'let's get cricket out there' spirit and was approved by cricket operations. Marketing then delivered its ideas to public affairs, which had to carry them out. By the time the plans were passed along to the national selectors and in turn to Ricky Ponting and Tim Nielsen, they had gathered too much momentum to be stopped. Suddenly, issues like Michael Clarke's fitness – he had pulled up with a back problem in the Sheffield Shield after his return from

India – and growing doubts about Nathan Hauritz were competing with a hard deadline for a televised squad announcement.

The squad in 2006 had been named during the final round of matches ahead of the Ashes, but in 2010 it was due to be unveiled three days earlier than that. The selectors, given a jolt in their thinking by Greg Chappell's replacement of Merv Hughes on the selection panel, wanted to delay naming the squad until after a Sheffield Shield round and an Australia A match against an England team in Hobart. Usually mild-mannered in his dealings with CA's other departments, Andrew Hilditch argued forcefully for the delay. Nielsen also protested, reckoning that 'it almost cut down our opportunity to pick someone else if they came flying out of the blocks; we were stuck in that squad come what may.' Jamie Cox remembers: 'There was enormous frustration. It took hours going through the various scenarios. Digger [Hilditch] tried very hard to change it, but it was what it was. I think we thought at the time, if not explicitly, that it was the beginning of the end for us. We knew how it was going to look externally and that's why we fought to have it changed. What it basically did was give an uncertain group of players a reason to be concerned. You can argue a group of professional sportsmen should have coped, but we were well aware at the time this was not going to have a good impact on our group.'

After an unseasonably wet start to summer and a creeping preponderance of grassy, result-driven wickets in the Shield, the announcement added to a sense of anxiety among the players. On the day, rain forced Hilditch and the players present to huddle under umbrellas. The chairman intoned, 'We haven't picked this squad for the whole series; it's just for this Test.' Incredulous facial expressions said more than any of the rote quotes trotted out for Channel Nine and a press pack that came close to outnumbering the forty or so onlookers who had braved the showers. Most poignant of all was the sight of Hauritz looking uncertainly towards the skies. Included in the seventeen, he was nevertheless omitted from the first Test, at the Gabba, and never played another Test. Instead, Xavier Doherty, Michael Beer and Steve Smith made Hauritz's efforts look supreme. Shane Warne called the decision to drop Hauritz 'dumb' and Cox conceded it was 'over-thought'.

Though it was Hilditch who faced most of the criticism for the event, English batsman-turned-journalist-and-commentator Mike Atherton pointed rightly to the dominant hand of marketing in Australia's squad announcement. Writing in *The Times*, he linked the timing of the squad announcement to Michael Hussey's earlier battle with CA over the Champions League: 'There was plenty to be gleaned from this nonsense, but it was not that Australia's selectors are clueless, or indeed that they have no idea what is their best team, rather that Cricket Australia has begun to get its priorities mangled. It used to be cricket before money; now it is the other way round, as Mike Hussey found out when he wanted to jump ship from the Champions League to join his Australia teammates for Test preparation in India, but was told to stay put.'

If any solace at all could be taken from the episode, it was that the day's sodden experience at Circular Quay was unlikely ever to happen again. 'Generally, what they do with those sorts of things is they'll plan it all before they tell you, because they don't want you to knock it on the head,' Ponting says ruefully. 'It goes too far and it's to the point where you can't change it before they let you know about it. And that's what happened with that one. I think there's been some lessons learned about naming extended squads instead of getting on the front foot about who you know is your best, and even if you're not convinced at least make it look like you are, so players feel settled. As it turned out the day itself was raining and no-one turned up. So that was bad. The Poms would have been laughing their heads off.'

English laughter would only have grown had all mooted plans been carried out. Among the ideas discussed in the CA marketing department was a gradual elimination of squad members following the initial announcement, with the seventeen being culled, one by one, to twelve by the day the squad convened in Brisbane. Mercifully, this brainstorm did not reach the selectors.

Assembling in Brisbane, the players should have felt a comforting sense of the familiar. They began with a miniature training camp at Allan Border Field before moving to the Gabba two days out from the Test. Yet there were numerous signs of unease. Batsmen and bowlers alike questioned elements of their preparation with coaching staff, while the presence of Chappell as selector on duty, quasi-coach and mentor-advisor for Nielsen left several players looking over their shoulders.

Chappell had interacted oddly with Hussey before Western Australia's Shield fixture against Victoria at the MCG before the Gabba squad was finalised. 'Greg came up to me and said, "You've got the place at the moment. We back you . . . But can you please just score some bloody runs?" So it was, "Okay, are you really backing me here?"' Hussey says. 'The uncertainty I had around that time was I knew Greg's philosophy and he was very open that he wanted to pick young players and find the next Ricky Ponting or the next Michael Clarke. Being an older player, it made me very nervous.' As Clarke wrestled with his back, Chappell made it known his preferred replacement would be Steve Smith, who had made his Test debut earlier that year batting at number eight in the two Tests against Pakistan.

What also became apparent was the blurring of lines between Chappell's role as selector and national talent manager and his job as head coach at the Centre of Excellence – Troy Cooley was slated to take the second role after guiding the bowlers through the season. Chappell had worked successfully with Shane Watson, among others, as a batting technician and theorist, but now he was a selector the players were uneasy about conveying to him their technical and mental worries or blind spots. Chappell made the suggestion that Ponting should consider moving down to number four in the batting order.

A sensible enough thought in isolation, it was an unsettling proposal to make a few days before the start of an Ashes series.

Among Chappell's better moves while at the Centre of Excellence had been to involve the former Test paceman Craig McDermott as a scholarship coach. Following a brush with infamy and a car-park get-away on Channel Nine's *A Current Affair* due to the collapse of his property business, McDermott had sought to reconnect with cricket and quickly shown himself to be an effective deliverer of simple advice to young pacemen. He worked briefly with the Ashes squad ahead of the first Test and by encouraging Peter Siddle to try a fuller length aided the Victorian's short-term progress in his first Test match since the preceding January.

However, not every instruction was taken to kindly by Australia's pacemen. Cooley asked his pupils to submit to some pitch map analysis in which they would either nominate or be asked to bowl on a certain line or length. This would seem a simple enough task for Test match bowlers in the week before an Ashes series, but several fast men were seen to react reluctantly and even angrily to the suggestion, wondering why their ability was being measured at a time when they were trying to find rhythm for the matches ahead. More than one member of the coaching staff was heard to observe, 'If you can't handle the pressure now, how are you going to go when the game's on?'

The support on offer to the players that week was not getting through as it once might have done. A fog of unease seemed to have settled on the squad, and any new ideas were construed as criticism rather than help. One former coach says of these sessions, 'I know what the plans were and I know Troy kept ramming it down their throats. It wasn't like the plans were bad, but it's the ability to communicate with influence that's important. Warning bells were probably going off at the time about that.' Cooley had been with the team for four years, strength and conditioning coach Stuart Karppinen three and Justin Langer two, while Nielsen's involvement with the team, either as assistant coach, Centre of Excellence chief or senior coach, was nearing a decade.

Another warning sounded in a conversation between Michael Hussey and Marcus North. Barely a week before the Brisbane training camp, North had been mentioned in the press as a candidate for the next captaincy. In his most recent Test match, he had sculpted a fine first-innings hundred against India. But his nerves were palpable: so much so that even the naturally edgy Hussey was taken aback. 'Coming into the start of the series when I was seriously under the pump he said to me, "I just hope they give me at least the first two Tests. If I don't get runs then they can drop me." I thought, "Are you serious? You got a magnificent hundred literally one Test match ago."

'Marcus liked to read everything, liked to know exactly what was being said about him. And because he never got a hundred on Australian soil there were always doubts with the public and possibly the press whether he was quite good enough. Overseas his record is phenomenal, but because he never nailed a big hundred here and showed Australia how good he was I got the feeling they didn't rate him as highly as we did in the team. Because he read everything and took everything in, maybe he sensed that his head was on the chopping block before others.'

Hussey's own self-doubt had reached a point of critical mass when he watched Michael Slater declare he must be dropped on television during the Australia A match that coincided with the last Shield round before the Gabba. Duly shaken, Hussey went out to bat against Victoria thinking he was toast and crafted a century that secured his place. Throughout an Ashes series in which he was one of few Australians to excel, he uttered the words 'Stuff you, Michael Slater' when tapping his bat. But whereas Hussey found a way to channel his worry, North and others were consumed by it.

Adrenaline, anxiety and the lure of the Ashes were enough to carry Australia through the first three days of the opening Test. Strauss was out to an airy cut shot from the third ball of the match, that single dismissal seeming to be the only evidence that the back-of-a-length offerings favoured by Ben Hilfenhaus that summer were going to take wickets. Siddle's tutorial from McDermott reaped the rewards of a first-day hat-trick, and Hussey took advantage of some overdue good fortune – an edge falling short of the slips first ball, an l.b.w. appeal from Anderson denied on the third morning – to put on a stirring 307 with a refreshed Brad Haddin, who was fit again after an elbow tendon complaint had kept him out of the Pakistan and India series.

Yet aside from those three displays, signs of trouble emerged. Ponting failed to make the Gabba Ashes hundred that had underpinned his dominant 2002–03 and 2006–07 tallies; Clarke was out of rhythm and struggling with his back; North was just as tentative as his words to Hussey had suggested. Take out the Hussey–Haddin partnership and the scoreboard looked far less healthy, as their parting allowed England to round up the final five wickets for 31. Hilfenhaus was innocuous and Johnson wayward in the first innings, and neither improved at the second time of asking. Doherty, chosen to spin the ball away from England's right-handers, saw only one wicket on days four and five. Left almost two days to bat in order to save the match, Strauss, Cook and Jonathan Trott barely broke a sweat doing so. If an image of the 1–517 scoreboard does not hang in their living rooms, it should.

Those final two days, during which Shane Warne was heard to criticise Ponting's tactics from the Nine commentary box, chipped away any of the confidence Siddle, Hussey and Haddin had built. Hilfenhaus and Johnson were then dropped, and Siddle's first-day lessons seemingly forgotten. Says Hussey, 'I think it was more than just the two days in the field. It was the realisation for us that they could compete in Australia. A blow to our confidence, a real shot to theirs.'

Relief passed across the face of Ponting when he won the second-Test toss, at Adelaide Oval. Bolstered by two apparently fresh pacemen in Ryan Harris and Doug Bollinger, he could now do what he did best by constructing a commanding first-innings hundred, guiding Australia to a tally somewhere in the region of 500 and then placing a tired England under pressure in the second act of back-to-back Tests. Meanwhile, a chastened Johnson could work on his technique and strength before returning, fresher, for Perth.

Only the last part of this scenario took place. Shane Watson and Simon Katich crossed wires in the first over, granting Trott a chance to throw down the stumps, which he gleefully took. Ponting pushed out hard at his first ball, edging Anderson's subtle away movement into an England cordon looking as impenetrable as Australia's once was. And in the third over Clarke, who had spent a long time with Ponting trying to iron out kinks in his technique on match eve, fell in similar fashion to his captain, pushing insistently at a ball that would have swung for only another hour at most. The score was 3–2. In the stands, Hilditch glumly realised the Test match had gone in an instant.

For two New South Welshmen, the five ghoulish days that followed were their last in Test cricket. Bollinger was still trying to regain fitness after his India side strain and had played only one and a half Shield matches by way of preparation. Alarmed to see Bollinger's pace drop about 20 kilometres per hour over the course of 29 overs, the selectors were never willing to choose him again. Katich was even less limber, carrying a sore Achilles into the match after two days of leather-chasing in Brisbane. Another 150 overs in the field at Adelaide left him limping badly, and he was barely able to run during a bloody-minded 43 in the second innings.

Defeat was so abject that even the heavens mocked Australia. The sun shone on the final morning, and England harvested the last six wickets in little more than 15 overs. To English glee and Australian dismay, a torrent of rain fell about two hours after the close of hostilities, and a larking Paul Collingwood was cheered on by teammates as he slid on the oval covers in his underwear.

*

Shorn of Katich, disappointed with Doherty and dispensing with North after the two-Test shelf life he had foreseen, the selectors opted for callow youth. Phillip Hughes was back in, despite precious little recent batting form, Steve Smith was recalled and Michael Beer was plucked from obscurity. Beer arrived in Perth looking about as stunned as the average lottery winner, while Smith and Hughes were paraded before the media as Australian cricket's future. Never mind that they had just been tossed into the maelstrom of an Ashes battle their side was losing. 'I've been told that I've got to come into the side and be fun,' Smith said without a hint of irony. 'For me it's about having energy in the field and making sure I'm having fun and making sure everyone else around is having fun, whether it be telling a joke or something like that.'

No such mirth was evident when Smith's outside edge dropped Australia to 5–69 on the first morning. England had lost Stuart Broad, but Tremlett proved himself an ideal replacement, offering swing, seam and above all sharp bounce. Hussey, Haddin and the recalled Johnson took the total from embarrassment to something like respectability, helped by the fact that both Swann and Finn were leaking runs more readily than England's plans allowed.

Johnson's return came after a two-week program of rushed technical work with Troy Cooley and Stuart Karppinen, plus a session in which Dennis Lillee essentially told the left-armer to believe in himself. When he took the ball on the first evening of the Test he appeared more relaxed, and on the second day he ran through England with a shattering spell of swing that still has the capacity to quicken the pulse, years later. But was it repeatable? 'When we left him out of Adelaide and then he got wickets in Perth they were trying to rebuild his action in a week, through an Adelaide Test and then in Perth,' Ponting says. 'When he got those wickets everyone said, "They've done a great job with him," but nothing had really changed; he just bowled better.'

The slinging technique certainly did not look too different, and Johnson's pace still hovered around 140 kilometres per hour, well short of his peak. Karppinen, himself a former swing bowler with Western Australia, agrees that the burst was as attributable to a helpful breeze as anything else. 'We dragged him out from Adelaide. He just needed work on his bowling action and his physical strength. But he had an easterly prevailing for four days, perfect conditions to get swing in Perth. The seam angle still wasn't perfect yet the ball was swinging. That to me was luck: one of those rare days when everything was right for swing bowling.'

Australia caught lightning in a bottle in Perth and at 1–1 seemed to be back in the race. Few could tell how little they had left in reserve for the festive-season sprint to the finish.

On Boxing Day morning, no-one in either dressing room was sure whether to bat or bowl first. No-one, that is, apart from David Saker, who had not only bowled on the MCG's capricious drop-in pitches but had also coached others how to do so. England's lack of certainty about the surface was assuaged in the hours before play when Saker encouraged Strauss to bowl on the basis that a moist drop-in was likely to play at its best on day two. Strauss sought reassurance from Anderson that he was happy to do so before walking out to the middle. Melbourne's famously changeable weather also played a part in the decision. Weak sun covered the ground when the coin went up, but clouds and the occasional shower were forecast.

Ponting had exhorted his team to retain the energy and passion that had infused their efforts at the WACA. At the toss he used the same words. 'We've got to play with the same sort of attitude and emotion that we did last week. I think that was the difference in us last week compared to Brisbane and Adelaide. The guys are aware of that.' Twenty-three years before, Australia had also chosen four fast bowlers and a spinning all-rounder for the Boxing Day Ashes Test, alongside a few chest-thumping words from Allan Border about taking an aggressive approach to England. The results proved much the same. The first day in Melbourne called for patience, but Australia offered dangling bats like nervous twitches.

Watson was surprised by Tremlett's bounce and taken in the gully off the shoulder of the bat. Hughes threw his Kookaburra at Tim Bresnan's seventh ball in Ashes cricket and was caught at gully the over before drinks. Ponting followed a prancing, seaming Tremlett delivery and edged into the cordon. Hussey, Smith, Clarke and Johnson all pushed out at well-pitched Anderson deliveries on their way through to Matt Prior. Haddin snicked a drive at Bresnan to second slip. Siddle and Hilfenhaus edged Tremlett leg cutters. All in less than 43 overs. Strauss recalled the ball barely beating the bat, but edges arriving more regularly than Nine commercial breaks.

Of course, any low score can offer the offending team's bowlers the chance to gain their revenge on a still-helpful pitch. But the sun emerged about the same time as Strauss and Cook went to the middle, where they feasted on a diet of short balls outside off stump and the occasional half-volley. It was dire stuff, leaving Ponting to stare aimlessly at the ground and sportswriter Robert Craddock to conclude in *The Courier-Mail*, 'Don't shed a tear over Australia's Ashes demise – the looming defeat could be just the kick in the pants Australia needs. While Australia has recklessly snatched at glory this summer, no team in 25 years has come to our shores better prepared or with a stronger collective focus than this England squad. An Australian victory in this Ashes series would have only served to heighten Australia's belief that its system is going fine when it's clearly not producing young players of robust Test match pedigree. It needs an urgent review of its set-up. If England win the Ashes, they deserve it.'

About the only thing wrong with Craddock's passage was the use of 'if' rather than 'when' in the final sentence. What followed was an extended victory lap through Melbourne and Sydney for Strauss' team, as Ponting's band were largely humiliated for each of the next nine match days. A fractured little finger, sustained when he tried to grasp an edge from Trott in Perth, meant that pain shot through

Ponting's body virtually every time he hit or caught the ball. His patience snapped when the umpires declined a decision review system appeal for a Kevin Pietersen edge, resulting in an eight-minute interruption while he debated the point with Aleem Dar and Tony Hill. For all his successes, Ponting's final Test as captain ended in an innings defeat by which he lost the Ashes and copped a fine for dissent.

The New Year's Test followed more or less the same script as Boxing Day's. Clarke did a passable job as stand-in captain but once more failed to make his presence felt with a major score. He was booed by sections of his home crowd when walking out to bat on the first day. Johnson weathered innumerable choruses of 'He bowls to the left; he bowls to the right; that Mitchell Johnson, his bowling is shite' from the Barmy Army and ended his series with a first-ball duck at the hands of Tremlett. England's greater attention to detail was evident even at the presentation ceremony, when Strauss had to ask event staff to find an Ashes urn replica when informed that all he had to hold up was the Waterford Crystal trophy.

At one point of the Test, Andrew Hilditch, Jamie Cox and David Boon walked together through the SCG members' enclosure behind the stands. Revered as a folk hero, Boon avoided most of the brick-bats. Relatively anonymous, not having played international cricket, Cox was similarly fortunate. But Hilditch was on the receiving end of 'just some ferocious, really angry, emotional stuff. The abuse for Digger was just unbelievable . . . Digger copped the lot.'

Hilditch did not help his case by uttering the immortal words 'I think we've done a very good job as a selection panel' during a media post-mortem. The chief executive, James Sutherland, also raised eyebrows when he argued that the team's preparation had not been at fault. 'I'm not discounting the fact we couldn't look at the way in which we prepared, but I think to point the finger at preparation is rubbish,' he said. 'We actually played more Test cricket than England did leading into the Ashes series. I know we all want to point the finger at someone or something, but there are lots of things that could have been done differently.'

By the time the limited-overs matches rolled around, the selectors and CA management had been locked out of Australia's dressing room. Arriving for a game against England, Cox was informed by Hilditch that the panel members were no longer welcome to take up their usual posts in the players' viewing area. Unwilling to schmooze in a CA corporate suite and reluctant to place himself among the same crowd that had torn his chairman to shreds a few weeks before, Cox walked into the downstairs lounge beneath the members' stand and watched the match on television.

Months earlier at the Australian Cricket Conference, numerous delegates had noticed something missing. As they had scanned the conference program of panel discussions and guest speakers on the first day, high-performance and cricket operations staff from CA and the six states had realised there was nothing that explicitly discussed their area: top-level cricket. Wider topics were covered, with a sharp focus on CA's strategy for attracting new followers and the need for the governance reform. But issues such as the mediocre performance of the national team and the standard of supporting competitions were absent. Says one official, 'A few of us thought that was a bit odd. That was symptomatic at that particular time of people not having a great grasp on how the Australian public viewed the team in terms of the success of the business. There were quite a few cricket people there and we all looked at each other and said, "Where's our bit of the conference?"' Research prior to the conference conducted by CA's strategy division had found that team performance was not perceived as a top issue by prospective attendees.

By January 2011, the significance of the oversight was clear. The margin of England's victory in the Ashes was so vast that the Gabba,

Adelaide Oval, MCG and SCG all finished deserted apart from joyous English tourists. The Australian public, stunned to be witnessing the disintegration of their team and the captaincy of Ricky Ponting, stayed well away as each match entered its final stages. Graeme Swann's sprinkler dance competed with Mitchell Johnson's wides, Alastair Cook's cut shots and groping Australian bats as the definitive image of the series.

Nothing about the Test team functioned properly. Batsmen were unprepared for England's plan, bowlers incapable of carrying out their own. Fielding and running between the wickets were never better than average, and often catastrophic. Ponting's form evaporated and his composure followed, while his deputy, Michael Clarke, fared almost as poorly. The coach, Tim Nielsen, and his assistants seemed unable to tackle the problems before them, whether through technical advice or sage readings of the team's darkening mood. And the selectors abandoned many of the players and the plans honed over the preceding eighteen months, leaving the likes of Phillip Hughes, Steve Smith, Xavier Doherty and Michael Beer to squint at the harsh light of Ashes exposure. Not surprisingly, none were able to conjure the miracles suddenly required of them.

Even so, Ponting's men were very much in the series when they arrived at the MCG on Boxing Day morning. The events of that day encapsulated the series, as a tally of 98 all out was followed by England's unfettered advance to 0–157. A crowd of 84 345 had thinned by the close, and as the days went by numerous Australian players felt like joining them. 'It's the closest I've come to being depressed,' says Mike Hussey. 'You wake up in the morning and you don't want to go to the ground. You just think, "I want to stay in bed all day. I don't want to come in today."'

13

One Cup,
Two Captains

FEBRUARY – MARCH 2011

ICC World Cup in India

Sri Lanka and Bangladesh

For about forty-five fraught minutes on 29 March 2011, Australia did not have a captain. Ricky Ponting had resigned of his own accord and Michael Clarke had been nominated by the selectors, but there was no consensus on the Cricket Australia board about the identity of the team's new leader. A telephone hook-up organised to approve Clarke's ascent had unearthed hitherto unspoken concerns among board members, and previously firm support for the vice-captain was now wavering. Whether listening in to the call or being kept updated on its progress via text message, planners of the Clarke succession were beginning to panic.

Only three months before, the board had rubber-stamped Clarke's appointment as the forty-third Test captain, albeit in a caretaker capacity while Ponting missed the fifth Ashes Test in Sydney due to a broken finger. Moreover, Clarke had been the heir apparent since 2008, from the moment he was chosen as vice-captain to replace the retired Adam Gilchrist. The chairman of selectors Andrew Hilditch had been adamant about Clarke's standing as the only choice to replace Ponting, stating the case in his regular updates to the board.

Around the team, coach Tim Nielsen knew Clarke was capable, having proven himself in numerous ODI and T20 assignments when Ponting was injured or resting. Their reservations about Clarke had been to do with the way he operated as Ponting's deputy, occasionally tuning out by donning earphones on the team bus or producing the odd scatterbrained innings. But they had little doubt that whenever granted the leadership, Clarke was better at it than anyone other than Ponting himself. Ahead of the fifth Test, Nielsen observed that Clarke changed noticeably when he was captain. 'Over the next couple of weeks,' he said, 'the Australian public will see a different Michael Clarke.'

On the morning of his resignation, Ponting had no qualms endorsing Clarke as his successor during an 11 a.m. press conference in the SCG members' dining room. Ponting's words were sure and sound. 'He's done a terrific job in almost every game he's had a chance to captain for Australia, starting with the T20 team – I thought he did a great job there. What he did with the one-day team in my absence not only through the summer but in other tours was absolutely first-class and I think he's certainly growing into those leadership roles every day, so I would totally endorse Michael Clarke as the next captain.'

Yet when the phone hook-up commenced an hour or so later, the fourteen-man board was far from unanimous. Clarke's former team-mate Matthew Hayden led the opposition, stating his conviction that Ponting's deputy was not the right man. Ian McLachlan followed Hayden by stating that, given the former opener's relevant experience of Clarke, his views should be heard. In the midst of this discussion, Geoff Tamblyn mentioned another possibility. Always keen to push the case of their highly successful state players, Victoria offered up an alternative nominee for Test captain: the Bushrangers leader and Australian T20 captain Cameron White. A hush descended on the dialled-in parts of CA's Jolimont office. This was uncharted territory.

*

Signs of the team's fraying fabric extended into the ODI series following the Ashes. As Ricky Ponting convalesced with his fractured finger and Michael Hussey had surgery to reattach a hamstring tendon, Michael Clarke led the side successfully against England. But members of the support staff were worried by the increasingly morose visage of coach Tim Nielsen, who seemed to be taking upon himself blame for the team's Test match failure. During an ODI in Hobart, the strength and conditioning coach, Stuart Karppinen, spoke with the head of cricket, Michael Brown, expressing concerns about how hard Nielsen was taking it. Brown observed the team for a few days before concluding that Nielsen was indeed struggling. He was prescribed counselling sessions with Marianne Roux, a human resources expert who soon afterwards joined the CA management.

'It didn't work,' Nielsen says. 'I was asked to do this sort of stuff, and I had to be big enough to say there are areas where I can improve and, yes, I want to get better at what I do. So I went and did it, but it didn't work for me. What I really needed was some time to sit down and not think about it for a month, get into a position where you're not so emotionally wound up and can make more sensible decisions. The team had been beaten, and in a performance-driven environment like we were involved in, everyone was concerned about their future. All of a sudden people stop playing for the team and start thinking about individual survival. We'd just lost an Ashes series 3–1; we'd been pounded by an innings in two consecutive Test matches; I was hanging on to try to maintain relationships and help players perform. But every day we picked up a paper it was talking about someone else being dropped.'

Still ranked the number-one ODI team at the start of the World Cup, in February 2011, Australia did little to suggest they would seriously contend for a fourth consecutive title. Inconsistencies in selection haunted the team once more, as the limited-overs combination that had performed so ably in 2009 and for much of 2010 was broken up to make room for a somewhat desperate ploy – an attempt to win a World Cup played in Bangladesh, India and Sri Lanka with fast bowlers. Brett Lee, Shaun Tait and Mitchell Johnson were central to the plan, while Doug Bollinger was also part of the squad until an ankle problem flared. His injury allowed the recall of Michael Hussey after a hamstring tear, even though he was initially told by Andrew Hilditch that he would not be considered.

Other absentees due to injury included Nathan Hauritz, Ryan Harris, Clint McKay, Xavier Doherty and Shaun Marsh, a list that made another omission doubly puzzling. James Hopes had been an understated but important member of the ODI squad during its aforementioned successes in England and India and at the Champions Trophy, and over five years he had built up a solid record as an all-rounder. He was also a highly regarded team man, noted for his good sense and even temperament. His case summed up the players' discontent with the selectors around this time, as they wondered what CA's plans actually were.

Hopes recalls, 'In India in 2010 Andrew Hilditch called me about 2 a.m. after the last one-dayer to say, "You're not going to be in the team to play Sri Lanka but that doesn't mean you won't be going to the World Cup." So I thought, "Okay," and went out and put together the best season I'd had for Queensland [winning Sheffield Shield player of the year]. But I never spoke to Andrew again until he called me to tell me I wasn't getting a contract and said, "This must be hard to take because you've had such a good year." I just said, "Well, what can I say, mate?" That was the only time I spoke to a selector during that period. There was no "You're not going to figure in the World Cup squad", none of that. A number of guys got turfed around. David Hussey got picked, dropped, then picked again right at the end. It was a bit of a nightmare.'

The nightmare extended beyond Hopes, since 2010–11 had been the summer in which CA had chosen to experiment with a split-innings limited-overs format. The idea, introduced because the organisation's marketing department felt the 50-over game had become tired, was met with howls of protest from the Australian

Cricketers' Association. 'The timing of it is not good. It raises the question of how the players will be rated when the selectors are picking the World Cup squad,' the association's chief executive, Paul Marsh, said to the *Sydney Morning Herald*. 'I've told CA that they've gone about this completely the wrong way – they haven't brought the players into the process properly.'

Others with reasons to shake their heads included that season's leading domestic limited-overs performers, Brad Hodge and Dan Christian. Darren Lehmann, by this point coach of Queensland, expressed his dismay at the balance of the squad. 'I find it amazing you can't find room for a Dan Christian and James Hopes as all-rounders and make a hard call on someone else,' he told *The Advertiser*. 'To go to India without a legitimate batting all-rounder with the way the wickets are surprised me a little bit.'

Ponting's finger recovered sufficiently for him to take his place in India, but it was not long before the frustrations of the summer and a curiously muted team environment on the subcontinent started to take their toll. A beaten-up story about Ponting trashing a dressing-room television after he was run out in the team's opener against Zimbabwe did not help, and against Canada a near collision with Steve Smith when the pair both went for the same skied catch had the captain hurling the ball into the ground, in the manner of Allan Border's worry ball after a one-run loss to the West Indies in 1993. Ponting began to merit the 'Captain Grumpy' epithet handed to his forebear as the team spluttered through minor matches. Border at least had the excuse that it was arguably the most important match of his career.

Nonetheless, Australia were equal leaders of their group until the final pool game, against Pakistan in Colombo, where a poor display with the bat dropped them to third. Symbolically, the defeat ended a run of thirty-four consecutive World Cup match wins stretching back to 1999. Its aftermath was also a significant reminder of the team's edgy state, though they had nearly a week until the play-off match thanks to the tournament's inordinately spaced-out schedule.

Harbhajan Singh celebrates India's victory over Pakistan in the inaugural World Twenty20 final, September 2007. 'I might have suggested that they needed to be a little more humble,' said Andrew Symonds, 'which didn't go over terribly well.' (HAMISH BLAIR/GETTY IMAGES)

Hamish Blair's photograph of spectators taunting Symonds with monkey gestures at Wankhede Stadium, October 2007. Australia's team manager Steve Bernard took the photo to the BCCI office as proof of racial abuse. (HAMISH BLAIR/GETTY IMAGES)

'We were made to look like idiots.' Symonds flanked by Ricky Ponting, Michael Clarke and Matthew Hayden in Adelaide's Federal Court building for Harbhajan's appeal hearing, January 2008. Dean Kino, Michael Brown and Peter Young sit behind. (AFP)

Players crowd around a prone Shivnarine Chanderpaul after he was knocked out by Brett Lee – the world's most feared fast bowler – in Jamaica, May 2008.

Phillip Hughes leaves Kingsmead in Durban after the second of back-to-back hundreds, in his second Test, March 2009. 'We were painfully slow to realise how proficient he was at the square cut,' said South Africa's coach Mickey Arthur.

(HAMISH BLAIR/GETTY IMAGES)

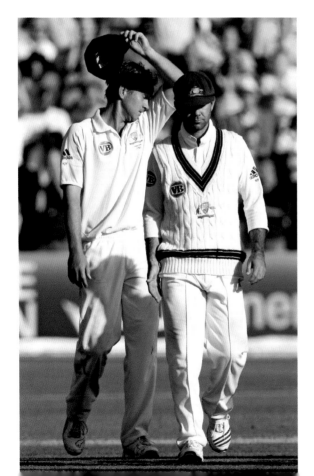

'One of the greatest disappointments of my life.' A drained Nathan Hauritz and dejected Ricky Ponting leave the field after England wriggle out of the Cardiff Test with a draw, July 2009.

(HAMISH BLAIR/GETTY IMAGES)

Ricky Ponting hands Steve Smith his Test cap before the Lord's Test against Pakistan, July 2010. Smith started as a speculative leg spinner but bloomed into a fine batsman and capable leader. (HAMISH BLAIR/GETTY IMAGES)

AUSTRALIA		Runs	B/F	Min
WATSON	c. PIETERSEN b. TREMLETT	5	12	14
HUGHES	c. PIETERSEN b. BRESNAN	16	32	59
PONTING	c. SWANN b. TREMLETT	10	38	51
CLARKE	c. PRIOR b. ANDERSON	20	54	88
HUSSEY	c. PRIOR b. ANDERSON	8	41	44
SMITH	c. PRIOR b. ANDERSON	6	15	18
HADDIN	c. STRAUSS b. BRESNAN	5	16	22
JOHNSON	c. PRIOR b. ANDERSON	0	4	9
HARRIS		10	23	39
SIDDLE	c. PRIOR b. TREMLETT	11	15	26
HILFENHAUS	c. PRIOR b. TREMLETT	0	8	10
EXTRAS	(5nb, 2Lb)	7		
TOTAL	10 for	98		

Australian cricket read the MCG scoreboard on Boxing Day 2010 and wept. 'It's the closest I've come to being depressed,' says Mike Hussey. 'You wake up in the morning and you don't want to go to the ground.' (HAMISH BLAIR/GETTY IMAGES)

'Every day we picked up a paper it was talking about someone else being dropped.' Tim Nielsen and his players endured this view of England lifting the Ashes urn at the SCG, January 2011. (HAMISH BLAIR/GETTY IMAGES)

Ponting leads his players from the field for the final time as captain after defeat to India in the 2011 World Cup quarter-final in Ahmedabad. (HAMISH BLAIR/GETTY IMAGES)

John Inverarity, Mickey Arthur and Rod Marsh, all Argus review appointments, get to know each other at Allan Border Field, November 2011. (HAMISH BLAIR/GETTY IMAGES)

'Test cricketers are expected to turn up and know how to do the job, but some do and some don't.' Craig McDermott's work with Peter Siddle paid off when he bowled Sachin Tendulkar at the MCG, December 2011. (HAMISH BLAIR/GETTY IMAGES)

Clarke and Shane Watson share a joke with Sri Lanka's Shaminda Eranga at the MCG, December 2012. (RYAN PIERSE/GETTY IMAGES)

Darren Lehmann's gregarious, hands-on approach to coaching Australia placed Michael Clarke somewhat in the shade, July 2013. (RYAN PIERSE/GETTY IMAGES)

Ricky Ponting and his successor Michael Clarke arm in arm after beating India at the SCG, January 2012. Both had made hundreds; Clarke went on to a monumental 329 not out. (HAMISH BLAIR/GETTY IMAGES)

Ryan Harris zips through Joe Root at Durham. Harris' highly skilled work revealed cracks in English batting techniques to be opened up further in Australia, August 2013. (RYAN PIERSE/GETTY IMAGES)

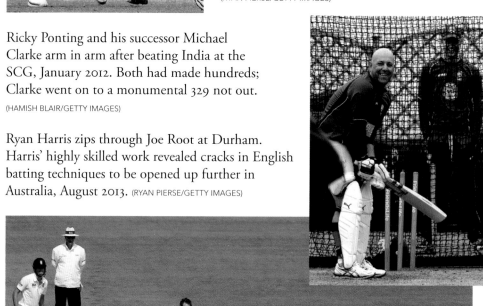

'It showed us they weren't that good.' Ashton Agar's last wicket stand with Phillip
Hughes revealed England's limitations when asked to think outside the box, July 2013.

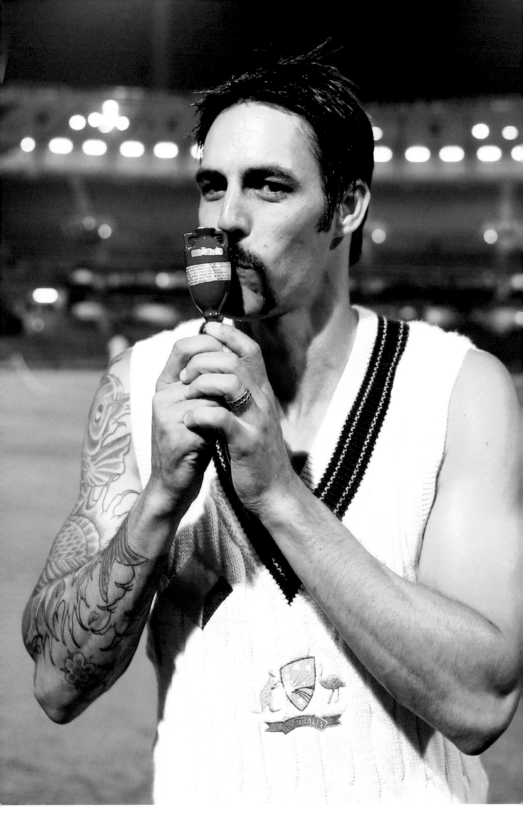

Cause and effect: Mitchell Johnson with the Ashes urn his bowling delivered,
January 2014. (RYAN PIERSE/GETTY IMAGES)

In Melbourne during the Ashes, Michael Clarke and Phillip Hughes had been criticised by James Sutherland for attending a Boxing Day breakfast function before the Test and had then been spotted at a Southbank bar on the penultimate evening of the match, after both had batted for the final time. Nielsen had defended the pair publicly, but headlines like 'Clarke and Hughes on Booze before Ashes Defeat' formed part of management's thinking in Colombo; Brett Lee claimed in his autobiography that the players were counselled against going out for a drink following the loss to Pakistan. 'I believe that the incident had a negative effect on the squad,' Lee wrote. 'It's all too easy for such decisions to snowball. If a player is told he can't do something that he considers to be quite reasonable, it's possible resentment can develop. Or alternatively the player becomes so worried about doing something wrong that suddenly he thinks twice about taking a chance in a match, for fear that his action might be seen as irresponsible. I reckon that guys in our squad became scared of doing everything from having a beer or two to playing a daring shot.'

Lee, Ponting and the rest tried to put all this aside for the semifinal meeting with India, in Ahmedabad. Several limited-overs successes against the hosts in recent visits to the subcontinent counted for little in a tournament that India's players were extremely driven to win, and they always appeared to have room to spare in the ultimately comfortable five-wicket victory. Ponting constructed one of his finest ODI hundreds but lacked sufficient support through the innings. Several players looked askance at Clarke's slog that was caught on the mid-wicket boundary just as he and Ponting had established a partnership. India won the cup.

On the night of the India match, Ponting barely slept. The thought kept recurring that his time as captain was over. The World Cup campaign had been poor, his own career was winding down and it was now more than two years away from the next Ashes series and four from the World Cup. He was resigned to the fact the team needed fresh direction, having seen the abysmal failure of his 'best I can be' example during the Ashes. That approach had not only loaded up pressure on Ponting, but had also left other members of the team feeling that if their captain failed, they had little chance of beating England. When the campaign for the urn fell utterly to pieces, on either side of the freakish result in Perth, much of Ponting's pre-series rhetoric was made to look awfully hollow, and his on-field leadership equal parts stubborn and sullen.

As a captain, Ponting's need to make runs increased the longer he continued, because his team was in decline. But that decline and the cycle of players into and out of the team also had a debilitating effect on his batting, because he had fewer hours in which to hone it. In some recent matches, such as in Johannesburg and Headingley in 2009, Ponting had still been able to produce innings redolent of his best. But the supply had become sporadic before cutting out altogether during the Ashes. The day before the critical second Test of the series, in Adelaide, Ponting had spent as much time advising Clarke on his technique as he had working on his own. Both were out cheaply the next morning.

Ponting was not prepared to move from his signature number three spot in the batting order while captain, nor to compromise on the aggressive style of play, winning the game off his own bat, that had made his reputation as the best batsman of Australia's dominant era. As a young member of the Australian squad in the 1990s, Ponting had felt that Steve Waugh should have batted at number three because he was the team's best batsman, and after his own retirement he was equally convinced that Clarke should be batting there. This view did not change.

Similarly rigid was Ponting's tactical view of the game. It is true that he had the odd excellent match or series as an on-field ringmaster, most notably in South Africa in 2009. Like Allan Border, he had become adept at ODI leadership, helped by his ability to station himself in the fielding circle and prowl for run-outs. But overall there was a methodical, plodding element to Ponting's captaincy that often had bowlers summoned at mechanical intervals of five or six overs. Former Australian captain Ian Chappell believes that Ponting's greatest area of weakness was an inability to take enough of his gambler's instinct onto the field, despite his ubiquitous nickname 'Punter' and well-known love of racing greyhounds.

This played out most often with spinners, a class of cricketer with whom Ponting always struggled to find sufficient common ground. Hilditch's selection panel shared the affliction, as the degree of care and understanding required of many spin bowlers was mistaken at times for softness. Neither captain nor selectors were helped by beginning their tenures at a time when Shane Warne was still twirling the ball at one end, attacking and defending simultaneously, setting his own fields, weaving his way into the subconscious of umpires as well as the opposing batsmen.

Hauritz concluded that neither Ponting nor the spin bowlers he worked with could quite see past the fact that no-one would replace Warne. 'What was hard for Punter was that for years he could just go, "Warney, there you go," and he'd come up and say, "I'm going to do this; this is what I'm thinking," and Punter would set the field. When he was working with me he'd be saying, "What do you think?" and I'd say, "What do you think?" and he goes, "Okay, we think this," and I'd be, "Okay, I'll do that," but sometimes I just wasn't good enough to do exactly what he wanted. Punter was an awesome captain and was always very good to me and helped me out as much as he could, but in the end I probably wasn't good enough to do what he wanted from me all the time. He backed me to the hilt, and I didn't back myself.'

But even Warne struggled with Ponting's fixed views at times. Often teammates heard him say, 'Mate, give me a bowl,' only to be turned back with the reply, 'Nah, it's only the 14th over.' Warne, throwing his head back in the way familiar to umpires and batsmen, would conclude, 'I should have bowled six overs ago!' As a pupil of Warne, Michael Clarke had no qualms about speaking his mind but was caught up in the complications of being not only Ponting's vice-captain but also the man so many expected to succeed him.

Therein lay another reason why Ponting's resignation, when it came, was timely. Most academic and business opinion has settled on the view that a chief executive's ideal job span sits somewhere between five and ten years, and by March 2011 Ponting had been at the tiller for seven. It is said that longer stints can result in several problems, notably the leader losing their once-clear head for the issues confronting them, due to overfamiliarity with the staff and surroundings. Also significant is the risk that the ambitions of other staff will be stunted, resulting in the loss of quality individuals to other entities or growing bitterness among those who choose to remain.

Aside from their lower-middle-class origins, Ponting and Clarke lacked points of commonality. This extended even to their sleeping patterns, with Clarke habitually in bed by 9 p.m. unless he had reason not to be, and Ponting often unable to sleep until sometime after midnight. When on tour, Ponting revelled in the closeness of the environment, the opportunity to spend time with other team members. When off tour, he was near impossible to contact. Clarke liked his own space on tour, often being absent from group dinners, but away from playing and training he was always up for a text exchange or phone call.

Ponting took great pride in keeping his mood steady, trying his best to treat triumph and disaster as the impostors that Rudyard Kipling once declared them. Clarke's emotions could swing, and his opinions were seldom far from being shared. Where Ponting cared little for public perception and took up public relations duties like his captain's diaries and newspaper columns with a sense of duty rather than enthusiasm, Clarke brought a professional gleam to such tasks, whether it be speaking sunnily but opaquely at press conferences or poring over the paragraphs of his own ghosted column. Ponting was never eager for interviews but unfailingly frank whenever finally cornered. As Gideon Haigh summed up in *The Australian*, 'They have replaced a captain who cared very little what people thought with one who cares a lot.'

Differences between the pair were noticed by CA but in some ways encouraged. There was a separation of powers inherent in their dealings with management. Michael Brown and James Sutherland had agreed upon a system by which the head of cricket operations would tell the chief executive everything that was going on in the team, but that Ponting would speak with Sutherland when he had issues to raise that went wider than the coaches or the selectors. This kept Sutherland in touch with the team and left the rest of the players to communicate through Brown. But it also meant that Clarke and Ponting took their queries to the board separately rather than together.

Attempts to forge a closer relationship commonly foundered on the rock of the sportsman's ego, though some felt more efforts could have been made. As one former staff member puts it, 'There was the opinion that they're big boys and it'll sort itself out, but what it ultimately showed is that it doesn't and they don't. You've got to sort it out and deal with it, and it wasn't dealt with. It festered and it was a problem.'

Despite all that, Clarke served as Ponting's deputy and heir for a full year longer than Mark Taylor had been Allan Border's vice-captain. During that time, Taylor had learned how difficult life could be in the copilot's seat. His run-making dipped, and critics made queries about his weight, his suitability for the one-day team and his ambition to replace a legendary predecessor. The experience allowed Taylor some empathy for Clarke, even if he had avoided a few of the more 21st-century potholes that the younger man struck. Among these was a poor public perception, based on his supermodel fiancée and purchase of a Bondi penthouse and sports-car package. There was peer jealousy too, stemming from a range of lucrative sponsorship deals that quickly outstripped the arrangements of more senior teammates.

*

Dialling into the teleconference that afternoon from his Sydney home, Mark Taylor had expected most of the time to be occupied by debate over the identity of Clarke's deputy. As the tenuous Ponting–Clarke alliance had shown, the choice of vice-captain needed to be given plenty of thought. Brad Haddin had served as Clarke's lieutenant in the SCG Ashes Test, and as a mentor and team man he displayed considerable abilities. But Shane Watson also had some claims, as he had seemingly found a way of keeping his body together while also emerging as the most authoritative – if not yet prolific – batsman in the side.

But then Hayden had spoken, followed by McLachlan, and Hayden again. He mentioned Clarke's uneasy relationship with Ponting, the perception of Clarke as a cause of trouble in the team, his flashy image being unbecoming of an Australian captain, his departure from New Zealand to break up with Lara Bingle, and his bust-up with Simon Katich on Hayden's final night as a Test cricketer.

Near enough to twenty years before, when substituting as Australia's ODI captain for an injured Allan Border, Taylor had held his hand up to the powerful coach, Bob Simpson, to let him know that he would address the players, thanks. During this crucial teleconference he was similarly decisive, making Hayden and others sit back in their seats. First, Taylor acknowledged the fact that the team had not been happy. He agreed that Ponting and Clarke were not close. But then he rejected the public perception of the Australian team as a bunch of great mates from numbers one through eleven. Taylor drew the distinction between a club team in which all players had grown up and lived their lives together and a national representative side in which individuals from different backgrounds all over Australia came together to play. The second scenario was far more likely to throw up personal differences. Taylor noted that Hayden's tight friendships with Ponting and Justin Langer had not appled to all members of a winning team during their years of dominance.

Taylor's second point was to flatly reject the view that Clarke's personality and lifestyle had been reasons for Australia's suffering performance after 2007. While declining to repeat exactly what he said on the board teleconference call, Taylor is happy to outline his opinion on this matter. 'It's just wrong, absolutely wrong,' he says. 'Sure, he thinks differently to Ricky Ponting, Shane Watson, Matthew Hayden and so on, but that doesn't mean he's always wrong. As a vice-captain you know what it's like, particularly if you're the vice-captain behind a very successful player as I had with Allan Border and I knew Michael would have had with Ricky Ponting. You say something that's against the grain, you're almost seen as "You're not with us, and if you're not with us you're against us." That's what I felt about that whole side. It got to the stage where you're either in the bubble or outside it. Michael wanted to be outside it – he moves on his own to a certain extent – but he also loves communicating. He doesn't want everyone to move in the same circles, but he wants people to be in touch all the time, which I think is great and how a representative cricket team should work.'

Taylor first met Clarke when invited to the Cricket Academy by Rod Marsh in 2001. Clarke was a scholar that year and was assigned the task of picking Taylor up at the airport. 'He had the peroxide hair and black roots; he was brash, cocky; but I loved his attitude, and we talked cricket a lot even then. I could see that he had a really good understanding of the game and curiosity about it. People never saw that with Michael; all they saw was Lara Bingle, cars, Bonds commercials. They didn't see that Michael Clarke's actually a pretty good player. Ricky was a better player, but Michael is a much better captain because he understands the game better.'

Others on the call remember that Taylor 'took control', calmly disputing Hayden's objections to Clarke and reassuring other board members in the process. In doing so he carried the day and allowed for Clarke's permanent appointment to be ratified.

Reflecting on the succession, Ponting says that the right decision was made, but wonders why the concerns raised on the call had not been discussed earlier. 'How did it get to that, anyway? He's been the Test vice-captain for three years; he was the T20 captain before that; he's already captained Australia in a Test match. What had the board been thinking for three years? It should have been debated before that. Before I stood down there should have been some questions asked so they weren't left in that position.'

Equally problematic was the appointment of Shane Watson as vice-captain, a decision rushed because the fourteen board members indicated they had to get off the call to continue their everyday lives. The deputy chairman Wally Edwards was not even on the call by this point, having lost phone connection from New Delhi where he was on a business trip and failed to retrieve it. The lack of care applied to this choice later rebounded on the team and the board in many ways. A line from the looming Argus review succinctly summed up the resultant situation: 'The captain should . . . actively seek and use the counsel of his vice-captain, which is an important role and should be more clearly defined.' As later painful experience showed, Watson and Clarke were unable to make this relationship work.

Assuming, like Ponting, that Clarke had the job in his keeping, most journalists had already penned pieces about the succession, completely unaware of the board debate. Peter Lalor, chasing a scoop for *The Australian*, went to the InterContinental Hotel near Circular Quay where he saw Michael Brown and CA's public affairs manager, Peter Young, hailing a cab late in the afternoon. Taking a leaf from his days as a police roundsman and crime writer, Lalor tailed them in search of their destination. When the cab reached Campbell Parade on Bondi Beach, he knew Clarke was the man. As Lalor reported in the next morning's paper, 'Ricky Ponting has endorsed Michael Clarke to take over the role as Australian captain and said he was happy to take a back seat in any future team. The Tasmanian-born champion stood down from the captaincy of the one-day and

Test sides yesterday, expressing a desire to remain in both as a batsman. The selectors have already ratified Clarke's ascension and last night CA's general manager of operations, Michael Brown, and Peter Young, manager of public affairs, went to Clarke's Bondi penthouse to tell him he had won the job.'

When Brown and Young left Clarke's home, the sun was setting over Sydney. It had been a long day, and a near-run thing.

14

Argus, Before
and After

JANUARY – SEPTEMBER 2011

Australia in Bangladesh

Australia in Sri Lanka

James Sutherland watched England's Ashes victory pageant with an uneasy grimace in the SCG's Victor Trumper Stand. As the margin between the two teams grew each day and angry headlines piled up, he began to ponder how change might be instigated. There were many things about the national team and its underpinnings that had fallen into disrepair, and a system that had once been visionary was now only second or third best in the world. The breakdown had been gradual and partly obscured by the greatness of the generation that included Shane Warne and Glenn McGrath, but its creep into the national team was now as vivid as the acres of empty seats on the final morning at the SCG – those not occupied by the Barmy Army.

As CA's chief executive, Sutherland knew his own job would be under scrutiny if things did not quickly improve. As well, he had to be seen to be seeking change, not merely encouraging it in the understated manner in which he had guided CA over the preceding decade. At the same time as England wrapped up Australia's final three wickets to seal the 3–1 scoreline with a third-innings victory, Sutherland had his first discussions with his head of strategy, Andrew Jones, about what was to be done. The words 'We've got to do something about this' escaped Sutherland's lips only a few minutes before Chris Tremlett bowled Michael Beer to end the series.

The 'something' that emerged was the Australian Team Performance Review, its independent panel chaired by the former BHP Billiton supremo Don Argus and including Sutherland's predecessor, Malcolm Speed, and the former captains Allan Border, Mark Taylor and Steve Waugh. While Sutherland decided on the composition of the panel, Jones spent much of January and February scouring ESPNcricinfo, CricketArchive and *Wisden* in search of background notes for the review. He would have found that Australia's Test side was mired in its worst series win:loss ratio since the retirements of Greg Chappell, Dennis Lillee and Rod Marsh, in 1984, having won only five series out of eleven since mid-2008. The team's ranking had slipped from number one to five. Its bowling performance was a major reason for the drop-off in results, as the pace bowlers' figures had increased by around five runs per wicket since 2007, while spinners' figures had blown out by more than 21 runs a wicket. The top-order batting decline was less pronounced but had been partly bailed out by improvements in tail-end batting. All-rounder Shane Watson and part-timer Simon Katich had better records over the period than most of the full-timers. Inconsistency was on the increase.

Introductory discussions for the review were followed by more than sixty interviews. Most key bases were covered, but others were left oddly unexplored. The new team manager, Gavin Dovey, fresh out of rugby, and Australian Football League premiership coach Mick Malthouse were consulted, but CA's scheduler-in-chief, Geoff Allardice, was omitted. Some were uncomfortable to find Sutherland in the room when they arrived to be interviewed, in his role as an ex-officio, non-voting member of the panel. In the words of one interviewee, 'I was thinking, "You're in the sights here; you're one of the people who has got to go. What are you doing here?"'

When Sutherland and the CA chairman, Jack Clarke, revealed the review's findings in August 2011, many of its conclusions drew knowing nods from those who had questioned the direction of the national team for some time. But there were still a few shaking heads, most notably about the appointment of the captain as a selector. By then, numerous roles had already changed hands. Some hirings and firings occurred while the review panel were still conducting interviews and thrashing out findings, many of them as significant as anything the Argus review ultimately handed down. Chief among these were the hiring of Craig McDermott as the national team's bowling coach, the recruitment of Dovey as its manager, the looming return of Rod Marsh and the sacking of Simon Katich.

McDermott and Dovey's first tour together was a ten-day sojourn in Bangladesh in April that was notable for being Michael Clarke's maiden trip as full-time captain. Ricky Ponting was also on the tour and adjusted smoothly enough to his new role as senior pro. The only awkward moment arose when he saw the scheduled team leadership meeting on his calendar. Not having been told if he was needed, Ponting poked his head around the door and was politely informed by captain, vice-captain, coach and manager that his attendance was no longer required.

While for Dovey this was a handover trip alongside the longtime manager, Steve Bernard, for McDermott it was more of an unofficial job interview. He quickly established a rapport with the likes of Mitchell Johnson and James Pattinson while honing the marriage of simple advice with rigid discipline. After his brief link with the pace bowlers in Brisbane before the first Test, McDermott had watched the Ashes with a sense of building frustration. After Melbourne and Sydney, he spent several evenings writing down his ideas on how the pacemen were falling down and what it would take to lift them. Statistical data available to him at the Centre of Excellence proved his point.

'They were hitting the right lengths about 27 per cent of the time, which for a Test attack was pretty dismal,' McDermott says. 'By the time we were getting thrashed in Melbourne in four days and in Sydney, we didn't make enough runs but we didn't bowl very well either; that's when I sat on my balcony and I wrote some notes on my laptop. Greg Chappell was my boss at the CoE at the time. I sent those off to him and I said, "This is what we need to try to implement with our Test attack but also our young guys coming through over the next five or six years. If we don't implement some of these things and hammer them home, our bowling attack will continue to struggle." That's where the momentum started to build.'

By 2011 it had been a decade since Rod Marsh had been poached by the England and Wales Cricket Board to run their academy. In that time he had been instrumental in England's resurgence, had been tripped up – as many have – by the strangely stultifying atmosphere of South Australian cricket and had then worked assiduously alongside Mudassar Nazar to establish the ICC's global academy, in Dubai. After winding down his ICC contract, Marsh had had retirement on his mind. His views of CA had been dimmed at the time of his departure, when his report on the flatlining of its talent stocks and the exodus of the game's intellectual property (as experienced players stopped becoming coaches) did not receive anything so much as a reply from the board or management.

The crux of Marsh's argument was that during Australia's years of dominance and increasing professionalism, the best players had lost interest in coaching and mentoring as a viable career path. This in turn had left room for a host of schoolteachers, theorists and others to jump into the gap. Having never or seldom played the game at the top level, they flooded theory into the Australian pathway, and were more likely to have their voices heard the more outlandish those theories were. All the while, cricket's immutable basics receded from view, referred to as 'assumed knowledge' for so long that by 2010–11 they had become a secret code of their own.

Marsh worried principally about the likes of John Buchanan and Bennett King, the Queensland duo who had minimal playing experience to call upon. This did not stop Buchanan from coaching Australia from 1999 to 2007, and King from replacing Marsh at the academy in 2002 then going on to an abortive tenure as coach of the West Indies. As Sutherland said soon after King's appointment, 'The fact he hasn't played Test cricket is not that important to us. The coach of the Australian cricket team hasn't played Test cricket either.' Both men benefited from strong talent bases, in Queensland and then with Australia.

King's elevation to replace Marsh was particularly troubling as it exemplified the fact that former cricketers were being overlooked, and consequently were drifting away from the game. Very few of Australia's best players were taking up coaching careers, because the money on offer was extremely limited next to that available as corporate billboards, commentators, or both. Shane Warne's casual role as spin ambassador was a compromise after he had baulked at CA's suggested remuneration for a fuller role.

Lastly, Marsh advocated a scholarship and succession plan, in which older players were encouraged to stay in the system by adding a coaching element to their state contract. Marsh's blueprint encouraged senior Sheffield Shield cricketers to start by coaching the best Under-12 and Under-14 players in the state through to their first representative side, and then follow through to Under-19s. From Under-19s mentor, that player rises to become an assistant state coach, perhaps to move states, perhaps become a state coach, and perhaps ultimately become national coach. Pay for these roles needed to be competitive with what state playing contracts offered.

But the concept had been largely ignored, and almost two generations of potential coaches drifted elsewhere. The exodus only increased when the Futures League was introduced, a system of affirmative action for youth that served mainly to push those players of a teaching age even further away from the thought of doing so. On that and several other issues, Marsh and his former Test captain Greg Chappell were philosophically at odds. Chappell had swayed many in CA's office to his views over time, and had another staunch disciple in Nielsen. So it was almost a kind of natural counterbalance when Marsh found himself looking over the CoE in Brisbane in early June.

He was there on the invitation of Troy Cooley, who had replaced Chappell as head coach of the centre after the Ashes. Liking what he saw but also pointing out several areas for improvement, Marsh crossed paths with David Boon, who had recently announced his intention to resign as a selector and become an ICC match referee. Following a conversation with Boon, Marsh met with Michael Brown in July and expressed his interest in becoming a selector. From that afternoon Marsh's resume was at the top of the pile for a prospective new selection panel, alongside that of his former state captain John Inverarity.

The likelihood of change resulting from the Argus review loomed ever larger from the day early in June when the list of CA contracts was announced. Like a lame-duck president stacking the United States' Supreme Court in the final year of his term, Andrew Hilditch's panel members were aware their days were growing short and had resolved to be as forward-thinking as possible. They were convinced that one of Simon Katich, Michael Hussey and Ricky Ponting had to be 'managed out', in order to eradicate the danger of all three quitting at the same time. As it was, Katich's culling unleashed a stream of fury from the public, the players and Katich himself, who could rightly state that no-one in the preceding two years had made more Test runs than he.

Katich's previous slights from the selection panel made him a most problematic choice. In 2004 he had been dropped for Andrew Symonds in Sri Lanka, despite making his first international century two months before in Australia's most recent Test match, against India. Later that same year he had been chosen in India and performed creditably as proxy number three in place of an injured Ponting. Jettisoned a second time when the home summer began,

Katich foreshadowed a reckoning to come. 'I've had a few people saying they probably think I've been too nice,' he told the *Sydney Morning Herald*, 'and on both occasions I think I've done the right thing personally because I think I've just kept my mouth shut and not done anything. But it's happened twice now and I think at some stage I'm bound to snap.'

Then there was Katich's strained history with Michael Clarke. Viewing the contracts list in the light of the two-year-old story of the pair's SCG dressing-room fracas, many fingered Clarke as the executioner. Not so, says Jamie Cox. 'One of the greatest public misconceptions was that Michael Clarke was behind Simon Katich not getting a contract. I've always found that quite staggering. There are conversations you don't know about, but I am very, very confident Michael was never consulted about that. It's bizarre that the public hold Michael Clarke responsible for Simon's demise. It was our decision.'

Many journalists contacted Katich's manager, Robert Joske, who had previously fought a notable battle with the selectors alongside another client, Steve Waugh. When Joske delivered his line that Katich was 'considering his options', most presumed those were retirement or playing on. In fact, the options were of the legal variety, as he seriously weighed up the possibility of suing CA for unfair dismissal. In the days after the announcement, Joske met with the headkicking Harmers Workplace Lawyers and was advised that an age discrimination suit stood a strong chance of success. After long conversations with the Australian Cricketers' Association chief executive, Paul Marsh, among others, Katich reached a compromise. He would not sue, and he would play on, but not before delivering the most stinging public critique of CA that it had ever received from a player.

Cricket press conferences are generally rote affairs, with one or two lines commonly emerging from the sea of clichés that can be turned around into headlines. Katich's appearance in the SCG's lecture hall on

11 June was nothing of the sort. Steeled by the presence of his batting mentor, Bob Simpson, in the audience, Katich tore into the selectors and CA management with a ferocity with which Clarke's neck was once familiar. A few of his observations are worth recounting.

On the selectors' part-time status: 'You pay peanuts, you get monkeys.'

On selection inconsistencies: 'A week or two before the Ashes a squad of seventeen was named. Now, in my opinion, if you can't know what your best eleven is a week before our biggest series then that to me reeks of indecision. The fact that we've had ten or eleven spinners in the last three years, that to me is another indicator of the inconsistency in selection. Rules for some and rules for others.'

On his four-minute dialogue with Hilditch, during which he was notified of his dismissal: 'As soon as he told me the reason, which was what was being trotted out in the press about wanting the opening partnership to be bedded down for the 2013 Ashes, that got me steaming.'

On criteria for selection: 'When I got picked for my first tour, in 1999, you got picked because of your performance. Now it seems that that's changed and it's not only about performance; it is about potential.'

On the possibility of a CA sanction over the press conference: 'Technically I'm still contracted until the end of June 30. So no doubt the phone will ring and I'll probably have to answer for this. But at the same time, I'm not going to stand up here and lie about it all.'

On the Argus review: 'Hopefully something good will come out of that review, because this might just be the straw that breaks the camel's back.'

This was sound and fury that signified much, and in many ways it replicated the sort of testimony being offered to Argus and his panel at the time. The players' frustrations had been building for some years but had been brought to the boil during 2010–11 as Greg Chappell's ideas on ushering in youth were given more or less free rein by Hilditch and CA management. Central to these ideas were the concept that great players learn by being identified early and playing Test cricket at a young age and the contention that first-class cricket was no longer a proving ground worth the name.

If sound enough in theory, especially when backed up by examples such as Ponting, Clarke, Warne and Sachin Tendulkar, Chappell's notions had two significant flaws. First, none of the aforementioned great players had been pitched into an Ashes series, whose demands often favoured settled experience over brash youth. Secondly, Australia's system was not producing young players of that level of ability anyway, and it seldom did. Amid the evidence unearthed by Andrew Jones in his Argus review research was a concept he termed 'the few, the very few': to mid-2011, only nine batsmen in Australia's Test history had averaged 50 or better (four since 1979–80), and only twenty-one bowlers had taken their wickets at cheaper than 25 runs apiece (three since 1979–80). Most players took time to learn their skills in first-class cricket.

The wholesale search for players who appeared so rarely in Australian cricket's history combined with the panel's often haphazard communication with players had left many feeling that teams were being chosen by roulette wheel. Says Jones: 'It's a bit like if you were queuing up for lunch and sometimes they serve the person at the front of the queue or sometimes they serve the person in the middle or the back of the queue. You'd be like, "Wait a second, what the hell's going on?" and you'd get annoyed about that happening at lunchtime – imagine if that's actually your career.'

As if to prove his point about age, Katich went on to play first-class cricket for longer – albeit by only one season – than either Hussey or Ponting. Jamie Cox has conceded, as did the CA chairman Wally Edwards eventually, that the decision to cull Katich may have been a mistake. But Cox also explained the thinking of his panel, which wrestled with the loss of Warne and McGrath in much the same way Ponting did as captain. By the time Clarke became captain and new selectors followed, the reality had sunk in rather better. 'With Katich, Ponting, Hussey we might have got the order wrong,' Cox says. 'But you have to have an order, you have to plan stuff; whether the plan is right or not is where you ultimately get held to account. You don't know how good a guy is until you've got him in and he's had time to settle. Ricky averaged 35 until about his fortieth Test. Matthew Hayden the same; then they just went bang. Gilchrist and Hussey aside, they all took their time to settle.

'The difference with our panel to their panel, and you're only right if you win, is we would have said to Phil Hughes, "Okay, Phil, unless you do something really dumb, you're in. The senior players are under pressure here, because if you're not performing it is the senior players who should cop a bullet before the younger ones." That got flipped on its head to where if you're coming in you've got to make an immediate impact, and if you've already made the impact they'll have faith in you. Not right or wrong, just different.'

Adding to the shock of the recent changes was the Argus review's announcement during the Australian team's tour of Sri Lanka, in August. It created a uniquely difficult state of flux for the team. Coach Tim Nielsen was set to join the rest of the tour party for a visit to the Australian High Commission in Colombo when Gavin Dovey called him aside. Michael Brown and James Sutherland were en route to join the squad. 'I thought, "There's only two ways this is going: great news or not great news,"' Nielsen recalls, 'and it'd be pretty unusual for them to stop me going to the High Commission if it was great news.' Three Ashes Test match defeats were paid for with three jobs: Nielsen's was spilled, Andrew Hilditch's ceased to exist, as he was to be replaced by a full-time national selector, and Greg Chappell lost his selection post though remained national talent manager. When the players returned from the High Commission a few hours later, they found Nielsen in tears.

Earnestly and doggedly as he had worked, Nielsen fared little better in the review than the selectors. His keyed-up, nervous state during and after the Ashes had been noted, as had his wider lack of gravitas due to his relatively modest playing career. Never a selector, Nielsen had commonly set up an 'us against them' dynamic when talking a player through how the two of them would work together to ensure Hilditch's panel could not wield its axe. Ultimately, though, the confidential words of the players in the conference rooms had done in the coach.

'How can you talk about team culture without being in the change rooms or being on a tour and seeing how training runs?' Nielsen still wonders. 'All Don Argus, and to an extent Steve Waugh, Allan Border and Mark Taylor, could go on was what was said in interviews. And people were undoubtedly ensuring they were covering themselves. That was one thing I was disappointed in. The things that hurt the most when you're talking about teams you're involved with are things like culture and behaviour. That's the only thing I still carry a bit at different times and still hurts, because I reckon a lot of the time we were in pretty good shape.'

The extension of Nielsen's contract as coach in August 2010 had been one of the more broadly questioned decisions of the pre-Argus regime and in many ways summed up the diffuse and unaccountable structure that had existed for years. At the time, Nielsen had wanted the additional tenure to put his mind at ease ahead of the Ashes and had put his request to Michael Brown. Not being directly accountable for the coach's job, Brown had queried the possibility with the players and coaches, who had been positive about the idea, before recommending the extension to Sutherland, who then did likewise to the board. By creating the position of executive general manager of team performance, Argus hoped to achieve the sort of accountability missing from that decision.

After getting over their initial shock, Nielsen and Chappell resolved to do their best for the remainder of the tour, fighting an inevitable sense of bitterness in the process. Most difficult was the fact that two of Nielsen's assistants, Justin Langer and Steve Rixon, had their eyes on the senior coaching job. Rixon had twice been passed over in years gone by but had taken up a role as fielding coach in mid-year and now felt his time might finally be at hand. Highly regarded by Clarke, he had also received a coruscating endorsement from Brett Lee at the team's mid-year training camp: 'Whatever Steve's touched in his life in coaching has turned to gold.'

In managing this situation while also guiding Clarke through his first Test tour, Nielsen earned a good deal of respect, even though by the time it ended, in late September, he had decided not to reapply. His wife, Bronwyn, who seldom toured, and their children joined him in Sri Lanka as he made the decision. 'I had time to think about it over the next three weeks, and I made a conscious effort to ensure it wasn't going to impact on how I went about my job,' he says. 'I didn't want to, by being bitter, break down those relationships I'd taken so long to build. I don't have a lot of contact with those blokes any more – time has gone on – but the one thing if I do happen to run into them: I know I can look them in the eye knowing that for every minute I was there I gave it everything. I wasn't good enough; that's why I'm not still there, and that's fine.'

The review's findings met with favour among the players, the public and the media, all groups reassured that CA was at least showing some interest in addressing the problems of the previous summer. If there were reservations about the elevation of captain and coach to selector status, the identity and thoroughness of the review panellists assuaged much of the anxiety. In the *Sydney Morning Herald*, Peter Roebuck summed up the reaction: 'The inclusion of the team leaders is contentious. Struggling players might not confide in a coach also called upon to choose the team. Doubtless Argus and company carefully weighed the pros and cons – they consulted widely – so their conclusion can more easily be accepted. Argus has also recommended the appointment of an overseer of cricket operations, the job so ably carried out by Hugh Morris in England. Selectors, coaches, captains and the rest will report to him (or her). It is a sensible move, calculated to ensure compatibility.'

Paul Marsh believes the announcement of the review's outcomes was the moment at which a dangerous drift of players towards cynicism about the national team was scotched. A sense of disillusionment had sprung up during Monkeygate and had deepened with the abundance of contentious issues such as the Champions League, Futures League, split-innings limited-overs format and blue-sky selection policies. 'In our player surveys we'd ask the question annually "Would you prefer a $1 million IPL contract or a baggy green?" and the numbers of a few years ago had slipped to about 66 per cent baggy green," Marsh says. 'Last time we did it, it was 92 per cent, and there's a few reasons for that. Our players are paid very well, far more from CA than any other players in the world, so we're more protected against the freelancing option. But I also think the Argus review had something to do with it. At that point there was this ongoing erosion of how important international cricket was, and the players felt that; they didn't think CA cared enough about it. Argus refocused Australian cricket on high performance. The players started to say, "This is how it should be. If they're prepared to commit and starting to put more money in, then so are we."'

As CA set about the search for a new coach, new selectors and a team performance overseer, Clarke's tourists put together a victorious journey through Sri Lanka. The squad was wisely chosen, with Trent Copeland providing the sort of seam-up control that Andrew McDonald had offered in South Africa two years before. The coaching staff also did their most constructive work in some time. McDermott elicited strong displays from Ryan Harris in the first and second Tests and from Peter Siddle in the third, after working with the Victorian to get him bowling more precisely after a poor display in a warm-up fixture. Langer's work with the young batsmen bore fruit in the form of a debut century for Shaun Marsh in Kandy and Phillip Hughes' first since South Africa 2009 in Colombo.

The senior players adapted to their new arrangements soundly enough, though Ponting missed the second Test to be at home with his wife for the birth of their daughter Matisse. He was otherwise the model tourist, allowing the new leadership plenty of room to breathe and giving up his number three batting berth following Marsh's head-turning entrance. Clarke worked reasonably with his new deputy, Shane Watson, who played a major role in the winning of the first Test on a parched Galle pitch by bowling the reverse swing he had first exhibited in India three years before.

Hussey found himself in the form of his life and won the match award in all three Tests on the way to 463 runs at 92.60 for the series. As vivid as any of his cover drives was the winkling-out of Kumar Sangakkara in Kandy, the result of the sort of tactical brainstorm at which Clarke was to prove adept. Vitally, Clarke also played two innings becoming of a new captain: a bold 60 took the game beyond Sri Lanka's reach in Galle, then a sturdy 112 secured the series in Colombo. Clarke's handling of Rangana Herath was masterly. 'Ricky was very supportive of Michael starting off his thing,' Hussey says. 'And when you've got a new captain it's like in the AFL when a new coach comes along: everyone lifts a little bit or wants to impress the new guy so you maybe improve a per cent or two inadvertently almost.'

After the team's earlier misadventures with corporate leadership schemes, Nielsen introduced something a little simpler and far more effective in Sri Lanka: each senior player paired with a junior as mentor and pupil. The most significant of these duos was Hussey's pairing with Nathan Lyon, the twelfth spin bowler tried since Warne's retirement. Lyon's classical off spin had turned heads during the Big Bash League the previous summer, and it was at Chappell's insistence that he was fast-tracked to Sri Lanka. Aided by some tremendous catching from Clarke and Ponting, in addition to the new captain's greater affinity for spin, Lyon claimed 5–34 in his first Test innings, immediately shedding the sort of anxiety that had haunted his predecessors.

Lyon was part of a winning team in his first match and first series. With the help of Hussey, he felt like he belonged. Much like post-Argus Australian cricket, Lyon had a long way to go. But both had made an encouraging start.

15

Just Like
Starting Over

OCTOBER – NOVEMBER 2011

Australia in South Africa

New Zealand in Australia

Change was taking place at speed, and not only around the national team. A CA board resolution to advance the Big Bash League for the 2011–12 season had left CA and the states to scramble for the requisite cash to launch the tournament with the sort of bubble and fizz the marketeers demanded, cutting considerable money out of state team programs as a result while opening up a gaping hole in the middle of the season, in which numerous Sheffield Shield matches had once resided. Simultaneously, CA's search for a new team performance supremo, selection panel and head coach needed to be both exhaustive and expeditious, two qualities seldom found to coexist. The sports consulting firm Crank Sports and corporate headhunter John Allen were hired to aid in the recruiting, backed up by a team performance budget suddenly more bountiful than before.

Michael Clarke's first Test tour had been a success, but he was in for an early shock ahead of a trip to South Africa in October, which the hosts had downsized to a two-Test series in order to fit in a more extensive limited-overs schedule. Alongside Shane Watson, Clarke asked the assistant coach, Justin Langer, to collate some anonymous feedback from the touring squad. Expecting a strong report card based on the team's results, Clarke was floored by a selection of less-than-favourable reviews, a reaction that set him back for some weeks.

Early in the South Africa tour, Clarke faced another rocky few days when he and the caretaker coach, Troy Cooley, censured some members of the team, including Michael Hussey and Brad Haddin, for going out to celebrate the wicketkeeper's birthday after an ODI loss in the quiet Eastern Cape town of Port Elizabeth. 'We were all sheepish, but later we talked amongst ourselves and felt aggrieved,' Hussey wrote in his autobiography. 'We didn't think we were doing anything wrong. We were treated like naughty schoolboys, and it put us on edge.' A win in the deciding limited-overs fixture eased some of the residual tension.

Clarke's expectations were high, and the first day of the Cape Town Test demonstrated why a few of his excesses needed to be forgiven. On a fresh early-season pitch, against Dale Steyn, Morné Morkel and the impressively poised debutant Vernon Philander, Clarke soared to 151, cuffing twenty-two boundaries along the way. Ponting called the innings 'one of the best I will ever see'. It was Clarke's finest hundred yet and seemed likely to be the performance of the match, exemplifying the sort of skill and courage the team needed to exhibit against heavily favoured opponents.

Moments after the lunch break on day two, Australia's reserve players left the Newlands dressing rooms for a gym session. As they wandered down the stairs, Graeme Smith and Hashim Amla were walking out to bat, with South Africa at 1–49. Little more than three hours later, the puffed and sweaty bunch returned to the team viewing area to find Smith and Amla still in occupation, the scoreboard appearing barely to have moved. At first, they wondered if it had been raining. Only gradually did it dawn that two entire innings had taken place. South Africa had fallen to 96 all out before Michael Clarke's team, believe it or not, had been obliterated for 47.

The speed with which Clarke's men had found themselves batting again after the South Africans' collapse seemed to inject the top order with a giddy sense of momentum. Sun on the Newlands pitch had encouraged some talk of the surface improving and even of scoring swiftly enough to send the South Africans back in for an over or two that night. The result of that eagerness, some nifty bowling by Steyn and Philander and a strip offering just enough movement to catch the edge resulted in the scarcely believable scorecard of 9–21.

Graeme Smith had made a point of calming his team down before they bowled at the Australians for the second time, telling them largely to follow the template of Watson's seam-up swing. 'Before we went out, we weren't emotional and "What are we going to do now?"' he says. 'We were actually clear in the change rooms with the guys, saying, "We're going to bowl this line, this length," and suddenly we got out there and it started to snowball. That was a key shift in our thinking that day. I remember looking up at the scoreboard showing 9–21 and thinking, "Is this a dream?"'

Watson, Clarke and Hussey all drove presumptuously, while Haddin's swish when walking down the wicket to Philander had to be among the worst shots played in Test history – not least because the card read 5–18 when he played it. As for Ponting, a tendency to fall across to the off side while playing balls angled into his pads resulted in a pair of near-identical l.b.w.s in the match, an endorsement of South African accuracy but a sign of the former captain's decline. Only Shaun Marsh had some cause for absolution, a painful two-ball stay at number ten more than should have been asked of him after his back seized up. Only the last men, Peter Siddle and Nathan Lyon, allowed Australia to creep past the lowest innings total in all Test matches, eventually settling on sixth worst.

Clarke's guard was down afterwards when talking to the press. 'Our shot selection was disgraceful. We nicked everything in sight, any half l.b.w. was given out, I can make a million excuses – the facts are we should not have been all out for 47. A lot of times in my career, as I just said to the boys in the change rooms, the bowlers seemed to get criticised for us losing games of cricket, but I can guarantee you we have done nothing but put ourselves under pressure because of our batting performance in this second innings. There's nobody else to blame.'

The team played out the rest of the match in a daze, as Smith and Amla each made a century in an eight-wicket victory that stretched the bounds of credulity. In the meetings that followed, Hussey had never seen an Australian team so panicked, so vulnerable. The extremes of Cape Town left many heads spinning, and Clarke's public words only hinted at some of the exchanges that occurred between teammates over the next forty-eight hours. Hussey was called out by other batsmen for his extravagant first-ball cover drive, while Haddin admitted to feeling he was 'really struggling'. In a way, it was the sort of honesty Ponting and Nielsen had sought from their earlier attempt at debriefs, but it took a cataclysmic event to draw it out.

On the theoretical fourth day of the Test, Justin Langer did his best to rally the batsmen. The prescribed remedy was a series of individual sessions at the Newlands nets and plenty of quiet, reassuring conversation. He spent most time of all with Ponting, who was suddenly confronted by the prospect of his international career ending well before he had envisaged. No longer able to rely on the selection safety net of the captaincy, a series of l.b.w. dismissals was playing havoc with his usually robust confidence. However, there was one factor that served to grant Ponting a little more time than he might otherwise have had – the changeover in selection panels.

Andrew Hilditch, Greg Chappell, Jamie Cox and the acting coach, Troy Cooley, were caretaking while CA identified a new panel to replace them. As Cox recalls, there would likely have been far greater will to move on from Ponting, either before South Africa or mid-tour, had Hilditch's panel not been disbanded. 'Our Katich, Ponting, Hussey plan fell foul of Don Argus. The tour of South Africa in 2011 came after the Argus review, and we were interim selectors for about two months. So do you reckon we were going to drop Ponting as our parting gesture to Australian cricket? No way. So that became picking Pat Cummins, Dave Warner – getting a few kids in. I honestly think the discussion with Ricky would have come very soon afterwards.'

Ponting could have retired at the same time as he relinquished the captaincy and concedes that there were numerous queries from within CA about why he did not do so. Don Argus, James Sutherland and Michael Brown all asked him why he was playing on. 'I was very conscious of making sure I wasn't stepping on anybody's toes and not looking like I was still the captain without being the captain,' he says. 'CA were worried about that when I stepped down, that "this has never happened before. We've never had a captain resign and then be in the team; we think this could be detrimental." James and Don Argus both asked me about it at the time.

'I just said, "If you think that about me you don't know me from a bar of soap. I can walk away now, but the reason I'm hanging around is to benefit the team – I want to be there to guide these young blokes through." I was a bit worried about what was going to happen when all those leaders were gone out of that group. Michael was a young captain, there was a new coach, and I was worried about where that was going to go. That's the only reason I hung around. If I'd retired two years earlier I would have been perceived as a whole lot better player than I am. I battled for the last couple of years and I probably could have finished on a better playing note, but it wasn't about me.' The even temper of Ponting and Langer in particular is remembered by many members of the South Africa touring party as a major benefit in the rapid turnaround that was achieved for the final Test, in Johannesburg.

Two days after the first Test, Cape Town awoke to shuddering news. Peter Roebuck, the Fairfax and ABC correspondent, formerly captain of Somerset, had killed himself by jumping from the sixth-floor window of his room at the Southern Sun hotel in Newlands after being confronted by police about allegations of sexual assault. The sudden loss of Roebuck hit the touring journalists particularly hard and was complicated by the circumstances and associated tasks, such as identifying his body, a duty conducted by Peter Lalor to spare *The Age*'s Greg Baum and the ABC's Jim Maxwell.

They were touched when Ponting, subject of one of Roebuck's most hot-tempered pieces in the aftermath of the 2008 Monkeygate Test, was among the players to approach them and offer condolences. Had Ponting read Roebuck's final column in the aftermath of Cape Town, he would have nodded at the wisdom of counselling against rushed judgements. 'It's no use ditching players for the sake of it, or in response to public demand,' Roebuck wrote. 'Apart from anything else the replacements might not be any better, or ready.' Roebuck also pointed out that Watson's role as an opening batsman and skilled bowler was unsustainable. Prescient words.

For most of the Johannesburg Test match, Australia hung desperately on to South African coat-tails. Both sides squandered strong starts to their first innings, but at 3–237 on day three Hashim Amla and A B de Villiers appeared to have taken the match into their keeping. But driven by the desire to make amends for Newlands and fortified by the poise and skill of the teenaged pace debutant Pat Cummins, Clarke's team clawed back the lost ground. When Cummins ripped out Philander and Morkel with consecutive balls on the fourth day, it appeared Australia might even be chasing less than 300. But the eventual run requirement, of 310 to win, looked a distant hope.

Australia's pursuit was sustained by a series of tenuous alliances in conditions still ripe for the ball to move around. Ponting fought his way to 62, largely in the company of Usman Khawaja, who played crisply and well after arriving at the crease for the third ball of the innings. Their union accounted for a little less than half the target, but at 6–165 on the final afternoon victory appeared about as unlikely as defeat had been before tea on day two in Cape Town. Brad Haddin, so crestfallen days before, and Mitchell Johnson, who has since confessed to needing a break from the game by this stage, after four years of uninterrupted cricket and wildly divergent results, forged the critical stand.

Haddin and Siddle perished with 18 still required, and the broadcaster's shot of a wide-eyed Lyon padded up ready to go in last conveyed Australian nerves in vivid terms. But Cummins completed a match to be remembered by helping Johnson stagger over the final few yards of the chase, finishing it off by shovelling an Imran Tahir googly to the straight mid-wicket fence. Given Australia's traumas in Cape Town, Smith remains puzzled about how South Africa managed to lose. 'We were set up on day one; maybe we relaxed at 1–0 up,' he says. 'Australia had to chase a lot of runs in the fourth innings and I still feel that Test match, with our bowling attack, we should have won. But sometimes you have to give credit: Australia really fronted up that day.'

Cummins' performance earned him the match award and has become steadily more mythical ever since, not simply because his seven wickets, one outstanding outfield catch and the clumping of the winning runs were so memorable, but because by the end of 2014 it was still the only Test match he had played. A heel bruised at the Wanderers turned out to be the early signs of a stress fracture, and a series of other injuries and efforts to remodel his bowling action kept him from returning. Baum summed it up in *The Age*: 'Cummins is an imposing size for an 18-year-old and looks indestructible, but so did Shaun Tait.'

Another injury, the foot ailment that befell Johnson, allowed the incoming selection panel to avoid an awkward decision. Including a nine-wicket Ashes burst at the WACA, Johnson's past three series had reaped 24 wickets at nearly 50 runs apiece. 'If I hadn't got the injury and I got picked – because there was concern that I wasn't going to – I don't think anything would have changed,' Johnson said in 2012. 'I don't think I would have retired, but I definitely would have stepped away from it a little bit. Before my injury I wasn't confident and didn't believe in myself. The first two months away from it, I didn't miss the game at all. I'd spoken to one of the coaching staff and said, "I'm just not interested in it."' The break did Johnson untold good.

Less helpful were hamstring and calf problems for Watson that accompanied the increased amount of bowling he found himself doing under Clarke. In some ways this was an issue created by Watson's own accomplishment as a seam and swing merchant, as proven on day two in Cape Town. But it was the cause of some disagreement between the new captain and his deputy, who went on to an endlessly frustrating home Test summer in which he ultimately played no part. The pair's efforts to build a constructive leadership were placed on indefinite hold.

Nevertheless, the Australian celebration at the team hotel that night was intense and prolonged, an outpouring of relief and tension shared by players, support staff and, on a rare occasion, the touring journalists. Haddin and Ponting, subject to plenty of fierce questions about their futures ahead of the match, shared drinks, conversation and even the odd good-natured headlock with Baum and Lalor. After the team's return to Australia, Siddle's jovial series summary felt appropriate, if not technically accurate: 'A good one-all series win.'

Australian cricket's new manager was to be the 'single point of accountability within CA for Australian Team Performance'. The role was modelled on that performed quietly and ably by Hugh Morris, the man who had lured Rod Marsh to the England and Wales Cricket Board in 2001 and worked smoothly with Duncan Fletcher and Andy Flower. Its particulars were designed partly by the head of cricket, Michael Brown, who had been frustrated at times by the range of things he was not empowered to do. 'No one person actually owned the Australian cricket team,' he says. 'I didn't appoint the selectors – the board did; I didn't appoint the captain – the board did. I had no power to sack or discipline a player without board approval.'

Brown recommended that the new man be based in Brisbane, linking with the Centre of Excellence and its forthcoming upgrade to the shiny new $29 million National Cricket Centre in 2013. There was also a desire for fresh perspectives on the Australian game, even if the Argus review's pages had emphasised a loss of fundamental basics at all levels as a major reason for the national team's problems. The result of all these factors and requirements, some at odds with one another, was the appointment of Pat Howard in mid-October. A former Wallaby, club coach for Leicester and high-performance director of the Australian Rugby Union, Howard had also worked as a pharmacist and a property developer. His inquiring mind was allied to a determined streak and a conviction about his high-performance background. He also knew precious little about Australian cricket.

The counterbalance to Howard's lack of ground-level knowledge was meant to be the coach and selectors. Howard was somewhat involved in interviews for these roles, though James Sutherland and the CA chairman, Wally Edwards, already had an eye on their preferred candidates. Rod Marsh had been interested in becoming chairman, but John Inverarity was ultimately considered the better figurehead and arrived with the endorsements of both Edwards and Hilditch. Inverarity was unwilling to move to Melbourne, and his Perth locale and its time difference raised some issues in terms of the communication he was expected to provide in what the Argus review had termed the role of 'HR manager' for the team. But his relationships with players, coaches and administrators as a longtime mentor, coach and thinker were strengths. Geoff Lawson was among the other interviewees.

The last piece in the appointments jigsaw was that of the coach, and numerous candidates raised their hands. Apart from Steve Rixon and Justin Langer, Tom Moody was also in contention. Ultimately, though,

CA settled on the affable South African Mickey Arthur. In his first season as coach of Western Australia, Arthur had made decent strides in shaking a complacent squad out of its torpor. His Argus review interview had impressed Steve Waugh and Malcolm Speed, notably with the suggestion that the coach needed to be empowered to draw some pressure away from the captain. Equally alluring was the fact that Arthur had advised Andy Flower on the setting-up of England's team when the Zimbabwean replaced Peter Moores in 2009.

'The advert came out and I thought, "You're in Australia – surely you've got to have a go at it?" So there was no contact from CA at all; I just applied,' Arthur says. 'Initially you got asked a series of questions and made an email presentation. Then there was psychometric testing, then only after that testing did we get asked to interview, in the Melbourne Hilton on the Park by Craig Mitchell from Crank Sports, James Sutherland, Pat Howard and Mark Taylor. They told me I had the job the next day [Friday 18 November].'

Arthur's broader ideas were attractive given that Argus had outlined a job description that took on not only the national team but also a strategic commission to formulate an aligned coaching plan for all the states. His preference for working as a manager who delegated individual coaching to assistants with help from senior players was looked upon kindly by the panel, as was his experience of cricket in another nation. During his time with Australian Rugby Union, Howard had recruited Robbie Deans from across the Tasman Sea to become the Wallabies' coach, and now he was eager for a fresh pair of eyes for the cricket team.

Arthur spoke well at the announcement of his appointment and denied he would encounter any difficulties as the first foreign overseer of an Australian dressing room. Sutherland declared, 'We're very, very confident that we have the right man.' But others were not so confident; South Africa's players told their Australian counterparts, 'This is not going to work for you guys.' Graeme Smith was astonished that his former ally thought he was ready for the task, after little more than a year in Australian cricket. 'I was surprised he took the job. He'd only just started in Perth; they had big challenges there, and he was starting to find some leaders,' Smith says. 'Mickey's strength is that he's a nice guy, outsourcing a lot of his stuff and having complementary people to work with him. I always felt if he was going to take the job he needed to be in Australia for a longer period. Work in Perth first and then get to the point where he's comfortable and really understood what it was about in Australia. Then he would have been in a stronger position to take it on.'

Little more than a week later, John Inverarity, Michael Clarke, Mickey Arthur, Rod Marsh and Andy Bichel wandered out into the middle of the Gabba and pondered their options against New Zealand. They were accompanied by Pat Howard, making an earnest start to his oversight role. Completed by the first-year team manager, Gavin Dovey, the Australian team's leadership looked more foal than steed. Plenty of stumbling took place as each appointee tried to work out where his job ended and the next one began. There was little agreement among the group about whether all the roles were complementary or even necessary. Howard made no secret of his intention to ask plenty of outsider questions, the sort not commonly heard among those who knew the game well. Among his first was 'Why do we have selectors?' The selectors had another: 'What is the captain doing here?'

Given the circumstances, the New Zealand series was never likely to be serene. Though Ponting and Haddin were retained, the new panel's first squad was heavy on youth, securing new Test caps for Mitchell Starc, James Pattinson and David Warner. (When Ed Cowan was later chosen for the Boxing Day Test against India, the number of debutants for Australia in 2011 had swelled to enough for an entire team.) Brisbane proved a typically helpful venue for the first Test, its pitch more lively than the one produced for the Ashes, and Pattinson emulated Cummins in the manner of his start: fast, full and swinging deliveries abounded, with a 10-wicket win the result.

Warner's emergence had been a significant development during 2011. First glimpsed as a T20 slugger against South Africa in January 2009, when he memorably pummelled 89 at the MCG, he had then drifted around the New South Wales second XI and T20 leagues for a time until Greg Chappell pointed out that his shot-making skills were allied to a better technique than many gave him credit for. At Delhi Daredevils, in the IPL, India's jack-in-the-box Virender Sehwag came to a similar conclusion, encouraging Warner to aim for Test cricket. With Chappell's cajoling, the Blues began to pick him for first-class duty, and he made enough runs in 2010–11 to be granted an Australia A berth for their winter tour of Zimbabwe, where he coshed a double century.

Those runs had Warner inked in as the team's reserve batsman, and he had been called up as a substitute for both Sri Lanka and South Africa in 2011. Shane Watson's injury allowed Warner to debut at the Gabba. He brought with him a pugilistic streak that had been missing from the team since Matthew Hayden's retirement. In February, Warner had exchanged abuse with the Tasmanian seamer Brett Geeves on Twitter. CA had threatened a heavy fine, and when Paul Marsh called to counsel the pair, he had received contrasting responses. Geeves was repentant, Warner nothing of the sort. Though disagreeing with Warner, Marsh also thought to himself, 'We might have a fighter here.'

At the second Test, at Bellerive Oval, Warner found himself in a fight as a fresh pitch and skilful bowling by Trent Boult, Tim Southee, Chris Martin and Doug Bracewell allowed New Zealand to close the gap with Australia. Though Ross Taylor's team achieved a memorable victory, Warner carried his bat for 123 and proved his worth as a Test opener. The fundamental soundness of his method contrasted with the jerky Phillip Hughes, who was squared up by Martin and caught by Martin Guptill in four innings out of four. Alongside Khawaja he was dropped, as Inverarity's panel demonstrated a more pragmatic mindset than Hilditch's had done. Based on another l.b.w. in the first innings and an unsightly prod to cover, Ponting might easily have gone instead.

Ponting would not have been surprised to lose his place at this moment. Instead, he, Clarke and the rest looked ahead to the arrival of the Indians, a team dealing with similar issues of time and tide. Thinking of playing Rahul Dravid, Sachin Tendulkar and V V S Laxman on one last tour, Ponting mused on their familiarity. 'It was as if,' he wrote, 'I'd been joined at the bar by blokes my age who were having the same problems at work that I was.' In delivering the annual Bradman Oration at Canberra's War Memorial, Dravid referred to the trio as 'creaking terminators'.

16

Indian Summer

DECEMBER 2011 – JANUARY 2012

India in Australia

A strange thing happened ahead of the fourth Test against India in Adelaide. The series had already been a runaway success for Michael Clarke's Australia, but when the squad assembled at the oval for their first meeting, all were reminded that there was still much for certain members of the team and those around them to learn.

Before Mickey Arthur stood to address the squad, he noticed in the dressing room an ageing man he had never seen before. 'Who's that guy? Gav, we've got to get him out of here.' The team manger, Gavin Dovey, similarly unaware of the unannounced visitor's identity, rose to remove him. 'Then Gav goes and politely asks him to leave, and the whole room goes into uproar. Justin Langer's come running to me and said, "No, no, he's Nugget," and telling me a little about him, so I say, "Of course, let him back in." For me, there's a guy sitting in the corner in our team meeting and I don't know who he is. Subsequently, I went and found out and learned all about him and I thought, "Wow, what a legend," but no-one told me about him.'

Barry 'Nugget' Rees is part of Australian cricket's furniture. Since the 1960s he has been ever present with the South Australian and Australian teams at Adelaide Oval and occasionally elsewhere, serving as team mascot. His place in the corner of the dressing room is unquestioned and welcomed. As Adam Gilchrist put it in *Australian Story* in 2007, 'That unique access to the team is rare but there's no second thought about it with Nugget. The Australian cricket team, whatever era it is, embraces him.'

Arthur and Dovey soon joined the embrace, but it was a telling moment. Key figures in the leadership of the Australian team had very little sense of its fabric or history. Had he been there, Pat Howard might have been similarly nonplussed. They were trying, but there was a lot to learn in a hurry. At the end of the Test, Brad Haddin and Ed Cowan presented Arthur with a T-shirt emblazoned with the label 'Aussie Mickey'. Arthur was grateful for the gift and the sentiment, but his description of it was also telling: 'It was almost acceptance.' Almost.

Selection debate for the India series was prolonged. For the first time, the Big Bash League meant there were no Sheffield Shield matches leading into the first Test, on Boxing Day, only a pair of warm-up fixtures for India in Canberra. As well, the poor display of the batsmen against the moving ball in Hobart and Cape Town had not engendered confidence that the likes of Zaheer Khan and Ishant Sharma would be comfortably countered. With Phillip Hughes and Usman Khawaja dropped as a result, debate focused on the top of the batting order.

Shaun Marsh had recovered from his back complaint but had no way of proving it apart from in the Big Bash. Shane Watson's calf strain had recurred, ruling him out. This left an opening berth vacant, and there was a preference among the selectors for a steady hand who could soak up pressure and help stave off the kinds of batting collapses the team had recently witnessed. Three contenders emerged: Chris Rogers, who had started the summer well for Victoria; Ed Cowan, in fine form for Tasmania; and the familiar figure of Simon Katich.

In contravention of the notion that he had been to blame for the left-hander's removal from the CA contracts list in June, Clarke pushed for Katich. He did so even though in November Katich himself had suggested that Clarke was behind his sacking, in a flustered, frustrated Shield press conference after making a century. 'If the consensus had gone to pick Simon Katich, Michael would have been very happy with it,' Arthur says. John Inverarity, who surprised many players by calling them for the sort of chat they had never enjoyed with Hilditch, spoke to Katich about the door not being closed when he joined the Perth Scorchers ahead of the Big Bash.

Eventually, Cowan won out, largely because while Rogers was heading back to club cricket with Prahran and Katich was in T20 mode, the youngest of the trio was completing a hot streak of four centuries in five matches, against the Indian tourists at Manuka Oval in Canberra. Cowan's inclusion represented the middle path the selectors were trying to take, choosing a batsman to fit a role for the present rather than storing up Test match experiences for the future.

Before suggesting Katich, Clarke had wanted Hughes to be retained. Overruling him did not always come easily. As early as 21 December, Inverarity stated publicly that the selector's role was creating extra difficulty for Clarke. 'It is obviously a very difficult situation; a captain needs to be supportive of his current players and Michael was exactly that,' he said of Clarke's support for Hughes. 'The pressures on an Australian captain are enormous, and with the current situation with the captain being one of the official selectors on the national selection panel, it is an extra difficulty, but that's the situation and Michael needs to cope with that.' Asked directly whether or not he was opposed to the arrangement, Inverarity was curt: 'That's a question I'll defer for the time being.'

Privately, neither Inverarity nor Rod Marsh felt that Clarke should be a selector. The reasons Clarke had been invested with the role were that Ponting had felt for some years that he should have been a selector, and that Don Argus was adamant about the concept that the most important people in any given management structure also had to be the most accountable. 'Every board presentation I had to do as captain, I'd go in there with the same thing at the top of my list, over and over again,' Ponting says. 'I stood down and what happened? The next Test match, the captain is a selector.

'It wasn't so much about not getting the teams, but if we talk about being accountable, you can't hold the captain completely accountable because he's got no say over who the coaches are, he's not picking the team; all he's doing is taking them onto the ground and trying to get a result. He can't communicate with them properly because he's not a selector, so how are you going to point the finger wholly and solely at him for what happens? The captain's got leadership but no ownership.'

Based on their own experiences, Mark Taylor, Allan Border and Steve Waugh were all uncomfortable with the idea but had conceded the point to Argus. Taylor and Waugh had brought about the opposite outcome in the past, firstly when the pair had told the Australian Cricket Board in 1994 that the coach, Bob Simpson, should no longer be a selector. Then, in 2001, Waugh had asked to be removed from the tour selection panel due to the hurtful process of dropping Michael Slater. 'I just felt you don't need that,' Taylor says. 'You don't need your captain or your coach to be a selector. It can allow the lines to blur. That's why when I took over the captaincy I was asked. That was my opinion then and still my opinion today. Now we've got the coach as a selector as a result of the Argus review I sat on, which means you don't always get your way on reviews!'

A tight alliance between Clarke and Arthur emerged, but so too did distance between them and other members of the team. Arthur had built his successful tenure as the South Africa coach on a close relationship with Graeme Smith, and on taking up the Australian job had likened the relationship between the team's on-field and off-field leadership to a marriage. As a result, he had spent much of his early time in Australia around Clarke, talking about cricket and life in the team hotels of Brisbane, Hobart and Melbourne. Meanwhile, the players were adjusting to the thought of not one but two selectors walking constantly among them. Hussey soon noticed an undercurrent of self-censorship whenever Clarke entered a room, and the following summer state players confessed to hesitation over whether they should be sledging a selector. Most agreed that the perception of a 'lurking executioner' was a problem for the team.

Before the start of the home series, Arthur assembled the top order, which was lacking any first-class match preparation for Boxing Day due to the Big Bash League, for a batting camp in Melbourne, where bowling machines were calibrated to mimic the lines, lengths and speeds of India's pace attack. 'It's just to get our unit of batters that we see playing in the Test match some sort of first-class batting practice,' Arthur said, 'without their techniques being compromised playing T20 cricket.' Shaun Marsh played only one match between Cape Town and the MCG, swinging his way to 99 not out for the Perth Scorchers against the Melbourne Renegades at Docklands Stadium. It was thought to be enough.

India arrived in Australia as warm favourites, but a 4–0 hiding at the hands of England earlier in the year had showed the frailties that could be exposed by decent seam and swing bowling on pitches offering a little movement and pace. That result had also suggested that M S Dhoni was not necessarily capable of rallying his team abroad if the hosts made a strong start. Rahul Dravid, V V S Laxman and Sachin Tendulkar had all tormented Australia in the past but were all past their best.

Even so, there were visible nerves among Australia's players on their return to the scene of the MCG Ashes fiasco a year before. Cowan did as he had been asked, nudging, nicking and occasionally driving and pulling on his way to a steady debut 68. That innings ensured a nervy batting order would not be shot out by India on an overcast Boxing Day, though it took a series of pesky lower-order partnerships to push the tally as far as 333.

The bowling attack was equally conscious of its failures the previous summer. Indifferent accuracy, wickets from no balls and flagging morale had affected the bowlers in 2010–11, and for the first four hours of India's opening innings there appeared some chance of the pattern being repeated. After the early loss of an out-of-sorts Gautam Gambhir and a blazing cameo by Virender Sehwag, Dravid and Tendulkar settled in. They had glided India past 200 and within sight of Australia's now meagre-looking total when Peter Siddle burst through Dravid's defence. However, the umpire's check on a foot fault revealed Siddle had transgressed, bringing the Victorian to his knees and drawing 50 000 groans from the crowd. All the work he had done with Craig McDermott. Wasted?

McDermott had cut a purposeful figure in Sri Lanka, convincing all the pacemen that they needed to be bowling fuller and on a more consistent line around off stump in order to take the wickets that the Argus review had pointed out as missing from the Test team's results. He had been notably pointed with Siddle, who bowled poorly in a tour match and lost his Test place as a result. 'Over there I really started to work things over and tried to get buy-in from senior players,' McDermott says. 'Michael had just taken over as captain and I certainly had his support for what my thoughts were about where we needed to pitch the ball, let alone the line of the balls we had to be bowling. It wasn't rocket science, but it was making sure we trained it bloody hard.'

McDermott had noted some scepticism similar to that earned by Troy Cooley's pitch mapping exercise. Most notably, Ryan Harris, who had been fairly successful in his brief Test career, needed convincing that he was not bowling full enough. 'The length we were brought up to bowl on, for me especially, was probably half a metre too short and you'd see the pitch maps on the TV that show your short, good and full lengths,' Harris said in 2011. 'We go by them and all the coding that's done on the games these days are done on those lengths. I got to Sri Lanka and spoke to him [McDermott] about that and I found it really hard to believe that we were not bowling full enough.' McDermott recalls that Harris 'never really came to me and questioned it, but when he got his first five-for the lights went on and he thought, "Hang on, this isn't a bad thing."' Slowly but surely, McDermott talked the bowlers around. He was helped by his own Test match pedigree and some instant results – the defeat of Sri Lanka in Galle. Little of what he said was new, but the way it was received marked a turned corner for the bowlers.

'I kept saying to [team analyst] Dene Hills, it's been happening since W G Grace, but we'd forgotten to coach it and to hammer it home to our senior players,' McDermott says. 'Test cricketers are expected to turn up and know how to do the job, but some do and some don't. If they don't you've got to have respect for them as a current Test player; they've got to have respect for you as hopefully a past Test player and someone who knows what he's talking about. Those two things were very visible between bowlers and me as a coach. Our relationship is very honest and frank and I respect what they've got to do. I know how hard it is.'

In Melbourne, Siddle was sustained by the memories of McDermott's advice. Returning to the top of his mark after the no ball, he charged in again and bowled a prancing off cutter that nearly cut Dravid in two, eliciting a roar from the crowd. Four overs later, another full delivery swerved in to Tendulkar and beat his slightly crooked drive. The delight of the Australians at the MCG contrasted with the eerie silence at that same moment right across India, for Tendulkar had crept to within 27 runs of his 100th international century. It was a point of pride for Australia's bowlers, and a measure of how the rest of the series panned out, that Tendulkar left the country at the end of the series without having reached this most hyped of all his milestones.

Ben Hilfenhaus, so ineffectual the year before, ran through India's middle order and tail the following morning, starting with a corking delivery to bowl Dravid. Ponting and Hussey combined for a staunch stand in the afternoon to establish a decent lead after the early loss of four second-innings wickets. India's fourth-innings pursuit of 292 on a still-lively pitch barely made it out of the starting blocks, as James Pattinson blasted out four of his own. Australia's rousing victory lifted confidence among all players, coaches and selectors, while visibly deflating India. There had even been a hint of intimidation – when Siddle and Pattinson confronted the touring tail, Clarke had pointed to the badge of his baggy green to suggest where his pacemen should be aiming.

If Melbourne was about the resurgence of the bowlers, Sydney was about Clarke, and preventative management. Pattinson had been so compelling at the MCG that Inverarity's panel chose to retain him for Sydney, even though Stuart Karppinen and Alex Kountouris indicated that the 21-year-old was at high risk of a stress injury due to the spike in his bowling load over three consecutive Tests. After Dhoni chose to bat, Pattinson found fine rhythm and charged through four of India's top six on a surface offering some early assistance. Siddle and Hilfenhaus followed up grandly, and Australia found themselves with enough time to face 26 overs in the final session. Early incisions by Zaheer brought Clarke in to join Ponting with the ball still new.

Clarke had been bowled twice in the first Test and took a few early swishes at the swinging ball, but, keyed up on his home ground, he found himself counterpunching fluently in the early evening. Ponting was similarly comfortable, having regained much of his poise over the course of a pair of 60s in Melbourne. Together they forged a major union, not being parted until the second new ball became due. In reaching his first Test century since January 2010, in Hobart, Ponting summed up the mud he had slogged through in the intervening months at one point by risking the sort of sharp single that had cost him his wicket several times as captain. Diving for the crease, he gathered a shirt and mouthful of SCG dirt, and took a moment to compose himself before warmly receiving the applause of a grateful crowd.

The audience was on Clarke's mind too as he carried on. Past 100, past Ponting's dismissal and Hussey's arrival, past 150, past 200, past 250, past stumps on day two. Seldom had an Australian captain been booed in the manner Clarke had been the previous summer, during the SCG Test and a handful of ODIs. Even his bat and clothing sponsor, Slazenger, had expressed a form of reticence by not renewing their long-standing deal with him. But with each boundary and milestone he achieved, he gained an increasing sense of respect among the populace, and among those who had ridiculed him at times through various media arteries.

Among those perched in the press box for the innings was Paul Kent, the *Daily Telegraph*'s irascible chief sports columnist. In February 2009, Kent had written that the Katich incident summed up discontent with Clarke and that former captains were 'openly appalled by Clarke's desire for Ricky Ponting's job'. In November of the same year Kent had penned a piece entitled 'The Problem with Michael Clarke', including the following passage: 'Michael Clarke is a tosser. Or, to give him an out clause, he *appears* to be a tosser. He might actually be an OK bloke, but how are we to ever know when all we see is the facade?' By way of crisis management, Clarke had signed with the newspaper as a columnist upon becoming captain.

So when Clarke addressed the media on the second evening of the Sydney Test, there was a priceless moment when Kent asked what this innings would do for the captain 'in the big picture'. The response included one pointed word. 'Hopefully, it helps me continue to earn *respect*.' Clarke went out the following day and carried on to 329 not out, stopping short of the Australian Test record and earning plaudits from Ponting for doing so. The innings secured his captaincy beyond all doubt and cuffed India's players into a state of weary submission.

The match was wrapped up inside four days, though not before Pattinson had bowled another 23 overs. To wry expressions from Karppinen and Kountouris, Pattinson confessed to foot soreness, and scans revealed the early stages of a stress fracture. His plight left the selectors far more open to taking the advice of the team's medical staff. 'Suddenly,' says Arthur, 'we thought, "Hang on, this isn't bulldust. They have a role to play here."'

Perth and Adelaide completed the rout of India on contrasting pitches. The WACA strip was as fast as the year before but greener, because the groundsman, Cameron Sutherland, had feared the forecast high temperatures would bake the wicket and lead to the kind of cracks seen in 1997, when Curtly Ambrose was run out after his bat became lodged in one. The Indians' anger about the surface and their conviction it had been watered at the request of the Australian hierarchy sowed the seeds for a dispirited surrender. It was followed by another at the Adelaide Oval, on a surface that should have been far more to their liking. It also gave rise to numerous instances of a warning delivered to Australia's players on the field: 'You're winning now, but wait until you get to India.'

Ponting and Clarke put together another major stand in Adelaide, both passing 200. The two innings were received rather differently, as Clarke's universal endorsements contrasted with garlands for Ponting that came with a sour twist: 'Wouldn't it be great to retire on top like this?' Well as Clarke had played, and comprehensively as India had been beaten, a major reason for the success had been the balance struck between an eager young captain and a trio of loyal older sweats. Ponting and Hussey followed Clarke on the aggregates, while Brad Haddin backed him fully as vice-captain, offering the odd piece of cooling advice. Without those three men, their knowledge and temperaments, the team looked far less solid. Shaun Marsh's series, at number three, was an unmitigated disaster, reaping 17 runs in six innings and leaving a vacant berth for the next Test assignment, in the Caribbean. David Warner played one domineering hand at the WACA but was otherwise flighty, and Ed

Cowan's middling return of 206 runs at 34.33 was an accurate reflection of his ability at Test level.

The man missing from this picture was Shane Watson, still shaking off a stubborn calf ailment that had been found to relate to wider nerve problems. In the prolonged celebrations that followed Adelaide, Pattinson's role was acknowledged when he was called on videophone to be part of the team song, of which Hussey led a lusty rendition inside the Adelaide Oval scoreboard. Later that night, Watson's more peripheral status was captured in a snatch of conversation at a nightclub. Asked when Watson was coming back, a player responded, 'We don't care.'

The extent of Australia's celebratory excesses in the aftermath of the India series was revealed a little less than a year later. In October 2012 the story emerged that one member of the Test team had been spoken to by CA after an episode that involved a cocktail of alcohol and cocaine. It took place that night in Adelaide and was relayed to team management through another player. When the limited-overs team convened in Melbourne, the player in question sat with Arthur and Dovey in the MCG dressing room. After admitting the veracity of the accusation, he was handed a heavy fine and also placed on a course of intensive counselling.

Formerly employed by the Australian Sports Anti-Doping Agency and England's Rugby Football Union, Dovey was far more conversant with the recreational drugs issue than he had been with Nugget's identity. The course of action was kept confidential and handled with a great degree of thought and care. The player concerned has not transgressed since and maintained his position as a consistent performer for the team. In its own quiet way this was a significant tick for the new regime, even if it was not the kind that could be boasted about.

17

Rumblings

FEBRUARY – OCTOBER 2012

Australia in the West Indies

Australia in England

Australia v. Pakistan in the UAE

ICC World Twenty20 in Sri Lanka

With the possible exception of Bill Lawry's 1970 South Africa tourists, already grizzled and gaunt after ten weeks in India, seldom has a more bedraggled collection of Australian players emerged from a plane than the limited-overs squad that touched down in Saint Vincent, in the West Indies, in February 2012. A schedule that left no room between the third ODI final in Australia and a departure for the West Indies was always going to tempt fate, and the loss of the second play-off against Sri Lanka had duly forced the third match. After grinding to victory in the day–night decider, the squad was up at five o'clock the following morning to begin the journey to the far side of the world.

'Honeymoon' had been an apt description for the India Test series, but the ODI triangular series that followed it had witnessed all the phases of drudgery, crankiness and flaws inherent in a longer relationship. Numerous potholes upset the delicate balance of egos and personalities that had been maintained during the Tests. These included a selection policy for ODIs that even the selectors themselves struggled with, the poorly communicated dropping of Brad Haddin, the premature elevation of David Warner to a leadership position, the use and abuse of Ricky Ponting in his final one-day tournament, various tensions among the coaching staff and emerging flaws in the management style of Mickey Arthur and Michael Clarke.

The limited-overs team that landed in the Caribbean was shorn of Ponting, while Clarke convalesced at home after pushing tight hamstrings too far in the closing stages of the triangular series. Leading in their place was Shane Watson, recovered from his leg troubles but re-entering a team and environment far removed from the one he had left in South Africa three months earlier. Within days of the team's arrival, Haddin flew home after receiving grim news about the worsening condition of his daughter Mia's health. The pitches in Saint Vincent proved to be perfect for the fiendish spin of Sunil Narine, and the West Indian crowds delighted in an ODI series that finished 2–2 with one match tied. The T20 matches were also split, and Arthur found himself under pressure not only from Pat Howard but also higher up the chain of command.

A more settled Test team roused itself from the slumber of under-preparation over the first three days of the first Test, in Barbados, to scramble to victory as the sun set behind Kensington Oval on the final evening. A draw in Trinidad and a sturdy victory in Dominica secured the series, also signalling the emergence of Matthew Wade as a combative batsman-wicketkeeper.

But a mid-year ODI visit to England was as dire as it was superfluous, resulting in a 4–0 hiding. The miserable team barely trained outdoors during the wet northern summer. Ponting and Michael Hussey were notable for their absence, and both Arthur and Clarke shared angry words with the team.

Further limited-overs assignments against Pakistan in the United Arab Emirates and at the World T20 in Sri Lanka were not so awful, but by then memories of the pleasant Indian summer had receded. The best way to sum up the prevailing mood was that by the time the team returned to Australia, in October, Michael Hussey was resolved not only to retire but to keep his thoughts about it to himself. Trust was missing.

Three years out from the 2015 World Cup, goals for the ODI team were hazy. Short of returning the team to the number-one ranking, there seemed room for some experimentation and planning. What grew in the vacuum was an idea of Pat Howard's that 50-over matches could be used not only as an end in themselves but as a proving ground for potential Test players. John Inverarity, Rod Marsh and Andy Bichel felt the notion had merit, but Clarke and Arthur were more reluctant, preferring the best team to be chosen. The test case was Peter Forrest, a neat batsman from New South Wales who had relocated to Queensland and emerged as a player of interest during the early part of the 2011–12 summer. He was included in the team during the late-summer triangular series with India and Sri Lanka.

'That was very much a Pat Howard initiative,' Arthur says. 'I didn't necessarily agree with it. I thought Peter Forrest was going to become a very good Test cricketer, not necessarily a one-day player. Pete got a hundred in Hobart, which was a very good innings, but on that wicket we ended up losing because we didn't have enough runs. Peter got his 104 off 138 balls, but that was a wicket where if you got a hundred it needed to be around a run a ball. I was glad for him – he showed he could play – but he wasn't going to play a role for us in the World Cup.' Forrest went to the West Indies but after a horrific run in England was dropped. His two highest scores were both mid-tempo tallies batting first in matches the opposition went on to win.

A further experiment was appointing David Warner as vice-captain, a flight of fancy exposed as troublesome when Clarke strained a hamstring three games into the triangular series. Watson was not yet ready to return, and Haddin had been dropped from the ODI team in favour of Wade. Inverarity had been clear to Haddin that his faltering form in the Tests and earlier limited-overs matches had forced the decision, though publicly the chairman indicated that the gloveman was being rested between Test series and needed to 'put his feet up'. Whatever the facts of the case, Haddin's absence meant that another leader needed to be found when Clarke felt the muscle twinge, compelling Ponting to return as captain only a year after he had resigned.

Initially, Ponting refused. Not unlike Haddin, he was drained after the exertions of the preceding Test series. Constant speculation about his place had not helped either, and in three ODI innings so far he had yet to reach double figures. Moreover, he wondered why Warner had been named vice-captain if the selectors had not considered the possibility of him actually leading. In the end, Ponting accepted the commission, but two games and two low scores later, with Clarke fit again, he was dropped.

For the first time since the late 1990s, Ponting discovered how little the selectors gave away in such situations. An epic ODI career worth 375 games and five World Cups, three of them won, ended shabbily. 'Never at any stage did they mention that my place was under threat,' he wrote. 'You might have thought they were ringing me to thank me the next day, but instead they were telling me I was done. That still annoys me. John Inverarity's new selection committee never gave me the chance to retire from ODI cricket . . . which I think I deserved. It had nothing to do with the fact Australia's next ODI was in Hobart. It wasn't about getting a lap of honour, just departing with dignity. Instead, they used me up.'

Arthur acknowledges that it was reasonable for Ponting to feel slighted. 'He was always under pressure, rightly or wrongly. I'm not going to abstain from any blame here but I always wanted Ricky in my team. I'll never forget sitting in my first selection meeting and Ponting was a massive discussion point. I'm on record backing Ricky right to the end; I wanted him to go through to the 2013 Ashes, but in one-day cricket was he going to play at the next World Cup? Probably not.'

Others noticed that the ODI team felt much less settled and more transient than the Test equivalent. Teams were being picked for brackets of three matches, and some players remember Arthur addressing the team about future fixtures while not knowing if they were even going to be flying to the next venue or returning home.

The anxiety was reflected in Ryan Harris' performance. He had been a strong contributor to the Test team in Perth and Adelaide but bowled as poorly as he ever had for Australia in the one-day matches before being dropped mid-series. The anxiety was also reflected in the team's results, which yoyoed through the triangular series and ended with an extra match that no player or coach wanted, and by Arthur late in one match, when a player found him sitting in the back of the dressing rooms, head in hands. 'I'm so nervous,' he said. Most tellingly, the anxiety was evident in Michael Hussey, who told his mentor Bob Carter that he was seriously considering retirement to avoid the West Indies trip. Carter talked him out of it.

In Watson, who led the ODI team to win the third and deciding triangular series final after Clarke sat out with a second hamstring strain, the players had a captain about as far removed from Clarke as it was possible to get. Now batting at number three, Watson seemed to have gained a more balanced view of his best fit for the team, using the extra breathing space granted by not opening to think more about bowling. Arthur spoke commonly of moulding Watson into Australia's Jacques Kallis.

But differences between Watson and Clarke, and the former's affinity with Ponting, were demonstrated in another selection conundrum that emerged in the Caribbean. Aside from challenging Australia's batsmen, the conditions also stretched the concentration of the bowlers, as the contrast was stark between Saint Vincent, where the first three matches were played, and Saint Lucia, host to the final two matches. Brett Lee had been taking wickets but at increasing expense. After the third match was tied, Lee bowled indifferently in the fourth, capping his display with a 50th over that was far too short. Kieron Pollard and Darren Sammy showed no fear of the pace Lee was trying to generate, thwacking him for 23 runs.

After the match, the tour selection panel of Inverarity, Watson and Arthur agreed that Lee was likely to be dropped for the final match but that they would keep their counsel until after training. Watson's compassion for Lee now overruled the cabinet solidarity required of selection panels, in which all members keep matters in confidence until speaking with the one voice at the required moment. Watson told Lee that he was in danger of losing his place and needed to smarten up – precisely the advice Ponting would have liked. Alerted to the state of play, Lee bowled immaculately at training and retained his place. But Inverarity was aghast and went home from the West Indies more adamant than ever that the captain should not be a selector.

At Andrew Hilditch's first selection meeting in 1996, Michael Slater was dropped from the Test team. He had played a wild swish to be dismissed in the second innings of a match against India in Delhi that Australia were battling to save. But he had also risen up fast in Australian cricket, riding one strong season for New South Wales into the 1993 Ashes tour and then three seasons of success, publicity and endorsements. Many felt that he needed to be taken down a peg or two. Fifteen years later, David Warner made a similar leap in the space of twelve months and was not shy in showing it.

The Australians moved to Barbados for the second T20 fixture, which the West Indies won narrowly. Test players, including the recovered Clarke, along with Ponting and Ed Cowan, arrived to find the coaching staff and all-format players looking and feeling a little more strung out than expected. Warner was among those rested from a three-day fixture at the picturesque Cave Hill ground, played on a desperately slow pitch. Reserve players are still expected to help out by running drinks and attending to various other dress-ing-room tasks, but Warner evidently showed little interest in doing so and began to irritate the likes of Ponting and Hussey. Eventually, Ponting spoke to Arthur but found himself worrying about the coach as much as Warner.

'Mickey, talk to him,' Ponting suggested.

'No, you do it. He's going to listen to you more than he'll listen to me,' replied Arthur.

'Mate, you're the coach of the Australian cricket team. I'm just another player in the corner. This is your chance to show some authority.'

Arthur felt it best to address Warner at a meeting with Gavin Dovey by his side at the team hotel. This took place later in the week, when Warner was asked to report in regularly to Arthur and was even put on a curfew that did not apply to other players. Looking back, Arthur reckons bestowing Warner with the vice-captaincy in Australia had not had the desired effect. Warner was a fighter and a useful on-field attack dog should Clarke require one, but qualities of leadership were still some years away. 'He was beginning to upset a lot of peo-ple. He got to a point where he might have started coasting a bit. He felt that he had made it,' Arthur says. 'After the vice-captaincy he sud-denly then thought he had become a permanent fixture.'

Less permanent, though for different reasons, were the places of the fast bowlers. Peter Siddle, James Pattinson and Ryan Harris were all wrestling with injuries of varying degrees, all of which could be traced back to the strains of the home summer. Having slogged through 343.3 overs across eight Tests, Siddle complained of back soreness after Barbados. Only recently returned from his foot stress complaint, Pattinson tweaked his back while making a throw off-balance from the Trinidad outfield. In this context, Harris was withdrawn from the fir-ing line for Trinidad after being man of the match at Kensington Oval, where he not only took five wickets and compiled a critical first-innings half-century, but also spent considerable time in the dressing-room toilet with stomach trouble. Irritated by the decision at first, Harris saw the sense of it when he returned in Dominica.

For bowlers and batsmen alike, the tour was a major test of patience. None of the top seven managed to average 40, and Wade's bold century at Roseau in the final Test was the only three-figure score. By the end of the series they felt frustration but also some sympathy for the increasing poverty in the West Indian Test team, which was missing Chris Gayle and Kieron Pollard. Australia's end-of-tour celebrations had a hint of weariness about them, as players hung out in a few disparate groups at a late-night party. As was typical, Hussey stood out for his enthusiasm, taking on the alter ego 'Maurice' that teammates saw emerge when a match or series had been won. It was his last time celebrating a Test win overseas.

Contracts were being renewed for both players and coaches during the Caribbean tour. Player deals were complicated by laboured negotiations between the Australian Cricketers' Association and CA, which stalled over the question of how much of the players' fixed percentage of Australian cricket revenue should be paid on a performance basis, as the Argus review had suggested. The man in the middle was Pat Howard, who had arrived in Barbados ahead of the first Test and had stayed down the road from the team at a different hotel. Howard's strong use of the Argus review as his battle plan was in many ways laudable, but in negotiating contracts he was placed in the awkward position of needing to be the team's voice at senior management and board level while also being tough with the players and coaching staff on the matter of their remuneration.

'There was an issue with the MoU [memorandum of understanding] negotiations, so that was a weird time for the players in the sense that you had a guy who was saying, "I'll fight for the team and everything you need I'll get," and he was also the guy CA were using to negotiate with the ACA, playing hardball on contracts,' Ed Cowan recalls. 'So the guys who were interested and engaged were asking, "Where does he sit in this picture? Is he with us or against us?" That was noticeable in the West Indies. And it was only after that MoU stuff had been resolved that they realised where he sat in the picture.'

The coaching staff were also at various extremes, whether in terms of their contractual status or desire to continue. Among those who had survived the rigours of the Argus review, feelings were mixed. The strength and conditioning coach, Stuart Karppinen, was thinking of leaving but did not want to do so until mid-2012. Well regarded according to his performance reviews but pressed to sign a new contract, Karppinen stalled until Howard informed him matter-of-factly that his job was to be advertised. Craig McDermott and Justin Langer, meanwhile, were encouraged to think about new deals more heavily loaded with performance bonuses, but the sight of Arthur's pressured visage in the West Indies gave them pause.

In the end, McDermott and CA parted ways by mutual consent at the end of the West Indies trip, largely because the schedule and time away had placed a strain on the bowling coach's family life and affected his demeanour on tour. His relationship with Arthur had also soured, meaning the senior coach's preference to delegate to his specialist assistants had become strained.

Though they had begun as rivals for the same job, Arthur and the fielding coach, Steve Rixon, operated together well enough, but there was a faint trace of disenfranchisement in their treatment of Langer. Some staff felt Langer's 105 Test matches were worthy of a little more deference and consultation. Says one member of the tour party, 'At times you'd have thought it was Steve and Mickey who formed the wonderful opening partnership with each other and scored a mountain of runs.' Arthur did not endear himself to Langer by comparing Australian players to their South African counterparts. If it was natural for Arthur to do so, Langer's counterview that Australia typically did pretty well against South Africa was also well founded.

By the end of 2012, Langer had moved on to coach Western Australia, and McDermott was setting up his own bowling academy. In their places were Ali de Winter and Michael Di Venuto, accomplished mentors for Tasmania who nevertheless lacked significant international experience.

In Melbourne, a series of awkward conversations was taking place. In the wake of the Argus, governance and financial reviews, and the departure of Michael Brown to oversee Australia's hosting of football's 2015 Asian Cup, James Sutherland changed the structure of CA's bulging management class, approving its reshaping into an Executive Leadership Team. Marianne Roux, who joined as human resources manager in mid-2011 before redefining her area as 'people and culture', had devised the model. The team was composed of executive general managers for commercial areas (Mike McKenna), game and market development (Damien De Bohun), business and advisory services (Kate Banozic), people and culture (Marianne Roux) and media, communications and marketing (former Southern Cross Austereo executive Ben Amarfio).

Notable absentees from this new 'top table' included the general manager of cricket operations, Geoff Allardice; the head of business and legal affairs, Dean Kino; the head of strategy, Andrew Jones; and the head of media rights, Stephanie Beltrame. Allardice's absence raised the most eyebrows, given he was the senior manager in the area of cricket itself, but other ambitions were also bruised. Jones' omission from a group meant to oversee strategy for the unification of Australian cricket seemed counterintuitive. Overall, the changes pushed CA further into the realm of a corporation, complete with a labyrinthine array of performance reviews and structures. Allardice, De Bohun, Jones, Roux and Kino have all departed since.

*

In early June 2012, Australia's ODI squad departed Sydney for England without Ricky Ponting and Michael Hussey – the first time an overseas touring team had been without one or other of them since New Zealand in 2000. While Ponting's absence was the selectors' choice, Hussey's was for parental reasons. Four weeks later, Clarke's team returned with another record: it was the first Australian tour since India in 1996 to fail to achieve so much as a single win. There was an undeniable link between the two missing players and the tour's result.

Many of Australia's players, Clarke included, had no recent cricket to call upon other than the IPL, about as far removed as possible from the damp surrounds of the 2012 English summer, which had all the rainy, cloudy, chilly triggers necessary for a bout of seasonal adjustment disorder. A pair of one-day county fixtures either side of a washout in Belfast were their only chance to adjust to the northern climes, and at Lord's an England side playing firm cricket under Alastair Cook confronted them. Clarke sent the hosts in to bat, but Cook and Jonathan Trott reprised their 2010–11 steadiness before Eoin Morgan blazed in the closing overs. The target of 273 was 16 too many.

The series was never again that close, as England stretched the margin with each match. Australian frustrations about the weather, the schedule and each other were illustrated at Chester-le-Street, where England sealed the series after winning a more than useful toss. Trott, Ian Bell and Ravi Bopara were seldom troubled in chasing down 201, as Clarke used eight bowlers and two substitutes. Lee and Watson were both injured, and when the latter trudged off the ground he argued at some length with Arthur, who felt the vice-captain should stay on the field even if not bowling. After the match, Watson was called into a lengthy meeting with Arthur and Dovey about what was expected of him. He did not appreciate the lecture.

Both Clarke and Arthur also delivered pointed rebukes to the team in the dressing rooms at the conclusion of the match, to the effect that players were not putting in and were costing themselves money in the

process. Arthur vented further anger when he met the press: 'I've chal-
lenged the players. I'll always be honest and I'll say it how it is. I'm
really looking for a response. I want to see a bit of mongrel, I really do.
I think we've been a bit submissive this whole series. We've allowed
ourselves to be bullied, and we're better than that.'

Arthur's desire for a response was not met at Old Trafford, which
quickly developed into another English saunter to victory. The tour's
complete failure left question marks in the minds of plenty of players, support staff, management and selectors. Though the team
had been playing out of season, its failure to be competitive grated.
England's ease also placed the previous results against India and the
West Indies in some perspective. Australia's successes had been merited, but did they demonstrate genuine improvement or simply the
beating of opponents who either did not travel well or were in a steep
cricket decline?

Two small positives did emerge out of the mid-year murk. Mitchell
Johnson returned to the team with a refreshed body, a remodelled
action and more robust confidence, after restorative training sessions
with Dennis Lillee on the expanses of Perth's Hale School. Notably,
he was baited by English crowds in the familiar style but was not anywhere near as perturbed as he had once been. Also useful was a meeting
between Inverarity and Chris Rogers, who was enjoying a typically
solid summer's run-making for Middlesex but was fearful of losing
his Victoria contract on the basis of age. Made aware of this anxiety,
Inverarity relayed his view to the Bushrangers that Rogers remained a
player of interest – in a year's time, his English experience might just
come in handy.

Biff, boom, bash. Shane Watson was back from injury and making
a mess of Australia's opponents at the World T20 in Sri Lanka: 3–26
and 51 runs against Ireland, 2–29 and 41 against the West Indies, 3–34
and 72 against India, 2–29 and 70 against South Africa. In a format as

hit and miss as T20 it was a startling sequence, but perhaps tellingly it took place while Clarke was in Australia.

The T20 side was captained by George Bailey, a thoughtful, gregarious Tasmanian who John Inverarity and Rod Marsh felt could fill some of the leadership vacuum they perceived behind Clarke, Ponting and Haddin. 'Michael's focus is perfection, train, win. If we lose, all he would say is "Train harder", whereas George is a little bit different,' Arthur says. 'George is a fantastic character, not to say Michael isn't, but George did exceptionally well with one-day and T20 teams. We picked George based on character: he was the guy we thought possessed exactly the qualities we were looking for in terms of our cricket philosophy, and we felt he was good enough to change his game and adapt, and history's proved it right.'

Well prepared for the tournament, Bailey's side ventured as far as the semifinal, against the West Indies. In that match, Bailey demonstrated a similar flaw to Ponting's when he placed inordinate faith in Xavier Doherty to subdue Chris Gayle and Kieron Pollard in the final over. Doherty was a friend and Tasmanian teammate of Bailey's, but this was a hard ask. In the space of five balls, 4–180 ballooned to 205, and Australian shoulders slumped. Bailey made the only score of note in the dispirited chase, Watson's earlier streak having tapered off.

A semifinal appearance in the World T20 following shared ODI and T20 series against Pakistan in the United Arab Emirates seemed to confirm that Australia were still a mid-table team, relying too much on the contributions of a few to be seriously considered as contenders for best in the world. Yet by a quirk of the rankings, Clarke and Arthur found themselves confronted by a tantalising scenario. Victory over Arthur's former team, South Africa, in a home series in November would allow the Test team to snatch the number-one ranking. The grumbles of the preceding ten months were momentarily set aside.

18

Last Goodbyes

NOVEMBER 2012 – JANUARY 2013

South Africa in Australia

Sri Lanka in Australia

On a brilliant October day in Sydney, Cricket Australia said all the right things to launch the 2012–13 summer. Under the banner 'Cricket's Back', the event at Circular Quay was polished and focused, not needing a premature announcement of the squad to face South Africa. Michael Clarke delivered a captain's address, laying out a plan to involve former players more actively in the team, with two or more invited to spend time with the squad at each Test. And Ricky Ponting, standing behind Clarke in the official photos with a look of grave determination on his face, spoke of how primed he was feeling, ready to dominate the home summer before going on to offer his vast experience to aid younger teammates in India and England in 2013.

This glossy picture of the national team and game a year after the Argus review did not hold together for long. The concurrent T20 Champions League once again conspired against the national selectors, as Shane Watson and Pat Cummins fell prey to injury off the back of the event. An injury chain reaction swallowed up Australia's chance of defeating South Africa and claiming the number-one Test ranking that Clarke, Mickey Arthur, Pat Howard and James Sutherland so coveted.

It carried on into the Sri Lanka series, worsening the relationship between Watson, Clarke and Arthur ahead of overseas assignments that could hope to be successful only with a united and seasoned team. All the while Brad Haddin stood curiously to one side, now considered Matthew Wade's reserve despite his leadership ability, years of experience, apparently refreshed skills and having been emboldened by time away from the game, albeit spent with his ill daughter. Clarke and the selectors witnessed a strength of character that allowed Haddin to sleep by his daughter's hospital bedside then return each morning to Bankstown Oval, in Sydney, for a Sheffield Shield match in which he made a century for New South Wales against Tasmania. But they did not deem him essential; the grass seemed greener with Wade.

Instead, much of the leadership burden was to be shouldered by Ponting and Michael Hussey, who at that moment appeared capable of going on for as long as Clarke and Arthur needed them. Yet within a matter of weeks Ponting had retired, having resolved not to let himself be dropped in the manner of his limited-overs exit the season before. By year's end Hussey had floored Clarke and Arthur by revealing that he too would not be making another tour. The manner of their exits was instructive about where the team truly sat, in a space far less gleaming than the front put on that day in October.

Arthur's insight into the South African Test side was expected to be one of Australia's major advantages. But he did not expect his views on each member of the touring team to be plastered across the front page of Brisbane's *Courier-Mail* on the eve of the first Test, accompanying a report by the tabloid larrikin Ben Dorries. 'Australia will engage Hashim Amla in a "psychological" sledging war and ruthlessly target leg spinner Imran Tahir, according to a top-secret dossier obtained exclusively by the *Courier-Mail*. In an explosive development on Gabba Test eve, the *Courier-Mail* can reveal the entire Australian game plan for each South African player.'

What followed was a rundown of each player's strengths and weaknesses, including Graeme Smith's susceptibility to l.b.w., and the contention that Hashim Amla might be unsettled by concerted sledging. It was the talk of Brisbane that day, but when Arthur was asked about it he said, laughingly, that 'there is no dossier'. He was right. The article's genesis, rather than a folder slipped under the wrong hotel-room door, had been a phone call by Dorries to Arthur weeks earlier. The journalist had requested that Arthur run through Smith's team with suggestions on how they might be attacked. Expecting a feature piece in the sport pages to be the result, Arthur was dumbfounded when he saw the newspaper at the team hotel. So was Smith.

'South Africa batted first and Graeme had been really frosty to me that morning,' Arthur says. 'I phoned the South Africa manager, Doc Moosajee, to just convey this was not meant to happen. Then Graeme got out and as luck would have it I'd gone down to pour myself a cup of tea underneath the stand. There was no-one else in the room, and Graeme walked in to get himself a drink. I said, "Sit down." We spoke and left the room after twenty minutes as we'd always been.'

Australian plans and their execution were notably precise over the first nine days of the series. They had the better of a rain-shortened draw at the Gabba before piling on a thrilling 5–482 on day one at the Adelaide Oval, its size reduced by the reconstruction work being undertaken to turn a picturesque cricket ground into a 21st-century Australian Football League stadium. Ed Cowan and David Warner swatted a century apiece, while Hussey hustled to a pair of hundreds. But the dominant force was Clarke, who dodged his share of short balls at the Gabba before ascending to 259 not out then appeared simply to resume the innings in Adelaide at an increasing pace while zooming to 230. He seemed capable of taking Australia to number one all on his own.

*

James Pattinson was sore: not so sore that he was unsure of playing, and not so sore that the team physio, Alex Kountouris, felt he needed a scan, but after a full Shield schedule and 53 full-blooded overs in Brisbane, there was a chance that he would be injured in Adelaide. At the Gabba, Pattinson had looked Australia's best bowler, well clear of Ben Hilfenhaus and Peter Siddle. Clarke, Arthur and the selector on duty, Rod Marsh, were eager for him to play in the second Test. With mild reservations, Kountouris gave the all clear.

Defending a tally of 550 that had been rattled up at better than five an over, Pattinson couldn't find his rhythm. His first four overs went for 26, including a trio of Smith boundaries in his third over and a brace for Alviro Petersen in his last. Aware that something was not quite right, Clarke let Pattinson cool off in the outfield for a while then returned him only for two-over bursts. The first and the second burst were wicketless, and the third was with the second new ball. After flinging down the first ball of his tenth over at Faf du Plessis, Pattinson reeled away in pain and clutched at his side. He was out of the series. As it turned out, so were Australia.

Lacking Pattinson's pace, power and reverse swing, Clarke's side could not press home a winning advantage. Even though South Africa lost four wickets on the fourth evening, they knew they had a chance if partnerships could be established. First with A B de Villiers, then with a ginger Jacques Kallis, du Plessis did exactly that. Having started life as a busy limited-overs player, du Plessis was suddenly monumental, his bat wonderfully straight, his concentration endless. Hilfenhaus was too mechanical, Nathan Lyon too quick through the air and through his overs. Siddle fought fatigue to throw himself once more unto the breach but fell two wickets short.

As South Africa's players celebrated the sort of draw that has buttressed their stay at the top as much as any victory, Siddle sank to his haunches, completely bereft of energy or reward for what he had expended. In the promotional campaign for the summer, he charged in at an unseen batsman, the words 'Come on, mate' on his lips and those of thousands of spectators. Life had imitated the advertising in Adelaide, lacking only the release provided by the final wickets. When Clarke went up to console his spearhead, Siddle quietly confided to the captain that he had nothing left for the final match, in Perth.

Shane Watson's early return from the Champions League T20 took place at the behest of Pat Howard and infuriated Stuart Clark, by that time the Sydney Sixers general manager. The plan, presumably, was to ensure Watson's fitness for the first Test against South Africa, at the Gabba. It failed. After the Sixers won the tournament, under Haddin's leadership, Watson suffered another calf strain while bowling for New South Wales against Queensland only days before the first Test. John Inverarity's preferred substitute all-rounder was Andrew McDonald, but with near-comic timing he succumbed to the need for hamstring surgery, underlining the physical demands of an all-bowling, all-batting role. Thrust into the team instead was the mature left-hander Rob Quiney, who followed a score of nine in Brisbane with a pair in Adelaide.

Gratified to have Watson back to something in the region of full fitness for the decider, in Perth, Inverarity's panel were addled by the loss of Pattinson, Siddle and Hilfenhaus as a result of Adelaide. The first two were injured, while Hilfenhaus was both fatigued and lacking the shape and speed of the previous summer. He returned to Hobart to regather strength and work on his action, leaving the team without an into-the-wind swing bowler. As Western Australian natives, both Inverarity and Marsh were eager for a steady type to soak up overs from the Prindiville Stand end.

The selection rankings of Australia's pace-bowling stocks at the start of summer had Cummins entering into the team in the event of any injuries, but he too had been felled, this time by a back stress fracture that had emerged during the Champions League. Next in line were Mitchell Starc, Mitchell Johnson, Josh Hazlewood, Jackson

Bird and John Hastings. Inverarity had been impressed by Hastings' returns of 2–57 and 5–30 in a 10-wicket canter for the Bushrangers. On the strength of that match, plus a controlled spell of 1–32 from 23 overs, including 12 maidens, for Australia A against the South Africans on a dead SCG pitch, Hastings was chosen in the squad alongside Hazlewood, Starc and Johnson. One would miss out.

Over the two days of training ahead of the match, Starc and Johnson found swing and speed to turn heads, eliciting the selection courage to choose two left-armers as likely to go for vast swathes of runs as they were to scoop armfuls of wickets. Alongside Watson, Arthur and Clarke favoured the younger, faster Hazlewood as their back-up, whereas Inverarity and Marsh leaned towards the older, steadier Hastings. Debate over the final spot lingered into match morning, until reaching a point of no return during animated discussion in the middle of the ground. Largely because of questions regarding how many overs Watson might be able to bowl, Hastings was handed a new cap.

Numerous players were dismayed by the team's composition. Though he had bowled well for Victoria, Hastings was not considered of the same rank as numerous others, notably the recently prolific Bird. Additionally, the selection of Starc and Johnson left the team exposed to a session in which all control of the scoreboard might be lost. 'It was very aggressive to put those two in, but that was also why Hastings played: to give us a bit of control,' Arthur says. 'The issue was picking two guys who leaked runs.'

The team for this match was perhaps the most baffling selection Inverarity's panel ever put together. Even if it was partly attributable to the pile-up of injuries, balance was lacking. 'If everyone in the team had written down a team, no-one would have picked the team the selectors picked,' says one member of the final eleven. 'Guys were confused; they couldn't understand how we ended up playing two left-armers of the same type, brilliant on their day but both likely to go for runs. Smith and Amla tore the game apart in that last session of day two, and it was just disheartening because we had bossed them around the park in Brisbane and Adelaide. We were exhausted from Adelaide, but as soon as we heard the team I think everyone thought, "If we win we're going to have to score a heap of runs," and that hadn't been the way in Perth. It had that flow-on effect.'

Having weathered a storm on the first day, when Starc, Watson and Hastings swung the ball, Smith's side essentially won the match by knockout on the second. Dale Steyn, Morné Morkel and Vernon Philander combined to raze Australia's batting, Steyn's late away swinger to dismiss Clarke the ball of the summer. Batting again with an unexpected lead, Smith and Hashim Amla tucked into Starc, Johnson and Hastings much as many had feared they would. As the lead stretched well beyond their range, Australia's players turned their thoughts to the hunched, weather-beaten figure prowling the field in a battered green cap. This rout was Ponting's last Test.

For the first time in his life, Ponting had found himself wrestling with doubts about his future. The speculation of the previous summer had weighed heavily, and in Brisbane he found himself thinking about all manner of issues in the instant before he edged Morné Morkel into the slips. It happened again on day one in Adelaide, when a Jacques Kallis away swinger left Ponting sprawled hopelessly on the pitch as the bails took flight. When he dragged Dale Steyn quite wretchedly onto his stumps in the second innings, Ponting decided it was time, but waited until he was with his wife in the sanctuary of their room at the team hotel to utter the words 'I don't think I can do this any more.'

In the airport lounge the morning after the second Test, Ponting told Clarke. The young captain had been eager for some time to forge his own team but was also aware of what Ponting's departure would mean. Both he and Inverarity asked Ponting to reconsider, something that gave him pause until Rianna reminded her husband of how broken he had seemed on the third evening of the Adelaide Test. So it was agreed that he would announce his exit before the Perth Test, allowing time for family and friends to fly in from around the country. When Ponting told his teammates, on match eve, he wept openly after a few words. When Clarke spoke publicly a little more than an hour later, he stopped himself from talking about Ponting, lest he cry too.

'I could understand Michael wanting to create his own era. But Michael also wanted to win, and he knew that Ricky playing well would allow him to win,' Arthur says. 'As we'd seen in one-day cricket, Ricky had a shorter period to show that he was going to play well. Ricky was always in our plans to go to England in 2013, provided his form held up. If Ricky had been averaging 35 over that period he'd have still got there. Anybody who saw his dismissals in the Adelaide Test match was probably at the point of thinking, "Yes, it's time." But one must always remember how much he was giving to the team: he was giving a massive amount to the team off the field. He was taking the young guys for dinner and talking to them about Test cricket. He was phenomenal.'

Tributes were many and varied, the match turning into a farewell pageant as much as a series decider. On the first evening, Rianna was among 20 000 spectators who rose to cheer the nightwatchman, Nathan Lyon, thinking he was Ponting. When Ponting emerged for the last time, on day four, Graeme Smith gave him a guard of honour. A brief stay was ended by the unassuming spin of Robin Peterson, and Ponting left the field with one final acknowledgement of the crowds in Perth and around the world. In the dressing room he struggled initially to come to grips with the end of it all, unable to respond to an attempt by the visiting Adam Gilchrist to offer consoling words.

When South Africa sealed the match, Ponting told the Australians that they needed to take on the striking example of Steyn, Smith and Amla on day two if they wanted to be the best. A few past teammates might have blanched at this use of South Africa as the archetype of success, given their many past beatings, but this time it was true. Throughout Ponting's later years they had been the best and most reliable of teams, if lacking the dynamism and aggression of Australia in excelsis.

Watson had suggested the team's gift to Ponting, a substantial gesture: forty-one bottles of Penfolds Grange to match his Australian-record tally of Test centuries, and each bottle's vintage matched to the year of one of those hundreds. Ponting's source of greatest pride was another number: 107. No player had played in more Test match victories.

That night, Gilchrist and his wife, Mel, hosted a farewell shindig in their Perth home. Food, wine, songs and stories flowed freely. Eventually, the party dwindled until Ponting, Rianna, their hosts and a handful of others were left. For a few hours they sat in Gilchrist's cellar, quaffing red and scoffing party pies freshly baked by Mel. By the time the party was halted, Gilchrist's children were stirring in preparation for school, and the sun had well and truly risen over Perth. If the Test match had been poor, Ponting's send-off was rich.

The toll of the South Africa series weighed down players, selectors and coaches in Hobart during the first Test against Sri Lanka. On a dead pitch, Australia suffered injuries to Hilfenhaus and Clarke, while Starc and Watson pushed their bowling workloads into the zone of high risk as a consequence. Increasingly desperate, Clarke threw the ball to Wade in mid-afternoon, before Starc summoned reverse swing to shut out the Sri Lankans in the final half-hour. Hussey's immaculate first-innings hundred was his seventh under Clarke's captaincy, and unlike Ponting he showed no sign of wavering. But late in the evening at a bar in Salamanca, he quietly confessed to a friend that this summer would be it.

'I'd done two stints beforehand of two months and three months and I just didn't want to go away any more. Looking at the schedule, the boys were going to be away for eight and a half months, basically. I knew in my heart I was dreading those tours. I was also apprehensive about telling anyone around the team because I worried the selectors would say, "Well, mate, if you're not going to be with us in the future you might as well finish now, and we'll get someone else in for three or four Tests to give them the experience leading into that." It's probably a selfish way of looking at it, but I really loved the Australian summer and I wanted to finish my Test career in Australia.'

Mickey Arthur had spoken to Hussey in the midst of Ponting's final bow at the WACA. 'I sat with Mike and told him how important he was to the whole set-up and the whole team and said, "You've got to really help us,"' he recalls. 'Mike's a lovely guy but he can be a bit withdrawn – it's not like Ricky where he's grabbing guys and bringing them in; he's not like that. His example was in the way he prepared. And he said, "Yeah, right, I'm really up for it," and gave me no indication whatsoever of his thoughts.'

Another disconnect was also reaching a critical point as Watson tried to recover from 47.4 overs in the first Test. The use of an external physio, Victor Popov, had been a major reason for Watson's improved fitness record in the latter days of Ponting's captaincy, but under Clarke the earlier problems had re-emerged, as the increasingly coordinated CA high-performance arm railed against the outsider. Kountouris, Clarke, Arthur and Howard were unhappy with the arrangement, particularly when the two physios conflicted in their advice to Watson. After Hobart, Kountouris favoured rest, Popov some light running. Watson ran – and felt tightness in his calf.

In public, Howard, Arthur and the selectors took a battering for the decision to withdraw Starc, a decision made after he had bowled more overs in his previous two matches than at any stage of his young career. Also of concern were bone spurs on Starc's ankle that had begun to cause him discomfort. Nonetheless, Starc was unhappy to be missing out on Boxing Day and said so. The selectors did not help themselves by declining to reveal the bowler's injury status, and later in the summer Inverarity scolded the Australian Associated Press's Greg Buckle for referring to 'rotation' rather than 'informed player management'. Whatever the semantics, for most of the summer the public went uninformed.

This noise diverted some attention from Watson, who was asked to undergo a fitness test on Christmas morning to show his capacity to bowl. He came through the examination well enough and watched Clarke train only mildly due to his own hamstring strain from Hobart. At the team's Yuletide function, captain and vice-captain concurred that both would need to manage their niggles carefully at times over the next five days.

As Kountouris treated Clarke's still-tender leg that evening, his concerns about Watson grew. Clarke felt Watson was fine to bowl, whereas Watson thought he was to be guided gently through the early part of the match before bowling later. Having worked with both players that day, Kountouris heard their divergent views so emailed them and Arthur to arrange a meeting for the morning. The four men met over Boxing Day breakfast at the team's Southbank apartments. Watson insisted he would be fine to play so long as he was 'looked after' by Clarke in the first innings. For his part, Clarke agreed to be considerate of Watson's still-healing calf. The quartet left breakfast seemingly on the same page.

Unbeknown to Watson, the selectors had asked Glenn Maxwell to come to the ground on standby that morning, delaying his departure from Melbourne for a Big Bash League match. The presence of another all-rounder at the MCG worried Watson and compelled him to bowl. Whatever Clarke said, the pair clearly had different ideas about what being 'looked after' meant. To Clarke it meant a few overs when Watson was fresh, and he duly handed his all-rounder the ball in the 11th over, with Sri Lanka already two wickets down. Late in his third over, Watson felt a familiar grabbing sensation in his calf. When the team left the field at lunch, Watson confirmed the injury, and Clarke fumed. Kountouris was unsurprised, Arthur exasperated.

Perversely, the procession of wickets and Australian runs that followed only served to increase the sense of unease about what had

occurred. Sri Lanka were bowled out for 156 and 103. The most overs
bowled by the Australians was a mere 22, the tally shared by Mitchell
Johnson and Jackson Bird. Underpinned by a stand of 194 between
Clarke and Watson, Australia's first innings of 460 was more than
enough. CA did not release the news that Watson was injured, though
players were briefed on what to say if the question came up. Ultimately,
the scoop fell to the unexpected quarter of former Australian Football
League player Matthew Lloyd, who tweeted about Watson's malady
after hearing of it at a CA corporate function.

An unusually tense atmosphere permeated the dressing room after
victory inside three days. 'We'd smashed them, and there was tension
in the change room after the game. I remember thinking it was a bit
weird,' one player remembers. 'We were having a beer and Watto was
having some kind of secret meeting out the back with Mickey, and
then Huss is having another one, after Michael and Mickey have been
in a selection meeting.' Arthur and Watson had sought each other
out, the former relaying a decision by Pat Howard that Popov was no
longer going to be allowed to work on Watson instead of Kountouris.
Watson replied that he had decided to give up bowling. Both decisions had been brought on by the events of the match, and both
pushed Watson further from the team's leadership.

A greater shock arrived when Hussey sidled up to Arthur and
Clarke following a selection meeting that settled on the squad for the
SCG and gave up his season-long secret. 'Sydney's going to be my last
Test match.' Clarke and Arthur were stunned, staring at the floor for
a moment before regathering themselves. In coming hours and days,
others shared the emotion. When Hussey told Nathan Lyon not only
that he was retiring but also that he had chosen him as the team's new
Test match songmaster, the off spinner shed a tear. 'I'd say Ricky was
the soul of the team essentially, and Hussey was the heartbeat. So in
the space of two months you had both being ripped out,' says Cowan.
'And that's not being disrespectful to Michael [Clarke] at all, because
Michael was the brains.'

Arthur felt a sense of dread pass over him. 'We'd gone from Ricky retiring to Shane saying in Melbourne that he wasn't going to bowl any more, to Hussey telling us on the same night he was retiring. Suddenly, all the planning for the Ashes was going up in smoke.'

Fittingly for a player who was often the less trumpeted batsman in a partnership, Hussey made his announcement on the same day that much-loved commentator and former England captain Tony Greig died. Greig had first noticed the symptoms of his lung cancer in Sri Lanka during the World T20 in October, and by the time of the Brisbane Test against South Africa, the following month, he had been unable to travel, signing off from Nine with a poignant televised message. Like Peter Roebuck's, Greig's internationalist viewpoint had added significant richness to cricket's coverage, even if his sharp observations on the game and its politics were sometimes submerged beneath a salesman's patter. His loss was keenly felt, and it led Channel Nine's news bulletin on 29 December.

A few minutes later, the world heard of Hussey's intention to retire, and the two events added a touch of the mournful to the Sydney match, which Australia won comfortably despite not playing near their best. Sri Lanka's best players – Kumar Sangakkara, Mahela Jayawardene, Rangana Herath – would all have won places in any Test side, but the depth beneath was lacking. Sangakkara had his hand broken by Johnson in Melbourne, and the rest melted away. Clarke was emotionally affected by Greig's death and also insisted that Hussey lead the team out on the first morning, over the retiree's hesitant protestations. This moment of modesty, indecision and unintentional rancour was repeated on a far larger scale at the end of the match, on Hussey's final night as an Australian cricketer.

Australia had won the series 3–0, but the achievement seemed a little hollow. 'The Sri Lankan series, we were winning because they were struggling. Mitch was brilliant, a few other guys were brilliant, but we didn't really get out of second gear and didn't really have to,' says Cowan. 'They didn't have the bowlers to capitalise on an opportunity, and if you knocked them over they were five out, all out. But there were times when everything started to fragment. It was a watershed kind of series, even though we were winning.'

19

The Boat

JANUARY 2013

Sri Lanka in Australia

'I'm not going.'

Not much can stop dead an Australian Test squad, particularly one merry from an afternoon celebrating a series win in the SCG dressing room and dressed up for an evening out on Sydney Harbour in one of James Packer's boats. But those three words, delivered by Michael Hussey in the mezzanine bar of the Quay West apartments that serve as the team's Sydney base, instantly knocked the wind out of twelve previously billowing sails.

Hussey's final night as an Australian cricketer had been a point of conjecture for the entire week and a headache for the team manager, Gavin Dovey. When Hussey had alerted the team that Sydney would be the venue of his final Test match, Dovey had thought of only two things: how is Hussey going to be farewelled, and what does his wife, Amy, think about it?

Having worked through several nights of the Perth Test match against South Africa to ensure Ricky Ponting's departure would be as fitting as possible, Dovey felt he was up to the task. He had secured the forty-one bottles of Penfolds Grange that recognised each of Ponting's Test centuries; Dovey and his fiancée, Carly, had individually tagged each bottle with a brief outline of the hundred it represented. The farewell party had also been a feat of logistics: after Ponting's wife, Rianna, objected to the idea of hiring a Perth bar or restaurant, Adam and Mel Gilchrist had worked with Dovey to cater for a suitably large party at their home and had then pushed it forward by a day when the Test ended early.

So Dovey's beeline for Amy Hussey was logical. Among his first orders of business was to inform her that Michael Clarke had organised the Packer boat cruise as an event to close the Test summer. Amy was uneasy about the boat – for safety reasons children would not be permitted – and she did not want the family to be separated on the night. Thinking about alternatives, Dovey then spoke to Hussey and Clarke, and the former indicated his keenness to go on the boat and said that he would speak with Amy. Clarke was open to diverting from the boat option but equally clear that any cancellation would need to be made with a reasonable alternative in mind.

Foreseeing potential trouble ahead, Dovey then spoke to Hussey's manager, Neil Maxwell. Like Hussey, he said he would speak with Amy, something he did without changing her mind. 'Certainly, Maxy was trying to persuade Amy at the match, saying, "You've got to go on the boat," and Amy was saying, "No, I don't want to go on the boat; it's not what I want to do,"' Hussey says. 'You can't make someone do something they really don't want to do. It was an awkward situation for Gav, no question about that. He's trying to manage the team and what's best for the team but he's also trying to manage my last Test match and keeping myself and my family all happy as well. It was a tough situation.'

Meanwhile, gifts were arranged for Hussey: a top-of-the-line watch, plus an in-person rendition of 'True Blue' by John Williamson after the Test. When Williamson walked into the dressing room, guitar in hand, Hussey was delighted.

Not having heard otherwise, Dovey had concluded by that time that the Husseys were settled on the cruise option. Few knew they had actually decided they would not be going. As the afternoon festivities made their way towards evening, Dovey stood up and announced the plans for the rest of the night.

During those hours in the dressing room, several players mentioned the harbour cruise to Hussey. Seldom eager to make waves or promote a confrontation, Hussey batted them away with homilies like 'I've had my time', 'It'll be a great night' and 'You guys will have fun', though never quite spelling out his intention not to go. Nathan Lyon, to whom Hussey had bequeathed the team song, had little idea that a long night's reminiscing and celebrating with Hussey was about to be cut short. When the players began to move off from the SCG in their usual assortment of minibuses, Clarke travelled home rather than to the hotel. He and his wife were to meet the team at the dock.

Shane Watson, who had not been in the dressing rooms but went to Quay West to see Hussey, waited in the mezzanine bar as the players and their partners slowly emerged from their rooms for an 8 p.m. departure. Settling in were several members of the support staff who also had children with them and would be staying at the hotel for drinks and pizzas. Hussey, Amy, their children and other family members soon joined the group and looked very much like a brood not intending to go anywhere. Nevertheless, the scene was made hazier by alcohol, and most of the assembling team were still convinced that Hussey would be joining them.

As a prelude to his announcement that it was time to go, Dovey was approached by one player's partner. 'We haven't decided whether we're going or not,' she said.

'Piece this together for me,' said Dovey, a little nonplussed.

'Mike's not going.'

Dovey, his eyes widening, walked over to Hussey, placed an arm around the retiree and asked, 'Are you ready to go?'

'Nah, I'm not going.'

'Mate, this is going to be a massive issue.'

'No, you guys go. I just want everyone to have a good time. It's not about me.'

'Mate, people aren't going to want to go without you.'

Dovey recognised what was about to happen next. His declaration of 'Let's go' caused the group to move towards the hotel's front door, until the question rang out, 'Coming, Huss?'

'I'm not going.'

Chaos ensued. The players declared en masse that they weren't going anywhere either. Dovey, Arthur and others countered that they could not simply stand up Clarke, his wife and the boat. Peter Siddle, who had turned teetotal after the previous summer, declared he would not go in any event. Lyon and Watson spoke similarly strong words. Hussey, realising the predicament, began to pitch for the players to go on the boat, saying how much they would enjoy it, and not to worry about him – even though it was his retirement night. Bizarrely, one of the most loved of Australian cricketers now found himself having terse words with his 'band of brothers', telling them they had to leave him be. After some coercion the team, minus Siddle and Watson, set off for the dock.

As often happens when a large group of revellers traverses Sydney's streets at night, the group broke up into sets of twos and threes, players and partners alike. Some players pondered turning back but were dissuaded by the fact their partners were already about 300 metres ahead of them.

They met Clarke on the boat, and the hubbub among players and staff continued. James Sutherland was also on board. Clarke was upset that Hussey and the others were not there, and soon phone calls began, attempting to get Hussey onto the boat at a later time, demanding an explanation. Hussey took numerous calls of varying degrees of dismay but responded to each with similar words, telling the players to have a great time and that it was not about him. It was clear throughout that most of the players cared little for the boat and wanted to be with Hussey. Only after Dovey explained that Amy Hussey had been opposed to going on the boat from the moment children had been barred did the rancour settle slightly.

Lyon was still disheartened by Hussey's absence, and numerous players spoke about the possibility of getting off the boat around midnight to return to Quay West. But, like so many well-intentioned suggestions made at the midpoint of a night out, it did not come to pass. Moreover, there were no navigators or helmsmen among the team. When midnight arrived, the boat had meandered over towards Manly, and a quick return was well out of reach. The drinks, the venue and the occasion all served to soften the earlier discord, but melancholy remained. 'At the time we were devastated,' says one player. 'It was like someone had killed him straightaway, like he didn't exist straightaway.'

The next morning, Hussey agreed to meet with Dovey, who was worried by some of the anger the episode had thrown up among the players. After the meeting, Hussey spoke with Siddle and Watson to reassure them that he had never planned to go on the boat and equally had never asked that the team stay with him. Siddle was content with this version of events, Watson less convinced. He reiterated his view that the team should never have left Hussey, who replied, 'Mate, we can't afford to have fractures in the team because of something stupid like this.' All were left with a bitter taste from a night that should have been as sweet as Hussey's cover drives.

Further irritation arose from an email sent around later in January that emanated from a Sydney financier who had overheard enough snatches of conversation in the SCG members' bar to concoct a story in which some events were faithfully recounted but not others. It alleged that Clarke had forced the players onto the boat by turning the event into an official CA function and had then abused Hussey over the phone when he did not join the team. Hussey addressed the email in his autobiography, publishing it in full to illustrate 'just how wrong it was'.

In isolation, the night was an unfortunate mess, born of poor communication, a diffident champion cricketer and his determined wife. But it also pointed to a wider malaise. If the team could not communicate effectively over a matter as straightforward as the retirement of Michael Hussey, what hope did they have in India?

20

Mohali

FEBRUARY – APRIL 2013

Australia in India

One by one, they filed in. Captain Michael Clarke, coach Mickey Arthur, manager Gavin Dovey, assistant coaches Steve Rixon, Michael Di Venuto and Ali de Winter, analyst Dene Hills, physio Alex Kountouris, strength and conditioning coach David Bailey, doctor Peter Brukner, masseur Grant Baldwin, media manager Matt Cenin, cameraman Adam Goldfinch, security manager Frank Dimasi, and psychologist Michael Lloyd. It was 7 p.m. on 10 March 2013, and the Australian team's management and support staff were meeting in a conference room at Chandigarh's J W Marriott Hotel to prepare for two days of training ahead of the third Test against India, in Mohali. They were not a happy bunch.

A scoreline of 2–0 to India was hanging over them all, most vividly the horrendous rush of wickets on the fourth morning of the second Test, in Hyderabad. A coaching decree to play as straight as possible had seemingly been forgotten, with the touring batsmen dismissed in a jumble of sweeps, swishes and crooked defensive blades. Minds were addled, feet nowhere. The bowlers had not been much better, unable to find a way of thriving in conditions many had never seen. The number-one spinner, Nathan Lyon, was not even playing, since Clarke and Arthur had grown frustrated with his inability to bowl consistently to a field in Chennai during the first Test.

To Clarke, the team's only remedy was to train, train and train in the relevant conditions. As the second match had ended on Tuesday 5 March, he had argued with Dovey and Arthur in the tunnel leading from the ground to the dressing room about cancelling two previously allotted days off in the week between the Tests. Often, Clarke got his way: among Australian captains, he was at this point uniquely powerful. But this time, Dovey and Arthur brokered a compromise. The team would train on Hyderabad's fifth-day centre wicket before the days off were taken, fortifying techniques then refreshing minds and bodies. To keep the players at least somewhat on the task, Arthur requested three points from each on how they would improve before the next Test – technically, mentally and as a team. Most agreed afterwards that Arthur asked for the work to be submitted by email, hard copy or text, or presented verbally, by Sunday night in Mohali. There was no hint of potential penalties for non-compliance.

Apart from the poor displays on the field, numerous members of the support staff were harbouring a growing sense of frustration with the players themselves. Transgressions were adding up: players late for meetings, individual wellness reports not filled out, players gaining weight, wrong uniforms being worn, change rooms left messy for the staff to clean up and an increasingly prevalent lack of respect. This was manifested not only in the way players dealt with team personnel, but also in their often caustic and occasionally abusive exchanges with local employees of hotels and restaurants. The new staff had little experience of how to push them back onto the appropriate track.

On the players' side, a sense of claustrophobia, anger and being constantly on trial had also built up. Some had sworn off taking naps out of fear they might miss a message or update to their electronic calendars. The presence of not one but three selectors – the selector on duty, the coach and the captain – had made players wary of talking too much, either to authority or to each other. The many challenges of Indian pitches were multiplying in panicked minds. Lacking Ricky Ponting, Michael Hussey, Justin Langer and Brad Haddin, all exemplars of how to behave and masters of the quiet word to ensure things did not get out of hand, players were rapidly losing a sense of how to conduct themselves.

There was one common denominator in all this. The majority of players and staff on the tour were new to the team, new to India, or both. Di Venuto, de Winter, Bailey and Brukner were all on their first overseas Test tour. Arthur and Dovey, in their second season as a management duo, were not far ahead of them despite experience in other countries and other sports. As an attempt to counterbalance the lack of experience, Clarke had found himself joining in meetings he would previously have left to Arthur. Their sense of haplessness was not new: in 1996, on his first major tour as Australian coach, Geoff Marsh had stated publicly in the aftermath of a heavy defeat in Delhi that his charges were training 'a little bit like millionaires'. But this time, in this room, things were building.

One source of optimism at the outset of the meeting was the homework assignment, which had been due that day. All members of staff were eager to hear what the players had come up with, how they felt the team might be able to extricate itself from the current morass. Even before proceedings began, Arthur was asked numerous times, 'What have they got for us?' After a little prodding Arthur spoke, his affable South African tones wavering slightly. 'Yeah, the feedback I had from twelve guys was brilliant, but four haven't done it.' The match was lit.

The tour had been beset by difficulties even before it began, as the national team's tight program meant half the Test squad and support staff arrived in India while the rest were still finishing off a home limited-overs series against the West Indies. Preparation for this most vexing of overseas assignments had been rudimentary, with only Ed

Cowan among the Test players able to find time for a decent amount of specific training, due to his lack of Big Bash League commitments. Even so, time in the Bellerive Oval nets was not the same as playing in India, no matter how useful the advice of the recently retired Ponting.

In assembling the squad, the selectors knew they were sending a decidedly green bunch of players and staff to places and conditions unknown. But denied the chance to choose Ponting or Hussey, John Inverarity's panel had also decided against calling up Haddin. There was no discussion of bringing him back as the team's wicketkeeper, for they were convinced of Matthew Wade's ability, in spite of the numerous chances he had spilled during the summer. Haddin was mentioned as a possible reserve batsman and squad member, but ultimately, the batsman chosen for his expertise in playing spin was the far younger Steve Smith. The spin department included Nathan Lyon, Xavier Doherty and Glenn Maxwell, plus one intern – a teenager called Ashton Agar, who was called up for a 'development tour' during the first two weeks of the trip.

When the full squad eventually assembled in Chennai for one warm-up match and then the first Test, players, coaches and selectors quickly discovered an enormous variation between pitches. Practice wickets were pristine and not spinning, the warm-up match strip was slower and spinning a little, but the surface at the M A Chidambaram Stadium was bare, pockmarked clay, ripe for India's trio of slow men and anathema to Australia's pace. In the space of 20 metres it exemplified both India's resolve to avenge their 4–0 humiliation in 2011–12 and the method by which they would achieve it.

England had ventured to India and won a series in late 2012 through the batting of Alastair Cook and Kevin Pietersen, plus the spin of Graeme Swann and Monty Panesar. But the wickets they had played on bore no comparison to those being cooked up for Australia. As an Indian selector explained to an Australian counterpart in Hyderabad, 'We were worried about England's spinners, so for those games we tried to prepare decent wickets. But we knew your inadequacies against spin, and our spin bowling was better than yours. We knew if we made sure the wickets were extreme you couldn't beat us.' In India, and more recently in England, this had become known as using home ground advantage. In Australia, it was known by another, less agreeable term: a stitch-up.

And so in Chennai the two teams and their relative strengths were displayed. Clarke and Moisés Henriques, the latter of whom debuted as an all-rounder due to Shane Watson's declaration that he was touring as a batsman only, sustained an otherwise shaky first innings of 380. After Cowan was stumped by a metre when charging down the wicket at Ravi Ashwin, others seemed hesitant to use their feet and were jammed on the crease. Phillip Hughes, chosen over the more fleet-footed Steve Smith, dragged a hesitant cut shot – his strength – onto his stumps. But when India batted, the surface suddenly lost its earlier treachery, as Sachin Tendulkar, Virat Kohli and M S Dhoni compiled innings of escalating importance.

Dhoni's 224 was masterful. He dismantled Lyon's off breaks with a brutal precision usually reserved for the later overs of an IPL match: from the 85 balls Lyon twirled down at him, India's captain ransacked 104 runs. Much of Dhoni's innings was played in the company of the number ten, Bhuvneshwar Kumar, their stand of 140 carrying away the match. Well as Henriques played in the second innings, India were never really in danger of being set a target to test them. The efforts of Clarke, Henriques and James Pattinson, returned from injury and admirably fast in the Chennai heat, came to naught.

Clarke's team found the task of recovering from this initial reverse to be beyond them. Lyon was dropped, and Hyderabad resulted in a far heavier defeat. The margin was an innings and 135 runs, but it felt even heavier when the tourists' ten second-innings wickets went down for 75 on the fourth morning, eight in the space of 32 overs. Within an hour of the defeat, Clarke decried the batsmen's shot selection as 'horrible', the two Test matches as 'unacceptable'.

During 'day five' practice, Arthur went into greater detail, discussing how the team had failed to follow instructions. 'Our whole conversation around this second Test match was about playing with a vertical bat, not a horizontal bat,' he said. 'So, when we lost two wickets to the sweep [David Warner and Phillip Hughes], I wasn't best pleased, put it that way. Especially as our briefing that morning had been "I hope you all noticed how Cheteshwar Pujara and Murali Vijay went about their business." When there's no fielder there, it's very easy to think, "I'm going to play my cards here because if I get on there, I score." I keep telling them there's a reason why there's no fielders there. They want you to hit there. You're putting yourself in danger.'

Finding themselves back at the team hotel in Hyderabad in the early afternoon on the fourth day, Clarke, Arthur, Dovey and Inverarity lunched together. It was not a selection meeting, but the sense of agitation was palpable. Various players were discussed, including the vice-captain, Watson, who had been at a growing distance from Clarke and Arthur. Issues of the preceding summer – the physios, the Melbourne Test, the refusal to bowl – had not been forgotten, and now a quartet of low scores from Australia's most seasoned batsman on the subcontinent brought them bubbling back. The talk was not merely of players being dropped but of more definitive action. Taken aback by what he heard, Inverarity counselled calm, citing the pitches and the inexperience of the squad. To act in haste now would be a mistake.

The following day, Inverarity left the tour. He was due to be replaced as selector on duty by Rod Marsh, who was flying in to India via Dubai. Neither of these two men, both steeped in the history and lore of Australian cricket, were on the ground in India over the next three days. There was precious little experience left in the squad to calm the mounting indignation.

On the BCCI-chartered flight from Hyderabad to Chandigarh on Thursday, Arthur, Dovey and a player sat together. The assignments came up in conversation. Dovey, as he was in the habit of doing, suggested sending a reminder text to all players a little closer to the due date. Arthur turned to the player. 'Do you think people have taken this seriously?' he asked.

'I'd like to think so,' the player replied. 'If your boss tells you to do something, you do it.'

'I'm not sure how it will be taken,' Arthur said. 'What if people don't do it?'

'Are you serious? You think people won't do it? If I was captain or coach and someone showed that much disrespect to a direct order I'd sack him on the spot.'

Arthur was a little startled. 'So you think it's that serious?'

'From my point of view,' the player concluded, 'yes.'

No reminder message was sent.

During the time off, on Friday and Saturday, some of the players' partners arrived. Various pursuits were indulged in to take minds off cricket. One game of basketball had an undesired side effect: Matthew Wade twisted an ankle and was ruled out of the next Test. Clarke spent one day away from the team, flying with his wife to Agra, where the pair took in the Taj Mahal. Minds drifted from cricket, from getting beaten up by India, from spinning pitches and from assignments.

By Saturday, Arthur had received around eight of the players' submissions. Others were reminded of the need to hand something in, though more by accident than design. For his own relaxation, Arthur played a round of golf that day with Warner, Maxwell and Hills. Somewhere on the back nine, the assignment topic came up. Neither Warner nor Maxwell had yet sent their suggestions in, but the conversation pushed it to the front of their minds. A pair of text messages buzzed their way onto Arthur's phone that evening.

The following afternoon, Henriques was taking it easy in his room. Remembering he had left something in the corridor, he ventured out on the briefest of errands clad only in his training shorts. As he turned back to the room, he heard that most unpleasant sound – the click of a hotel door shutting with his wallet and room key still inside. Cursing to himself, Henriques ventured somewhat sheepishly down to reception in search of another key. At the desk he bumped into Cowan, who reminded Henriques about the assignment. 'Oh yeah, forgot about that.' Shane Watson, Mitchell Johnson, Usman Khawaja and James Pattinson weren't quite so lucky.

Once Arthur revealed there were four assignments missing in that night's staff meeting, much tumbled out. All the aforementioned examples of poor behaviour, corners being cut and backchat. As with the lunch in Hyderabad, there was an underlying sense that something had to be done. As head coach, Arthur was the man expected to do it. Arthur, the friendly mentor and delegator, had not expected this. The level of anger in the room surprised him, even though there had been plenty of times on tour when he had felt similarly irritated.

The trouble was, Arthur's true thoughts often stayed hidden beneath the smiling exterior; they were occasionally shared with Clarke, but not others. Only twice before, in Adelaide and Chester-le-Street in 2012, had Arthur delivered a 'spray' to his players, the sort of sharp, direct communication the Australians were used to – and needed, even if they did not say so. In the words of another support staffer, 'I liked him as a bloke, and as a coach I thought he had some good ideas. But he was a nice guy and didn't have it in him to be a real bastard at times, which occasionally the Australian coach has to be.'

Arthur admitted later that he should have been firmer and more consistent in his directives, but also offered up the fact that much of the blunt talk he witnessed down under would not have been smiled upon in South Africa. 'In South Africa . . . you had to package everything in very politically correct ways. Maybe I needed another way with the Australian boys. A lot of the time I sweetened the message, and that's a criticism I could look back on and say maybe it should have just been hardcore, straight and direct and leave it at that. Perhaps there was a cultural disconnect there, and I realise that in hindsight. That's fair enough criticism. If I coached in Australia again I certainly would go about it in a different way. But you've got to understand I'm also feeling my way because I don't really know those guys yet.'

When the staff had finished having their say about problems they saw around them, and how the four missing assignments reflected slipping standards, the discussion moved towards a question of remedies. How might the team be shaken out of their present rut? What did people think? What examples could they raise?

Brukner, who had recently finished a stint with the storied Liverpool Football Club and had also served with a broad range of sporting clubs in Australia and the national Olympic team, spoke from his experience. He reckoned a fine would be meaningless, and mentioned what the Liverpool manager Rafa Benitez would have done if instructions were not followed: four players out, four in. Others in the room immediately took up the idea.

Arthur knew this was unusual territory for him, but he was moved by the depth of feeling among his staff. Of the fifteen people present, only one raised a strongly dissenting voice – Kountouris. Not in charge of the team's discipline, Kountouris was nonetheless a useful man to measure its mood. Having worked for Sri Lanka in the late 1990s and then in Australia since 2003, he was also the most experienced cricket staffer in the room. After hearing those pushing for players to be suspended, Kountouris expressed his concern that such a course of action would be difficult to communicate publicly. It would blow up, he contended, into the sort of storm almost impossible to contain or control – an assertion that was backed up by the media manager, Matt Cenin. In short, the costs outweighed the benefits.

Kountouris was also concerned by the way the possible suspension of four players from a Test match, action unprecedented in Australian cricket history, had sprung up from a meeting in which it seemed as though new staff and temporary members of the tour party were having a say in determining the course of action equal to that of the full-time and more experienced members. Lloyd had flown into Mohali alongside the executive general manager for people and culture, Marianne Roux, on a prearranged mission to take the players through shared CA values and beliefs – the sort of corporate exercise many players struggled to take seriously, let alone swear by. Individuals lacking proper insight into the workings of the team on this tour were thus added to the jury that delivered a judgement on four of its members. Kountouris was not alone in feeling that for matters of this kind only Arthur, Clarke, Dovey and perhaps Howard should have been deliberating.

Asked for an alternative plan, Kountouris indicated his preference for a stern warning delivered to the four players in question, without any action taken. Pressed for 'something to be done', he suggested a fine, kept in-house. This option appealed momentarily to Arthur, but he could also feel the expectations of others rising. Things had been allowed to drift – he had allowed them to drift – and he was now required to take a decisive step in response. Through all this, Clarke spoke, listened and agreed with the prevailing mood in the room. Arthur leaned towards suspending the players, telling the staff he would sleep on it before making a final call.

'I thought about it a lot. I hardly slept that night,' Arthur says. 'And I kind of knew what the implications were. The management team were fairly rigid on it, but ultimately it was my decision and I could have pulled the pin on it at any stage, so I'm not dispersing responsibility for it. But I did know our management team were massively in favour of it. Even if I was really uncomfortable with it, it did gather momentum in that management meeting, and the minute it was raised, a lot of guys who weren't going to have their necks on the line said, "Yeah, that's what we would do."'

As Arthur struggled for sleep, others went about their business. Dovey alerted Howard and the selectors that four players were to be made unavailable for the third Test, while Cenin plotted the public dissemination of the decision. His initial plans called for Arthur and Clarke to announce the suspensions together, but they were overruled because Clarke felt player discipline matters were Arthur's to announce.

Sitting in his hotel room at around the same time as the meeting had taken place, Watson spent half an hour thinking over the assignment. He had no recollection of a deadline, or that a written or verbal presentation needed to be delivered. In Watson's mind, his ideas for the team's improvement could be relayed to Arthur at training the following morning. He was eager to play in the third Test, as Mohali had been the venue of a rare Test century for him in 2010. Watson's wife, Lee, heavily pregnant with their first child, had refrained from telling him how imminent the birth was because both felt Watson should play in Mohali. Confident he had something worthwhile to offer his coach and captain, Watson went to sleep.

When Pat Howard and John Inverarity awoke to the messages left for them during the night, 'surprised' would understate their reaction. While Howard tried to contact Sutherland, eventually informing him of the decision when the chief executive excused himself from a media-rights meeting in Sydney, an appalled Inverarity left messages with Rod Marsh, then in transit to India via Dubai, and also with Marsh's wife. When Marsh landed in Dubai, his phone spluttered into life with message upon message. Marsh called his wife first and was informed that he had to call Inverarity urgently. Wondering what was up, Marsh dialled the selection chairman, who relayed the decision of the team management.

The pair instinctively sensed a major mistake was about to be made. They reasoned that as selector on duty Marsh should call Arthur and Clarke. During a pair of animated debates, each lasting around an hour, he attempted to convince the coach and captain that the path they were taking lacked common sense, was toying with the careers of the players and was bound to result in a public relations disaster for them and CA. He also strongly suggested that it was up to the selectors to make such choices. Marsh's words were strong and insistent, punctuated by plenty of colourful language. But neither Arthur nor Clarke was moved to reconsider. The previous night's meeting remained in their minds, as did the results in Chennai and Hyderabad.

'That morning Gav came to my room and I sat there saying, "This is going to be massive. You've got to understand this; guys will lose their jobs around this," and I remember Gav saying, "It's the right thing to do. It's what this team needs right now." Once the decision was made, I did feel a lot of pressure to act on it, because I would have let a lot of the management team down. They were watching to see how I reacted, to see me make the massive decision. Everybody felt we wanted a strong line in the sand, and I needed to back them up on what they were feeling.

'Would I do it again? I would like to think so, because I was trying to make a real stand. And it's not about the four guys who didn't do it; it's about the twelve guys who did actually give it some thought. So if we went, "Twelve guys fantastic; these guys forgot but they'll come and tell me today," the others will think, "Well why did I bother?" If we just brush it over then they'll think they shouldn't have bothered either.'

That morning, Watson and Johnson sat together at breakfast. It had become a habit for these two older members of the squad, fellow Queenslanders, to do so. There was some talk around the team that Pattinson might be rested after his heavy load during the first two Tests, and Johnson felt he had a chance to come into the team. Having watched the batsmen flounder so badly in Hyderabad, Khawaja also thought he might be brought into the side.

But something had come up. Johnson asked Watson if he had received a message about a one-on-one meeting, and the vice-captain replied in the affirmative. Both were required to see Arthur, Clarke and Dovey. What was going on?

A few minutes later, Watson walked over to the hotel lift and made his way to the team meeting room, where the decision to suspend the quartet had been made the night before. Arthur spoke first, then Clarke. Watson had failed to hand in the assignment asked of him and, as part of a decision to draw a line in the sand about team behaviour, would not be playing in the next Test. Watson reeled, saying he had missed around fifty Test matches in his career through injury, and now was having one taken away from him for this? Growing in anger as he heard a reiteration of why he was being suspended, Watson rebuked Clarke and Arthur and complained that the team's greatest problem was a crippling lack of experience.

With that, he returned angrily to his room. A few hours later he checked out of the hotel, having decided to fly home to be with Lee for the birth of their son. Three of the touring correspondents – Peter Lalor, Peter Badel and Chris Barrett – came across Watson on his way out of the hotel. Succinctly, he conveyed his disillusionment. 'Any time you are suspended from a Test match, unless you have done something unbelievably wrong, and obviously everyone knows what those rules are – I think it is very harsh,' he said. 'In the end I have got to live with it. That is the decision they have made and at this point in time I am at a stage where I have to weigh up my future with what I want to do with my cricket in general. I am going to spend the next few weeks with my family and weigh up my options as to exactly which direction I want to go or keep on.'

Watson's words of dismay were clearer than much of what Arthur, looking agitated and weary, said when informing the world of the suspensions. His explanation of the 'line in the sand' focused primarily on the failure to deliver the assignment itself and appeared to undersell the other transgressions. The wider world soon took a very similar view to that of Kountouris, Inverarity and Marsh. Most concluded immediately but inaccurately that this was a hit on Watson by a vengeful Clarke. Past Australian players were in uproar, their dismay summed up most pointedly by Darren Lehmann on Twitter: 'Adults we are, not schoolboys. Please let's act properly and make good decisions in India! Need these boys playing.'

Graeme Smith, in Cape Town, could not believe what he was hearing. 'Mickey was never that sort of guy with us. He wasn't a huge disciplinarian. He's a really outstanding man with really good values, but the biggest part of coaching sometimes is that coaches do things because they're under pressure, and that's the worst thing you can do. A huge part of doing the job and captaining or coaching is to make decisions because that's what's right, not because it's going to look good on the outside or "I'm going to justify my job." India shocked me because that wasn't Mickey Arthur to me.'

Witnessing the storm in Australia while the team trained, Sutherland questioned Howard over whether this was the right direction for the team. He also called Clarke to insist that the captain speak publicly to explain the decision. Clarke's words, and subsequent stories by the touring press, served to articulate the fact that the suspensions were not merely for 'homework' and to settle a little of the earlier outrage. But only a little. 'I want the public and the media to understand it's not just about one incident,' Clarke said. 'There has been some stuff off the field that's unacceptable for the standards an Australian cricket team needs to present itself to achieve what we are trying to achieve. We can't accept mediocrity here. Maybe I am biased, but there is a big difference between this team and other cricket teams. If you play for Australia there is a lot that comes with that, and standards, discipline, culture are all a big part of what we're talking about.'

Pattinson made a tearful public apology, while Khawaja and Johnson wondered whom they could still trust. Though Arthur made the decision as much out of respect for the twelve men who had delivered the assignment as out of discipline for the four who had not, in practice the suspensions left many members of the squad wondering whether they could also now be suspended and publicly humiliated for a similarly minor matter. Was being late for the bus now a sackable offence? Eating the wrong thing at breakfast? Wearing odd socks?

One fresh pair of eyes witnessed the shambolic scenes. Brad Haddin had joined the team on the Sunday afternoon as cover for Wade and awoke after his first night's sleep in India to find himself consoling jittery teammates that things would not always be this way. To players cowed by India and then shocked by the suspensions, Haddin's straightforward manner and ability to get others in his presence to relax had a soothing effect. 'That wasn't the Australian cricket team that I knew when I flew in to Mohali,' Haddin said later in the year. 'That was a unique situation, which in all seriousness I can't really explain. Guys jumping at shadows and the insecurity around everything that was being done. It was uncomfortable, walking into it.'

Though the decision was designed to have long-term effects on behaviour, it had little impact on short-term results. India won comfortably in Mohali and again in Delhi, albeit by slightly reduced margins. Perhaps the only ground gained through the suspensions was the inclusion of Steve Smith, who showed how far he had come since the 2010–11 Ashes by playing with a level of skill and patience that put others to shame. Lyon also bowled well in Delhi, aided by the worst pitch of the series.

Clarke, Arthur and Dovey remain convinced that they made the correct call. Arthur believes the decision had a marked effect on younger players in the team, raising standards of thoroughness and discipline. Equally, Watson, Johnson, Inverarity and Marsh did not retreat from the view that it was a major error. Either way, Arthur admits, it was the beginning of the end for his coaching tenure. 'It could have been done better,' he says. 'Pat and management had always said "no surprises". Well, we surprised the board and Pat and James [Sutherland] with that. We didn't give ourselves enough time to massage that decision. If you look at all the young boys now, the way they train, the way they eat, the way they prepare, well, yes, it made an impression. It had to start somewhere. But I felt a definite change in attitude to me from James and Pat, without a doubt.'

Others were critical that Clarke had allowed the decision to be taken, Ian Chappell among them. 'How an Australian captain could have allowed that to happen is just beyond my comprehension,' he says. 'How it got to that point is the other thing you've got to question. You can only assume that Clarke didn't have his hand on the tiller. If you're spending some time with your team, you've got to be able to gauge the temperature, and you've got to know something's going on, something's not right: let's find out what it is. One of the things I said to the guys in 1972 before we went to England was, "What I don't want is three guys in that corner of the room whispering, another three here and another three there. If you've got a problem, come and see me and we'll sort it out."'

Speaking for the players, Paul Marsh agrees: 'Every time you have a line-in-the-sand moment is through poor management. If you'd been looking after it along the way you don't have this build-up of issues. We refrained from really giving it to CA publicly at the time but we certainly did so privately. I think it humiliated Australian cricket. It humiliated the players, Shane Watson in particular, and was just so avoidable. I've spoken to the four involved and they believed it wasn't communicated as well as it could have been. One thing I would say about all this is that when you look back it was a positive, a catalyst for change, because everyone knew it wasn't right.'

The night before the Mohali Test began, Rod Marsh met Allan Border for dinner. Border was in India as a commentator, but he had also been a part of the Argus review panel. Apart from expressing their shared bewilderment over what had just befallen Watson, Johnson, Pattinson and Khawaja, the pair spent much of the night discussing how the team had progressed since the review. This brought Marsh to the topic of why Clarke had been enshrined as a selector, and he asked Border about it. The revelation that Border, Mark Taylor and Steve Waugh had reluctantly let the concept take hold despite their own better judgement was new to Marsh, and he enlisted Border to help take the matter up with Clarke.

Day one of the match was washed out, affording Marsh and Border valuable time to talk to the captain. On the covered seats in front of Australia's dressing room, the two elders counselled that Clarke needed to stand down from the panel. After a lengthy conversation about the role and where it had hurt the team, Clarke agreed to do so, informing Howard and Sutherland of his intentions when he flew home early from the tour due to a recurrence of his chronic back trouble.

Howard had endured his own heat, from both Watson and Sutherland, when he had defended the suspensions as a part of high-performance sport. Howard's line that Watson acted in the best interests of the team 'sometimes' had also left a scar.

During his time at home, Watson told Howard he did not think it appropriate for him to carry on as Clarke's deputy. Yet when Clarke was injured, Watson found himself returning to India as captain for the final Test. It was a task he performed creditably, impressing the other players with how much more engaged he became as leader – precisely the change many had witnessed with Clarke whenever he had stood in for Ponting. But when Watson began to reconsider his earlier position, Howard told him it was too late, and that a new vice-captain would be installed for the Ashes. After the Indian debacle, greater experience was belatedly being sought. Haddin was back in.

Trial by Television: the Media Rights

MARCH – MAY 2013

Australia in India

James Sutherland's head was in a different game when the 2013 tour of India went into meltdown. The decision to suspend four cricketers for a Test for failing to submit a simple homework task was unprecedented, but so, too, was Sutherland in uncharted waters as he stood in the Sydney offices of Credit Suisse, the investment bank hired to guide CA through the sale of its media rights. For the first time in thirty-four years the sport inextricably linked with Channel Nine and the late Kerry Packer had put those rights on the market. Sutherland took a call from Pat Howard explaining the issue, but his response would have to await the conclusion of the richest television rights deal in Australian cricket's history.

The landscape had changed since the expiring arrangement with Nine, worth $315 million over seven years, was inked. In 2011, the Australian Football League announced a five-year, $1.25 billion deal with Channel Seven and pay-television giant Foxtel. All games would be live, but only half would be guaranteed free-to-air coverage each weekend. The Australian Football League deal held limited relevance for cricket given almost all of Australian football's television money came from the domestic market (compared with about 65 per cent for cricket) and because government anti-siphoning rules prevented international matches from going exclusively to pay television.

Also, the country's dominant football code had stolen a march on cricket by promoting competition between the networks since 2001, when Seven's monopoly ended, while the summer game had preserved its emotional attachment to Nine, distinguishable through the voices of Richie Benaud, Bill Lawry, Ian Chappell and, until his death in December 2012, Tony Greig.

While bonanzas for the Australian Football League and National Rugby League took a billion dollars each out of the market, they reinforced the networks' appetite for 'premium sport', even in a weak advertising climate. 'As much as the networks maybe can't afford the rights, they can't afford to lose them, either,' says an official involved in the cricket deal.

The real game-changer for CA was the Big Bash League. If the inaugural 2011–12 season threatened to resemble a series of *The Bachelor*, straining to grab the attention of fans with a look-at-me launch party at Sydney's Carriageworks for which Sydney Sixers materialised out of pink Hummers, there was method to the marketing madness. The reason for the BBL's existence was to develop a source of revenue beyond international matches; Sutherland had told the Australian Cricket Conference in 2010 that the sport was unique in that it derived little money from its domestic product, leaving it to rely disproportionately on India and Ashes tours. So when just one of the eight new BBL teams, the Shane Warne–fuelled Melbourne Stars, turned a profit in the first year and the combined losses amounted to $1.85 million, CA pointed to the endgame – the sale of the media rights to the tournament in 2013 and beyond.

On several occasions, it was possible to question whether this end would be justified by the means, never more than when the day after

Warne was embroiled in an ugly exchange with Marlon Samuels during the Stars versus Renegades derby at the MCG in January 2013, Sutherland seemed far from upset that it had taken place. 'To be honest I thought it looked like two teams playing in front of a very big crowd in a highly charged environment with a lot at stake,' he said. 'Whilst we can stand here and say we don't condone anything that happened last night, this sort of thing is probably something that only inspires a greater rivalry between the Renegades and the Stars and creates greater interest for the Big Bash League.' No such thing as bad publicity, then. In *The Australian*, Gideon Haigh commented: 'Sometimes, when the best cricketers are involved, the BBL is as enjoyable as the old Big Bash. But that's not enough, and this is where the BBL really "is at": CA is so desperate to primp and plump it for sale to the highest television bidder that its chief executive sees "passion" in what looked as contrived, and not nearly as diverting, as rock'n'roll wrestling. There is indeed a lot at stake. But James Sutherland has more at stake than either Shane Warne or Marlon Samuels.'

Away from the circus, CA's general manager, media rights, Stephanie Beltrame, and Dean Kino, the general manager of business and legal affairs, headed the negotiating team. A subcommittee was also formed to oversee the negotiations, chaired by Deutsche Bank's Steven Skala, with strong links to the board through chairman Wally Edwards and independent directors David Peever and Jacquie Hey. Peever, as managing director of Rio Tinto, was a formidable negotiator with government on matters such as the mining tax, while Hey's background with Sony Ericsson and SBS meant she had specific insights into the growing digital field.

Beltrame weighed Nine's iconic history with cricket against the need to show the market the sport was willing to cut the cord. If CA didn't prove it was open to change now, the other networks would always question whether it was serious, and its ability to maximise the value of its rights would be diminished. 'It wasn't a bluff,' Beltrame said at the time. 'We felt comfortable that if the [Nine] scenario didn't work out, we were prepared to go down that path.'

As talks continued in the boardroom, there were hints of tension in the working relationship between Nine and CA during the last summer of the existing deal. During the 2013 Sydney Test, the vexed issue of rest and rotation as a means of managing players through a hectic schedule came to a head. Team performance chief Pat Howard held two meetings with Nine head of sport Steve Crawley and commentators Benaud, Chappell and Michael Slater. Crawley had publicly questioned how Nine was meant to sell the forthcoming ODI series without the just-retired Mike Hussey, the injured Michael Clarke and the resting David Warner. When Howard produced on his mobile phone a set of statistics illustrating the impact of Warner's workload on his one-day performances, Chappell said he didn't need statistics to know whether a bloke could bat or not, and stormed out. Later, he told Crawley, 'Crawls, forget the television side of it; from a cricketing point of view it is total crap.'

When a public slanging match developed between acting ODI captain George Bailey and Nine's executive producer of cricket, Brad McNamara, it was not difficult to imagine the game's long association with the network coming to an end.

In fact, CA's media rights work behind the scenes was detached from these conflicts, guided instead by meticulous research into cricket's strengths as a television product and equally thorough investigations into the strategies of the three free-to-air networks and Fox Sports, which was paying $6 million a year for the BBL and other domestic games. Every move was calculated by the rights subcommittee before it was relayed to the board, and had to pass a key test: was it a win for cricket?

Sutherland took a hands-on role with the network chief executives. When the chairman of Network Ten, Lachlan Murdoch, paid a personal visit to CA's Jolimont offices in March 2013, three weeks after the homework fiasco, it was obvious that Ten wanted a piece of the action. In May, the network stunned Nine by lodging an audacious bid of $550 million over five years for all cricket. When Nine invoked its right to match the offer for Tests, ODIs and T20 Internationals, keeping international cricket on its spiritual home, network boss David Gyngell described the $450 million price tag as an 'ouch moment'. 'If Nine lost the cricket it was going to cause significant damage to the Nine brand,' Gyngell told the *Australian Financial Review*.

That left Ten with the BBL. The cash-strapped network needed to build its ratings and rebuild its reputation after a flirtation with reality shows like *The Shire* and *Being Lara Bingle*. A major sport would help and Ten's core demographic of 18- to 49-year-olds was precisely the audience CA was trying to woo. While the city-based T20 league had found a comfortable niche on Fox Sports, which had built up the new colours and rivalries with insightful, lively commentary, the governing body had its heart set on more exposure with at least some free-to-air coverage for its flashiest domestic product.

In its first season on Ten, the BBL blew away expectations both within CA and Ten, attracting an average of 930 000 viewers with 1.4 million tuning in to see Shaun Marsh propel Perth Scorchers to victory over Hobart in the final. Ten boss Hamish McLennan hailed the network's $20-million-a-year investment as 'the deal of the century for Cricket Australia and Ten'.

In June 2013 at the MCG, Sutherland unveiled deals worth a colossal $590 million over five years, an increase of 120 per cent on the previous agreement. There was also a $40 million joint venture with Nine for the digital rights to Australian cricket, which would see CA aggressively spruik its mobile phone app and relaunched news site. The benefits would flow through to players and to cricket's grassroots. With the Ashes tour about to get underway in England, Sutherland could return his full focus to the machinations of the Australian team.

22

The
Silver Bullet

Early in the hours of 24 June 2013, James Hopes and his wife were woken up by the sound of his phone buzzing in their Brisbane bedroom. In the middle of the night, in the middle of the off-season, Hopes ignored it.

Then it buzzed again with a text message, and again with another call. Peering over to the bedside table, he saw the calls were coming from Darren Lehmann, his state coach, who was in England as an assistant for Australia A ahead of the Ashes tour. A little grumpily, Hopes called back and momentarily thought his coach had become the latest transgressor in the recent series of misbehaving Australian cricketers. 'I was half asleep, and I could have sworn he said, "I've been sent home." I asked him, "What have you done?"'

Seconds later, Hopes became the first person in Australia to hear that Lehmann was to replace Mickey Arthur. Lehmann was advising Hopes as captain of Queensland, but also as the friend who had previously raised the possibility. During the summer, Hopes had run the question of the Australian coaching job past Lehmann and received a dismissive response. Now the plot twist arrived. 'He said, "I want to tell you first because we've talked and I said I wouldn't do it. But I'm going to be announced as Australia coach tomorrow, and I just walked out of lunch now with it." We spoke again next morning to make sure I hadn't dreamed it.'

The unexpected phone call illustrated the suddenness of the decision and the unprecedented nature of its timing. Plenty of influential figures in Australian cricket had begun to wonder about the direction of the team under the leadership of Mickey Arthur, Pat Howard and Michael Clarke during the previous summer. Those figures had been doubly concerned when in India they had responded to poor results and slackening attitudes by summarily suspending four players in order to set an example for the rest. But no-one expected James Sutherland to act as brutally and decisively as this two weeks out from an Ashes series.

Grumbles predated India. Shane Warne's was the first voice to cry out, from the Big Bash League in January, that the Australian team was not functioning as it could be. Angered by the composition of the Test side that had played South Africa in Perth the previous year, and particularly by the absence of Peter Siddle, Warne penned a series of articles for his website. He advocated the removal of Arthur, Howard and John Inverarity, among others, and nominated New Zealand's former captain Stephen Fleming as coach, with Darren Lehmann next in line as assistant. Publicly, Sutherland defended Arthur and Howard, but he also met with Warne in February, spending near enough to two hours hearing the views of his former Victoria teammate.

'I let James know what I thought,' Warne says. 'I think they had a bit of a plan in mind too and were keeping a close eye on things. I wasn't happy with the situation the team was in. I don't think the players had confidence with all the chopping and changing that was going on – there was no confidence in anything. And you could see from the way the team was playing at that time, they were playing like they were all playing for their spots. A few people in the background at CA who were close to the team said, "Mate, have your say." It's interesting how since I wrote that, a lot of it or close enough to it has happened, which showed my nose was on the right track. I like to think I helped in some regard to make people aware of it who weren't thinking along those lines.'

Sutherland did not rush to judgement, not least because he had appointed Arthur and Howard, and both were under contract until 2015. But the Mohali suspensions and the manner of their handling left him wondering about the team and called to mind many of the issues raised by Warne earlier in the year. When Howard informed him of the suspension decision Arthur, Clarke and Gavin Dovey had made, Sutherland questioned the verdict and the process by which it had been reached. Howard went to India and in Delhi conveyed to Arthur that a big call had been made and that its rightness needed to be demonstrated pretty smartly. In other words, 'This had better work.' Following the conclusion of the tour, Sutherland met Arthur and Dovey in Melbourne, telling them a repeat would not be tolerated.

'Personally I'm disappointed we got to that stage,' Sutherland said publicly in May. 'I'm supportive of the decisions that were made at the time and I'm a really firm believer in the fact that those decisions will ultimately stand us in good stead as we build to sustained performance at the highest level. I think it's pretty well understood internally what I think about it, and the need for us to ensure those things are dealt with better before they ever get to that stage.'

Arthur was out of sight if not out of mind at the Sydney Ashes team announcement in late April, though Steve Waugh and Mark Taylor were present in an effort to summon the spirit of the triumphant 1989 tour. The squad itself represented a backtrack on the attitudes that had informed selection for India. Brad Haddin returned not only as wicketkeeper but also as vice-captain, while Chris Rogers was drafted in as a ready-made opener with a wealth of experience. His selection followed years in domestic purgatory, when all he had known was that Australian players seemed united in their distaste for him, based seemingly on a vague perception of him as a troublemaker. In one Sheffield Shield match a senior player had taken Matthew Wade to task for talking to him. 'Wadey and I were having a joke and he just turned around to Wadey and said, "You don't like that bloke, do you?" and he said, "I love Bucky. Why?" and he goes, "Nah, you don't fucking like him." I thought, "Huh. What have I ever done to him?"'

Clarke spoke about the attributes of the best teams in a more balanced manner than he had done before India. 'The best teams I've seen in the world have a good mix of youth and experience,' he said. 'I think this squad has that mix. I'm confident we have a good group of players who can learn from one another as well as utilise the coaches we have.' Shane Watson was happier with the composition of the squad and for his part had returned to bowling after a fretful Indian experience. Inverarity was careful to refer to Watson as 'a batting all-rounder' when he announced the sixteen.

Players prepared for England with regular trips to the Centre of Excellence, in Brisbane, where two significant events took place. The first of these was the reconnection of Craig McDermott with the pace bowlers after a year apart. McDermott's advice to the bowlers was typical: he urged them to bowl an accurate full length with the added spice of an occasional bouncer, and they appreciated his counsel on issues such as the Lord's slope. The second event was the reinstitution of a team fines committee, a long-time source of jokes and team drinking money that had disappeared from the Australian team in recent years. It was to be run by Wade and Phillip Hughes, and it eventually had ruinous consequences for Arthur.

At a sunny Edgbaston, in Birmingham, Australia resumed cricket contact with England in their first match of the Champions Trophy, in June. Like the 2005 T20 meeting at the Rose Bowl, in Hampshire, this contest could be viewed not only as an end in itself, but also as the first skirmish in a long war that spanned ten Test matches across two hemispheres: this Ashes series, during the English summer, was to be followed up by another just six months later, in Australia. Some members of the Australian hierarchy reckoned that under Andy Flower, most of this England team's great achievements might now be behind them. Inverarity told an Australian Cricket Society lunch at the MCG, 'England in 2013 won't be as good as England were in 2011 – I think they've peaked.'

Yet what unfolded in Birmingham suggested that Australia would struggle to get close. Their warm-up fixtures had gone in the wrong direction, with a comfortable win over the West Indies followed by a hiding at the hands of India. Now, lacking Clarke due to back trouble that confined him to London for treatment, they put together a timid performance. Mitchell Starc and Mitchell Johnson posed little threat with the new ball, as England strolled to 269. On a fine afternoon this should have been attainable, but the innings was strangled by the accuracy of the English bowlers and a curious lack of impetus at the top of the Australian order – none of David Warner, Shane Watson or Phillip Hughes was able to strike at better than 60.

England's technocrats did very little special that Saturday, yet they won by 48 runs. The pragmatism of Flower's method, carried out faithfully by Alastair Cook's team, was summed up by George Dobell for ESPNcricinfo, and much the same could be expected during the Ashes: 'England play, by and large, percentage cricket. They are not pretty. They are not exciting. What matters to them is that they have a method they trust and understand. While other teams can thrash and heave, England will nudge and accumulate. While other teams attempt the killer punch, England pick up points and refuse to open themselves up to danger. They apply pressure and look to make fewer mistakes than their opposition.'

Players and staff from both England and Australia were invited to a function organised for CA and ICC personnel that night. England's players had reason to celebrate, Australia's rather less so. Nonetheless, after a few drinks at their hotel, six members of the Champions Trophy squad ventured out: Warner, Hughes, Matthew Wade, Clint McKay, Mitchell Marsh and Glenn Maxwell. Of this group, Warner was the most senior player, the only solid member of both Test and ODI teams. Their destination was the Walkabout, a cheesy Australian-themed chain pub that Warner had already visited that week. It proved a suitably sordid venue for what followed.

After a few drinks, and a few contained conversations, English and Australian players mixed. Whether on or off the field, Warner had always been capable of picking a fight, and at about 2.30 a.m. he took offence at England player Joe Root's use of a party wig as a fake beard. He spoke to Root, may have received a verbal rejoinder, then took a swing at the other man's momentarily bearded chin. The blow was glancing, and the players quickly made up. It was witnessed by numerous players and staff from Australia and England, but none reported it immediately to management. Warner sent apologetic messages to Root the following day and thought the matter closed.

For nearly two days it remained a secret shared, and even joked about by Australia's players and by staff members who had been present, yet unknown to Arthur and Dovey. Most agreed that after the misadventures of India, this was an episode best kept quiet rather than played out in public view. But as the team trained in Birmingham on the Monday, ahead of their next match, events took a turn.

Wade had been eager in handing out fines and now called up Watson for wearing a batting vest in the nets rather than the full training shirt. No longer holding any official leadership role, Watson had grown increasingly irritated at the way the likes of Wade and Warner were dictating events, and spent his time with older players such as Johnson. In the words of one player in the squad, 'You either went out for dinner with one group of people or the other group. It didn't bother me which group I went out with, but I knew it wasn't going to be all together; it had to be one or the other.' In this environment, and after his suspension in India, Wade's nitpicking set Watson off. He refused to pay up. Feisty at the best of times, Wade called Clarke in London to complain that Watson would not take heed of the fines committee. Both complained about Watson to Arthur.

Arthur called Watson into his hotel room for a meeting that evening. He told Watson that fines committees worked only if all members of the squad agreed to participate, and that he hoped Watson as a senior player would set a better example for others through his attitude, adherence to rules . . . and wearing the correct attire. Indignant at being called in for the meeting, and annoyed at Arthur's words, Watson responded by saying he had bigger issues to worry about, though not elaborating on what they were.

Once the meeting ended, Arthur asked Dovey what Watson had been referring to. As manager, Dovey had been entrusted with the task of looking after the team's values, a task customarily shared by senior players. In this moment, it became clear that among those stated values, honesty needed some work: he had no idea what Watson had meant. A few conversations later, Dovey relayed the events of the Walkabout to Arthur.

In responding to this news, Arthur was torn between two factors. Having stressed India as a line in the sand, that the players must uphold standards and that all had to move on from Mohali in a new spirit of accountability, Arthur needed to take strong action. There was also the fact that Warner had been fined $5750 in May for abusing the senior cricket journalists Malcolm Conn and Robert Craddock on Twitter. But Arthur had over the preceding eighteen months taken Warner under his wing, rightly believing the combustible but talented opener was critical to the team's success. When questioned about Warner by CA management in the past, Arthur had assured them he would guide his pupil to maturity as a cricketer and a man. Staff who had been at the Walkabout begged to differ.

Eventually, Arthur chose to place Warner on 'amber', a team warning meaning that another transgression would result in punishment.

Both the acting captain, George Bailey, and selector on duty, John Inverarity, agreed with this decision, as neither wanted to lose Warner from the team for the next match, which was against New Zealand. Confronted by Arthur and Dovey, Warner admitted to the punch and spoke contritely. The amber status filtered through to Jolimont and all but sealed Arthur's fate.

Sutherland acted swiftly in response to what he saw as a soft response to Warner's transgression. A phone hook-up with England was organised for Wednesday at 7 a.m. Birmingham time, during which Sutherland and Dean Kino took the matter out of Arthur's and Dovey's hands, stating that Warner was unavailable for that day's match and that he had to submit to a code-of-conduct hearing. Bailey found out Warner would not be available when over breakfast he was asked, 'So what are you going to do with the batting order without Davey?' In the circumstances, Australia played well against New Zealand, only to have any chance of a result cruelled by rain.

The County Court judge Gordon Lewis, who had already ruled against Warner on the Twitter issue, levied a fine of $11 500 and suspended him from all cricket until the first Ashes Test, on 10 July. Lewis' judgement effectively banned Warner from the first two matches of the series due to a lack of cricket. The following day, Sutherland called a press conference in Brisbane, where he tore into Warner and the rest of the team. 'David Warner has done a despicable thing but I also hold the team to account,' he said. 'There were other people there with him. Those that were there need to take responsibility for that, but so does the team and the management group as a whole as well. There is not a lot of good that happens at two-thirty in the morning in a pub or a nightclub.'

No-one thought to ask Sutherland his thoughts about Arthur, which was probably just as well. Sutherland, his chairman, Wally Edwards, and Pat Howard had much to ponder. All were due to fly to the United Kingdom the following week. Before departure, Edwards and Sutherland met with Paul Marsh and Greg Dyer, chief executive and president, respectively, of the Australian Cricketers' Association, to hear their assessment of what was happening. Marsh was also bound for England, and once there he met members of the team, who were by that point in London for their match against Sri Lanka. Needing an unlikely 254 from 29.1 overs to reach the semifinal, they slid predictably to elimination. Marsh spoke with Sutherland again in London, relaying a frank picture of the team's anxieties and divisions.

By Saturday 22 June, Sutherland and Howard had completed their investigations and came to their conclusion: Arthur was to be removed and the job offered to Lehmann. In this dual action, they felt the team's results could be improved, while off-field ructions would be salved by Lehmann's universally strong respect and rapport among the players. That evening, at the Royal Garden Hotel in London, Sutherland told Dovey, then Clarke, who was utterly shocked. 'My head went so light I thought I was going to fall off my stool,' he wrote in his diary of the tour. 'It was the last thing – the absolute last thing – I thought the meeting was going to be about.' Following his resignation as a selector, Clarke's lack of say in the coaching choice demonstrated a significant reduction in his power. 'Michael wasn't consulted,' Howard later said, 'but he was told.'

At six o'clock the next morning, Sutherland and Howard informed the CA board via teleconference of their recommendation, which was approved with minimal dissent. Howard then set off for Bristol.

Not knowing matters were now out of his hands, Arthur remained upbeat, even defiant, in his pronouncements about the strength of the team. Warner's suspension created a gap at the top of the batting order, and Arthur and Clarke had decided to send Watson back to his preferred opener's berth, with Ed Cowan to bat at number three. After the premature end to the Champions Trophy campaign, Arthur ventured to Bristol, where Australia A were playing Gloucestershire.

This parallel tour had been running as well as the ODI campaign had gone badly. Helped by the joviality of captain Brad Haddin and batting assistant Darren Lehmann, players were enjoying themselves and performing, while the selector and tour manager, Rod Marsh, was struck by Lehmann's thoroughness. Years before, they had fallen out badly in South Australia when, as the grumpy old pro, Lehmann had objected to Marsh looking for new leaders in the Redbacks squad. On the day of his retirement in November 2007, Lehmann said, 'I think Rod as a player is one of the guys who I loved and idolised; his views and mine differ on the way to manage cricket teams. That's probably all I'd like to say on that one.'

Tim Nielsen had remained close to Lehmann, suggesting him for assistant coaching roles more than once. But there was suspicion about Lehmann at board level, given a disciplinary record less than spotless, a tendency to speak his mind and his long-time role as the president of the players' union. He had even been put up as a candidate to coach Australia's Under-19s team at the 2010 World Cup in New Zealand and rebuffed by the board as 'not the sort of man we want to teach young Australian cricketers'.

Nevertheless, Marsh had patched up their relationship in the years between and now saw how Lehmann's larrikin persona hid the habits of an exceptionally motivated, organised and ambitious coach – the embodiment of the player-driven coaching scheme he had advocated for more than a decade. Haddin was also swayed by his first experience of Lehmann the coach, much as the players from Hyderabad's Deccan Chargers and then Queensland had been. He had vivid memories of Lehmann's ways as captain of South Australia. 'As a captain – and South Australia weren't very good; let's be honest – Darren was all about winning cricket games,' Haddin said early in the Ashes tour. 'He thought the best way for young cricketers to get better was to put them under pressure and play on the last day for a result.'

On the final day of Australia A's match in Bristol, Lehmann helped the batsmen in warm-ups as usual and assisted the tour's head coach, Troy Cooley, until around midday, when Howard arrived and asked him out to lunch. Lehmann was a little surprised at the invitation, and with some reason. For a long time he had been among Howard's most vocal critics. His dislike for some of the more scientific extremes of player management and wellness reports was well known to Queensland's players. Due partly to their close proximity to CA's high-performance arm at the Allan Border Field, the Bulls took pride in doing things their own way, often ducking CA's recommendations.

Few Queensland players were chosen for Australia, yet over the preceding two seasons Lehmann had guided them to trophies in all three formats. After the national team's disastrous results in India, and little better in the Champions Trophy, Howard's approach to Lehmann was an admission that this anti-establishment maverick and others like him might actually know better.

After talking through a handful of topics over lunch, Howard cut to the nub of things. 'How would you like to be Australian coach?'

Misreading it as a blue-sky conversation starter, Lehmann responded, 'Oh, I dunno, maybe in a few years, that might be nice.'

'No, I mean now.'

Lehmann's wife, Andrea, and their children were in Bristol, as the family had planned a holiday in Scotland following the Australia A tour. He hurriedly conferred with them, before accepting Howard's offer. The Lehmann family's 2013 northern summer trip would go on without Dad.

Mickey Arthur, John Inverarity and Rod Marsh were wondering where Lehmann and Howard had disappeared. Australia A were on the way to a narrow victory, characterised by aggressive batting, swing bowling and some doughty spin into a strong breeze by the leg spinner Fawad Ahmed. A few pre-Ashes meetings had taken place that day, including one at which Arthur had informed Cowan he would be moved down the order. Unable to get a taxi in the crisp early evening, Marsh called his wife for a lift back to the hotel. Once there, the trio were to have a selection meeting in the hotel bar, but they waited for Howard.

When he arrived, Howard seemed agitated and distracted. He had no interest in the selection discussion, which revolved around the addition of Steve Smith and Ashton Agar to the squad. After a few minutes, Howard said simply, 'Mickey, I need to see you.' In that one moment, as Marsh and Inverarity took their leave, all the day's events and mysterious absences made horrible sense to Arthur. 'Pat said, "Mate, we're moving you on. The board said the David Warner incident was the final straw, and we're giving you three months' salary," and that was it,' Arthur says. 'Lasted thirty seconds.'

Arthur walked to his room in a daze but then went back down to see Howard and Sutherland, who had arrived from London and checked in to a hotel that was a short walk away from Arthur's. Sutherland told Arthur that if things were misconstrued in the press he wanted to be clear that he, Sutherland, had the utmost respect for Arthur and simply felt that it was the best decision for Australian cricket at that moment. The trio shared a drink while chatting, and when Howard indicated he was hungry, the dead man walking and his two executioners ate steaks together.

Next morning, the players went to Arthur's room for what was in several cases a tearful farewell. Though Clarke spoke warmly, two absentees said much for the problems CA hoped to cauterise: Watson and Haddin. Soon after, Arthur gave a press conference in which he fired no bullets at CA before taking the journey to Perth via Heathrow. Arthur's mother died in Cape Town while he was in transit, and within a few hours of returning to Australia his whole family flew to South Africa.

In Arthur's few hours in Perth, one of his friends arrived to offer commiserations and condolences but also to run a critical eye over his contract. Noting the meagre three months' severance pay for a deal originally meant to last until 2015, he reckoned the payout had to be contested. Having almost taken CA to court over Simon Katich's dismissal in 2011, Harmers Workplace Lawyers finally had a chance to rattle cricket's cage.

Details of Arthur's legal case were leaked to the press in the days before the second Ashes Test, at Lord's. The leak served an unfortunate but necessary function. At Trent Bridge, Clarke and Arthur spoke every day over the phone. But after some of Arthur's more colourful legal claims, which included an allegation that Clarke had described Watson as a 'cancer' in the team, were spilled in a Channel Seven news report, the relationship fractured. Neither Arthur nor CA was responsible for the leak, but the fallout meant Lehmann's union with Clarke had room to grow.

Looking back, Arthur has only one major regret: that he did not get the chance to run the team with the autonomy he had enjoyed in South Africa. In the earlier job, Arthur had reported directly to the chief executive and the board, making quarterly statements but otherwise building the program as he saw fit, in consultation with his captain, Graeme Smith. Though he had seemingly been granted more power as Australian coach than anyone since Bob Simpson, Arthur had also been forced to answer to a far broader and deeper bureaucracy, with Pat Howard at its centre. In Michael Clarke, he also dealt with a captain of strong opinions who did not have the robust senior player relationships Smith had been able to call on.

'I felt with Australia I never had the freedom to do it, simply because I always felt suffocated,' Arthur says. 'I felt there were so many people touching the team – and I said this numerous times to Pat – I wanted the freedom to run the team the way I knew I could, and I never, ever felt I had that freedom. When I ran South Africa there was a selection panel, but I would pick teams and had a lot more freedom. At CA I felt every decision we were going to make I had to make five phone calls to five different people, whereas with South Africa I just made my decision, put it in my report and told the board at the next meeting.'

Significantly, Arthur was not alone in thinking the coach had been driven to run the team a certain way. Ricky Ponting often felt Arthur was doing the bidding of others. 'I was in England playing with Surrey when Boof [Lehmann] got appointed,' Ponting recalls. 'Pat Howard rang me and said, "We're going to be appointing Darren." I said, "Yep, go and do it. Don't worry about the timing; just do it. Can't afford to wait another week." But I also said, "Please, if you appoint Darren Lehmann, let him coach his way, let him do it the way he wants to do it. Don't get in his way at all."'

Days earlier, when Sutherland spoke to Paul Marsh in London, Lehmann's name had come up. Marsh had worked closely with Lehmann when he was president of the Australian Cricketers' Association, and now Sutherland was wondering about how Lehmann might fare as national coach. Echoing Ponting, Marsh said that if Lehmann was to be hired, he had to be allowed room to operate in his own way. 'I cast back to the whole discussion we had in Perth during Monkeygate in 2008 and the image of the team,' Marsh remembers. 'I said to James, "Darren's strengths are the way he goes about it and the way he builds relationships and they're not necessarily aligned with the direction you've been taking CA and the behaviour of the team and all the rest of it. You've got to let him do his own job, because that's his strength." I'd worked with him at the ACA and I know what he's like, and if they'd tried to control him and cast him in the CA image it wouldn't have worked. They had to let him loose and let him be who he is and let him go about it. They've done that and hello, the Australian public's fallen in love with him.'

Sutherland and Howard ultimately concluded that Lehmann would be able to do the kind of authoritative job Arthur had not been capable of, but circumstances also played a part in the two coaches' fates. Arthur had arrived in a new role when all around him were finding their feet and as a non-confrontational personality occasionally left a vacuum that others, namely Howard, Dovey and Clarke, came to fill. When Lehmann was offered the job, it was at a moment when Howard and the others were looking for expeditious results and were therefore more willing to meet whatever demands the new man made. Instantly, Lehmann held more cards than Arthur ever had.

'I've spoken to a lot of people and they say Pat's hardly ever around now,' Arthur says. 'When I was there he was there every minute of every day. Everything I wanted is what Darren has, and Darren's now running it the way I ran South Africa, and I'm really chuffed for him because that's the way it should be. I missed that because everyone was trying to find role definition and clambering over each other to find their sense of authority. The roles were all blurred and intermingled. The one thing the sacking did was that the roles then got clearly defined, because they realised that mistakes had been made. I was the fall guy for Darren to get total autonomy over the team, which is great because that's how it should be.'

Arthur's dismissal and Lehmann's appointment had happened so quickly that the Queensland chairman, Jim Holding, had to wait ten hours after James Hopes' unofficial call, on the morning after his overnight conversation with Lehmann, to receive an official communiqué from Sutherland. The story broke in Australia about 10.30 a.m., via near-simultaneous reports by Jesse Hogan in *The Age* and Malcolm Conn in the *Daily Telegraph*.

In Bristol, a trio of press conferences took place, by Sutherland and Howard, Arthur, and then Clarke and Lehmann. Facing questions about the embarrassment of the moment, the rotting of Australian cricket and whether he had considered his own position, Sutherland made a statement uncharacteristic in its boldness. 'We're grasping the nettle and making a decision to make change,' he said. 'Perhaps ahead of where public expectation might be, because we're not going to let things remain the same – the status quo's not good enough and we need improved performance, improved accountability and we expect to see that over the coming months. We're really confident we're making the right decision right now, really confident the team will respond positively under Darren Lehmann and we'll see an effort going forward that all Australian fans will be proud of.'

Sutherland denied that Lehmann was the silver bullet, but in that moment he sure looked like one. Next to a somewhat shaky Clarke, Lehmann radiated confidence from the moment the cameras began to roll. The first question put to him as Australian coach was simple. Can Australia still win the Ashes? Lehmann flashed a smile. 'Yes. Definitely.'

23

Getting
Them Back

JULY 2013 – JANUARY 2014

Australia in England

Australia in India

England in Australia

Forty-eight hours before Pat Howard and James Sutherland began their move on Mickey Arthur and Darren Lehmann, a quintet of Australia's Ashes squad members took to a platform under the gaze of Tower Bridge for a choreographed game. A marketing stunt designed to sell tickets for the home summer, it created a somewhat incongruous scene. Michael Clarke, Shane Watson, Chris Rogers and others padded away questions about their apparently grim prospects of regaining the Ashes in England while CA illustrated their firm focus on the return bout that followed it.

The swiftness with which Arthur was removed for Lehmann allowed the new coach a series to settle in. Relationships could be established and deliberations made on players, coaches and tactics. Had Arthur been retained and the Ashes lost in England, as was likely, pressure to make a change with only weeks left before the home series would have been almost unbearable. Instead, Lehmann and Clarke had the chance to put together a method for defeating

England in Australia and to manage their resources with that end-game in mind.

For Andy Flower's England, this scenario looked decreasingly inviting the longer the players pondered it. Lehmann's appointment meant that they would not be up against a similar philosophy to Flower's in the opposing team – after all, Arthur had helped Flower put his own team structure in place – but instead a sharply contrasting approach that placed faith in players to be aggressive and instinctive, rather than keeping things tight and awaiting a mistake. Writing in *The Times*, Mike Atherton had identified the gap between Flower's methods and those favoured by many Australian players when the 'Warnifesto' was unleashed in January. 'What is interesting about Warne's no-nonsense blueprint is that in many areas it runs exactly counter to the direction England are taking. The Argus review, upon which much of Australia's current thinking rests (and into which [Mark] Taylor amongst others had a big input), was based in no small measure on England's system, which has brought them Ashes success at Australia's expense, and which Warne wants dismantled. Copying English cricket is bad for the soul, clearly.'

In England, Australia's players discovered that the seemingly unflappable androids they had encountered down under in 2010–11 were now older, wiser and louder, but also shakier. James Anderson, Stuart Broad and Matt Prior in particular had developed into verbal attack dogs after the fashion of Matthew Hayden and Andrew Symonds. But their cricket did not have quite the same quality to back up the cussing. Alastair Cook, a solid leader respected by his players, was tactically wooden and heavily reliant on Flower's advice at breaks in play.

This all came to light at Trent Bridge, when the left-field selection and unresearched batting of Ashton Agar caught England's planners completely unawares. His 98 not only brought a disbelieving Australian public along for the ride, but also hacked England's carefully calibrated analytics with remarkable ease. Though relying heavily on a pair of 10th-wicket stands, Australia fell only 12 runs short and might have won if not for umpire Aleem Dar missing a clear edge by Broad off Agar's bowling at a critical moment of England's second innings. 'It showed us,' says one player, 'they weren't that good.'

The end of that match also illustrated how the Australian team had begun to function more effectively and organically off the field. In the evening, a group of Australian players could be found in Nottingham's Revolution nightclub, letting off some steam. They were mainly younger types who had not played. But the man overseeing it all and making sure none came to the sort of grief David Warner had done at the Walkabout was Brad Haddin, returned as vice-captain and the last man out earlier that day. Haddin's days of hell-raising were largely past, but his presence as a team elder was an example of the sort of traditional senior player influence that had been momentarily missing in India and the Champions Trophy.

Warring factions were also calmed. The 'instant respect' Lehmann commanded as a former player was powerful, and so too was his capacity to put the squabbles of the year's first half in perspective. Players, he often told them, get only around ten years to make their international careers count, so it was imperative that they did not waste that time. In marked contrast to his two predecessors, Lehmann was also able to engender confidence without then taking it away with his own nervous visage. The anxiousness of Arthur and the intensity of Nielsen had often been passed on to the players. Lehmann's effect was quite the opposite. 'Players feel under pressure a lot of the time either externally or from themselves because they're high achievers,' says one member of the team's staff. 'So they appreciate somebody who just settles the mood down.'

Lehmann's understanding of the dressing room was informed by the experience of so many. In his autobiography, *Worth the Wait*, Lehmann had explained his shock at going from the relatively quiet South Australia squad to the ever-combustible Victorian team, where Simon O'Donnell and Dean Jones were but two of many egos: 'It often resembled a volcano that was boiling away under the earth and could explode at any moment. The other interesting thing was that the coach, Les Stillman, was more often than not the person adding fuel to the fire instead of being a calming influence.' In Lehmann's first year, Victoria won the Sheffield Shield, but from there the fabric began to tear badly. 'We had a team good enough to win two or three Shield titles,' he wrote, 'and perhaps we would have if the leaders in the group had been more united.'

Clarke's influence was reduced, but even here Lehmann used an artful tactic to build the relationship. Shane Warne was Clarke's best friend, and he was made very welcome in the rooms by Lehmann. By series' end Clarke privately conceded to a friend that 'I just work here now', but he had been allowed to concentrate on his fortes: tactics and run-making. Australia remained unpredictable, their performances lurching from the fleetingly brilliant at Old Trafford and the Oval to the indescribably awful at Lord's and Durham. But they were learning all the time and closing the gap in terms of matchplay if not the final margin.

The team's tactical romanticism was not to everyone's taste. Clarke's generous declaration on the final day of the series at the Oval so incensed the selector on duty, Rod Marsh, that he stormed out of the dressing rooms in a show of anger at how a Test match might have just been given away. Warne's influence on this decision and plenty of others, as he shared an almost equal amount of time in the Sky commentary box and the Australian dressing room, was considerable. What could not be debated was how Australia reclaimed the antipodean way of playing the game, at times speaking disparagingly of England's grey functionalism. 'It's not the type of cricket I'd play,' Lehmann said after the series. 'We've found England's cracks and worked out plans for next time.'

This was not to say the Australian approach lacked precision. Bowling plans for each batsman were detailed and required a high degree of skill. Lehmann's directives for the batsmen focused greatly upon reducing the threat of Graeme Swann by stacking the top order with right-handers not shy of hitting an off spinner for six. Though each man played in England, Ed Cowan, Phillip Hughes and Usman Khawaja found themselves surplus to requirements by the end of the series. Emerging in their stead were Steve Smith, who grew in stature and skill with each innings in England, and George Bailey, an ODI fixture and an intelligent, self-aware team man. Lehmann advocated hitting Swann straight and occasionally doing so first ball of an over or spell to throw him off balance.

The blueprint also included Mitchell Johnson, who returned for the ODI series that followed the Tests. In the space of his first few balls his hot pace roughed up Jonathan Trott, creating doubts that enveloped numerous Englishmen. Johnson's speed and venom, brought to perfect pitch by two years of regeneration and self-education, hit England's batsmen with the sort of intensity that none of Flower's metrics could have calculated. 'Speed defeats reactions' was the way the England fast man John Snow had once summed up the power of a bowler such as Johnson, whose speed also defeated the bravado that had built up around the English team, rendering empty many of the verbal threats made by Anderson and company.

Behind Johnson were Ryan Harris and Peter Siddle, bowlers of the requisite quality and endurance to hammer away consistently and skilfully following plans that emphasised getting batsmen out rather than simply starving their scoring. In one of the more pointed departures from English thinking, boundary sweepers were taboo. In the words of Jason Gillespie, Lehmann's disciple and Yorkshire's coach, 'I'm continually educating our bowlers to make sure, if you get your skills right, that bloke at deep point is out of the game. You're setting a field for a bad ball. You dry up scoring by bowling well, and challenging batsmen to play shots they don't want to play. I can cop a few boundaries.'

Despite Gillespie's wise words, when England arrived in Perth at the end of the year they still hung on to the belief that cold pragmatism could win out for one more series. But Australia had found their spearhead and regained their voice. They were also focused across all levels by a simple truth: everyone was sick of losing to England.

Clarke's exchange with Anderson in the closing minutes of the first Test, at the Gabba, was not the most pivotal moment of the return Ashes series. That honour rests with Johnson's dismissal of Trott shortly before lunch on the second day after roughing up England's usually unflappable number three. But the confrontation between Australia's captain and England's number-one agent provocateur was certainly the most symbolic.

Anderson's tendency to shoot from the lip, often with a threat of physical violence, grew out of his experiences as a young English cricketer cowed by domineering Australians such as Ricky Ponting, Matthew Hayden and Andrew Symonds. He learned to take on a manufactured nasty persona on the field and combined it with developing skills to become one of the least pleasant bowlers to face between 2008 and 2013. As the shadows lengthened on the Gabba, Australia's looming victory not in doubt, Anderson tried to steal a small measure of consolation by inflicting some damage on Bailey, the debutant at short leg.

'I don't know what it is about you, but out of all the guys out here you're the one I want to punch in the face,' Anderson said to Bailey before the start of a Johnson over.

Bailey, an equable character, responded with a smile and an inaudible reply.

Anderson continued to address him and began to delay the first ball. The umpires wandered over, as did Clarke. Amid a bout of finger-pointing, Clarke fired, 'Face up. Get ready for a broken fucking arm. Face up.'

Clarke's words were heard around the world as a curious Channel Nine momentarily – they claimed inadvertently – turned up the stump-microphone fader, in contravention of their agreement not to do so whenever the ball was dead. The broadcast earned Clarke an ICC fine in the region of $3000 but also demonstrated how Australia's players were responding to England's aggression, reclaiming the kind of unbridled hostility that was once the team's trademark.

For most of the period between 2006–07 and 2013–14, many of Australia's players and coaches had felt they were playing with one hand tied – not so much behind their backs, but to a corporate billboard selling cricket as 'Australia's favourite sport'. As one player noted after some years of attending players' camps and meetings in which values were espoused, 'It's been all about the kids and the families and the mums watching and making sure that cricket is Australia's favourite sport, so we want to be nice, we want everyone to like us.' While this was hardly a bad thing, the reining-in of the team's aggression had created something of an identity crisis. Australia's players were not politically correct and were often outright boorish, but it was part of how they won, and they knew it.

Ricky Ponting and Tim Nielsen had fought this corner for much of their shared leadership tenure. 'Having CA talk to us about the way we had to be perceived to be playing cricket was difficult,' Ponting recalls. 'I always said, "If you keep toning us down, toning us down, you'll make us the same as everybody else, and as soon as we're the same as everybody else we become as vulnerable as anybody else. What do you want? Do you want us to win, keep winning games and be the best cricket team in the world, or do you want us just to be like everybody else?"

'The point about Clarke and Anderson in Brisbane was the way the team played. We were told for the last four or five years of my captaincy we couldn't play that way. With Boof back as coach that was always going to change. What happened last summer? We win. But do you reckon they're telling them every day, "No, boys, you can't play like that"? Maybe they did have a crack at Pup after Brisbane, but they shouldn't have. They should have been patting him on the back and saying, "Well done."'

In the weeks before the Gabba Test, anxiety was palpable around CA about what might result if Australia lost again. Though the board chairman, Wally Edwards, offered as strenuous a public defence of James Sutherland and Pat Howard as was possible at the annual general meeting in October – headlines of 'Sutherland to Stay Even If We Lose 5–0' summed it up – there had been discussions of what might come to pass given another poor result. Howard would almost certainly have been replaced before his contract was due to expire, and Sutherland may not have been permitted to continue after his own deal concluded, in 2015.

Unsure what kind of backing he had from above, Howard resolved to give Lehmann, Clarke and the team the most support he could offer. This was demonstrated by acquiescence to most requests from the team, including the reinstatement of Craig McDermott as Test bowling coach, the employment of the Queensland strength and conditioning expert Damian Mednis and the provision of the spin coach John Davison to work with Nathan Lyon at four of the five Ashes venues. But the most significant message Howard delivered to the team was about attitude, aggression and verbal confrontation, the kind that had been discouraged for most of the past seven years. 'We were told by Pat that we'd be looked after; we wouldn't be hung out to dry if we went really hard at England,' a player says. 'That's the brand of cricket that everyone knows we have to play to be successful. We're not there to step over the line, but they want us to play at our best, whatever that is, and if something happens then we're going to be protected.' So it was that when England's players delivered their usual round of sledges in Brisbane, they found it returned to them with interest. It came as a shock almost as unexpected as the resurgence of Johnson.

'If you talk to people in the England system, they were blown away by the physical and verbal aggression of Australia,' Gillespie says. 'That England squad just didn't react well to that, and they openly admitted that threw them. They had no answer for it.' The physical threat of high pace ran closely alongside the verbal one dished out by the slips cordon and others. In Brisbane, David Warner pounced on Jonathan Trott at a press conference, referring to the batsman's 'scared eyes' and the 'weak' manner of his second-innings dismissal. But just as Howard had promised, there was little CA hand-wringing when Clarke's remarks were aired on Nine, even though Sutherland spoke to the captain and the ICC stepped in with a minor sanction.

Moreover, precious few high-minded columnists materialised to decry Australia's tactics. Rather than spanning emotions from outrage to support, as had been the case in Monkeygate, this time there seemed a greater acceptance that yes, right or wrong, this is how the Australian team wins. As television and radio presenter Waleed Aly concluded on the ABC's sports show *Offsiders*, 'I am in the school of thought that this Australian cricket team and Australian cricket generally is at its best when it is at or beyond the edge. That's just always been the way that it's worked, and the minute we try to pull back, we're not like that, and we just don't win. You can lament that but I just think that's the way it is, and that's how Clarke leads this team.'

The unshackling of Australia's players went a long way towards making England feel uncomfortable and unsettled on the field and attacked from all sides on tour. It helped that Johnson was also pushing the limits, though in a far more visceral way.

Sledging did not convince Kevin Pietersen of Mitchell Johnson's new credentials; it was the bowler's lack of words that unnerved him. After swinging Johnson to the fence between fine leg and deep square on the second afternoon, Pietersen spoke. 'I said to him, it's me or you, buddy, and believe me, I'm less scared of getting out than you are scared of giving me a lot of runs,' he wrote in *KP: The Autobiography*. 'He looked at me, just stared at me, he didn't say anything back. He kept starting and walked past. Shit. Shit. Shit. On so many occasions in the past Johnson has always bit back: shut up, KP, fuck off, shut up, big shot. This time he didn't say anything, and immediately I knew he was different.'

This quiet, even solemn self-assurance had also struck McDermott when he returned to work with the team ahead of Brisbane. Between Ashes series, Lehmann had spoken with the fast bowlers about who they wanted to guide them, and McDermott's name quickly came up. Ali de Winter had done a creditable job, as evidenced by the fact England had not reached 400 once during the northern encounter. But McDermott had retained the links forged in 2011–12 and had often been contacted from England: on the first morning of the Lord's Test, James Pattinson had called to ask which end to bowl from. Before England arrived in Australia, Howard, Lehmann and McDermott met out of sight of the National Cricket Centre at a cafe in Ascot and quickly reached terms.

McDermott's last real sight of Johnson had been in South Africa in November 2011. Johnson had been worn down by constant cricket and low on motivation. His action had grown ragged and was lacking in the sort of pace he summoned at his best. Bizarre as it seems now, Johnson bowled fast-medium swing off a short run in Johannesburg. He suffered an injury while batting. Two years later McDermott made it one of his first orders of business to fly to Perth to catch up with Johnson. What he saw was a higher bowling action, a stronger body and, above all, a refreshed mind. 'He's in a really good space mentally,' McDermott said before Brisbane, 'very confident about what he's doing and that's a great place for him to be.'

Johnson spoke with a similar level of confidence at the Gabba on series eve. In the reign of terror that followed – over eight Test matches against two opponents – many wrote of how remarkable and unforeseen it all was. Johnson, though, could clearly see the way ahead. 'I guess there's been a lot of talk that we're going to just bowl 155 clicks, bowling bouncers every ball. That's all just media hype,' he said. 'I know what I need to do, we all know our roles in the team, we're all different bowlers, I can't give too much away in terms of plan, but it's not going to be all-out bouncers, it's picking the right times and being smart. If it's not swinging conditions and I'm getting that good bounce then that's all that really matters to me, seeing it go through to the keeper.'

Australia's gloveman, Brad Haddin, took plenty of balls above his head over the next six weeks, as Johnson tallied 37 wickets and almost as many English bruises. With the exception of a handful of deliveries, he barely swung the ball. But his pace remained consistently high, invariably nudging 150 kilometres per hour, and Clarke used him in bursts of two, three or four overs to maintain it. England's batsmen failed to cope, and their bowlers gave away all pretence of pride. Pietersen heard Broad, Anderson and Swann concede how fearful they were when facing Johnson, while in Adelaide, from short leg, Bailey witnessed Monty Panesar's desperate attempt to concentrate. 'He was muttering away to himself to watch the ball; it wasn't pretty. I was just trying to get him to get his elbow out of the way, for starters.'

Numerous factors contributed to Johnson's success, not least his natural ability and the maturity that comes with experience, advancing years, marriage and fatherhood. He worked with Dennis Lillee on his strength and technique and with the Special Air Service Regiment's Victoria Cross winner Ben Roberts-Smith on his mental application – specifically a soldier's ability to carry on with highly challenging, exhausting and life-threatening tasks irrespective of what emotions bubbled underneath. But none of these markers of progress could have been achieved or even contemplated without the nine months he spent out of the game, in 2011–12.

For Ponting, who witnessed Johnson's earlier ups and downs, it was the decisive factor and a powerful argument for the strategic resting of players for a few months, rather than days, at a time. 'There's one thing that's turned Mitchell Johnson's career around – getting away from the game,' Ponting says. 'This is where cricket is so far behind. How do you ever work on your technique as a professional cricketer?

In the lead-up to the game or in a game, and who is going to do that? Is Tiger Woods tinkering with his swing at the Masters? No. You might do things slightly differently in your preparation, but Mitchell had to make significant technical changes. The only way he could do that was with time away from the game. Now he's a technically different animal, he knows his action; and you put some confidence with that, he's bowling well.

'He used to be very insecure about not being able to get the best out of his ability and about not knowing if the ball's going to spear down the leg side or go wide. But Mitch had to have eight or nine months away from the game to sort that out – if he'd stayed in the game and around the team he wouldn't have fixed it. And if he'd been out of the Australian team and playing first-class cricket he wouldn't have fixed it either. It was the fact he got away for as long as he did, thought about giving up altogether and came back refreshed. That's the thing that cricket doesn't understand.'

The understanding had been growing, however. CA's management of the ODI series in India that preceded the Ashes was an example of shrewd and strategic thinking. Lehmann had missed the tour in order to spend time at home between Ashes assignments, and Clarke had also stayed in Sydney, citing a relapse of his back trouble. Johnson had toured but was pulled out of the final match in order to be home in time for Shield duty. As significant were the omissions of David Warner and Steve Smith, which had allowed Australia's two young batsmen to find rhythm and form on home pitches in domestic competitions. Warner was not initially thrilled by the decision and even faced disciplinary action from New South Wales when he missed an October grade fixture in favour of a morning's training and an afternoon at the races. But Warner, Smith, Lehmann, Clarke and Johnson entered the Ashes better for the time at home, as subsequent results proved beyond doubt.

*

It was in Johnson's company that Haddin carved out the partnership that gave Australia a foothold on day one at the Gabba, after a nervy start by batsmen who all went on to contribute over the series. Clarke, Warner, Watson, Smith and Rogers each tallied at least one century during the five Tests, and when they did not Haddin was invariably there to steady the innings. Haddin's performance had an air of providence about it, as though the trials of 2012–13 had been endured in return for a bountiful reward the following summer. Spectators lost count of the number of times a Haddin edge or miscue flew through the hands or fell just out of reach of England's fielders, but they also became used to the wonderfully brazen strokes that arrived in between those chances.

The confidence Haddin drew out of others was similar to the effect wrought by Lehmann. Having shepherded Johnson in Brisbane, he accompanied Clarke in Adelaide, then Smith in Perth. And it was not just with the bat that he built a sense of shared purpose, but also in the field. The major beneficiary both in England and Australia was Nathan Lyon, who had built a relationship of considerable trust with his wicketkeeper. Lyon's sense of worth had been battered through 2012–13 by failure to bowl South Africa out in Adelaide and by a steady trickle of catches and stumpings missed by Matthew Wade. Haddin took a higher percentage of chances and offered reassuring words on a consistent basis.

'For a while there Lyono was creating at least one chance an innings that didn't get taken, whether it be a stumping or a caught behind,' says one teammate. 'If you're a finger spinner with no mystery variation, there's a big difference between 0–80 and 2–80. If you take two wickets an innings, four a game, you're in the team every time. If you're taking no wickets more often than not, you're out of the team; and that's what happened in India. Now he has confidence from a keeping point of view and a technical point of view. He'll go, "What's my pace like?' and Hadds will say, "Stop worrying about it; just bowl." Hadds probably saved Lyono's career.'

*

Once the urn returned to Australian hands after the third Test, at the WACA Ground, Melbourne and Sydney played out in an uncannily similar way to their 2006–07 equivalents. Like the team of Ricky Ponting, Shane Warne and Glenn McGrath, Clarke's team played spotty cricket at times but rode on the wave of confidence created in Brisbane and built upon in Adelaide and Perth. Cook's England resembled their forebears in being swallowed up by the doubts, insecurities and divisions brought to the surface in defeat, even though they put themselves in decent positions to win each of the final two matches.

The contrast with seven years before was this: England had been the team trying to make one final victorious bow amid much talk of legacies and retirements. Instead, it was Australia, the fresher and hungrier team, that rose up. As one victory mounted upon another, Clarke's men took no little delight in the fact that a series they had expected to be a scrap to the final day in Sydney had become the kind of pageant their lauded predecessors had specialised in. The extra days' rest won by bowlers who never allowed England to reach 300 in an innings even granted the selectors an unchanged team throughout – a luxury beyond dreams.

Lyon, to whom Michael Hussey had entrusted the team song in January, sang it for the first time in November, then another four times in little more than a month. Clarke and Watson put their differences aside while walking arm in arm around the SCG after the series. Rogers proved himself as the leading run-maker on either side of the world over ten Tests, Harris as the most prolific wicket-taker, on knees and hips held tenuously together by his 34-year-old frame. Lehmann took it all in jauntily, the CA outsider finally allowed to operate the team in his own way. And Howard and Sutherland breathed with the relieved air of two administrators who had come close to the precipice and survived.

In Haddin's characteristically blunt words, 'There were signs we were getting there in England. But the work leading into the home campaign was massive . . . and we destroyed an era of England cricket.' More poetic were the images summoned by Greg Baum after he witnessed Australia take a 4–0 lead in Melbourne via the usually studious but suddenly rollicking bat of Chris Rogers: 'I tried to see the future, but couldn't, any more than anyone could have seen this all-conquering present forty days ago. So I settled for an appreciation of that present and the blooming roses that too few modern players or fans stop to smell. They don't get any rosier for Australians than an Ashes series walkover. Through rose-coloured glasses, I saw hope for the Socceroos at next year's World Cup, and St Kilda in the AFL, and even me on a surfboard, and I heard Rogers speak for all when he said: "This is what dreams are made of." And I thought I saw Santa.'

England's final surrender in Sydney unfolded so rapidly on the third afternoon that a planned end-of-series party, at the Vaucluse family-mansion compound of the hotel and hospitality millionaire Justin Hemmes, had to wait twenty-four hours. Clarke's victorious team thus spent most of the night in the SCG dressing room, scene of so many farewells and dramas over the preceding seven years. Some went on to the Kings Cross nightclubs, retracing the giddy, and occasionally regretted, steps taken by many cricketers before them. In the early hours of the morning they were lauded in song by delighted revellers, as the elation of long-awaited victory washed over them.

A CA setpiece celebration event on the harbour was organised for the following morning and attracted so many wellwishers that the players were presented twice to crowds, on either side of the Opera House. Rogers was late, and fined by Lehmann, but also enjoyed his moment with a shimmying dance for the masses. At the moment Clarke lifted the urn to the crowd, a passing ferry tooted its horn in serendipitous acknowledgement. That night, at Hemmes' compound, the players, staff and friends shared a lavish barbecue, while Rai Thistlethwayte from Thirsty Merc strummed his band's signature tune, 'In the Summertime'. It's no masterpiece, this song, but it spoke fittingly of a summer in which everything did, at last, go right.

24

As Good
as It Gets?

FEBRUARY – SEPTEMBER 2014

Australia in South Africa

ICC World Twenty20

Australia in Zimbabwe

High above the bowler's arm at Newlands, in Cape Town, Wally Edwards watched Australia's dominance of the deciding third Test against South Africa, followed by their desperate scramble for tail-end wickets on the final afternoon. Mitchell Johnson had ambushed the world's number-one side in the first Test, on a Centurion pitch seemingly made to his orders rather than those of South Africa; its pace and uneven bounce making life hellish for the host batsmen and still worse for their bowlers. But a slow, dry surface in Port Elizabeth had helped Graeme Smith's men to level the series. Now they were fighting obstinately to replicate the Adelaide draw of 2012, see off their retiring captain and preserve an unbeaten record stretching back to Australia's 2009 visit.

In his three years as CA chairman, Edwards had witnessed a few peaks and some major troughs. But in South Africa he could see the national team straining to return to the top-of-the-world Test match rankings for the first time since 2009, while at the same time helping to firm up a patchwork of bilateral touring arrangements that were at the heart of a rather Thatcherite new era for the game's global governance. Cricket South Africa had been on-field leaders for much of the period but were becoming marginalised in the ICC boardroom by enmity between the BCCI's supremo, N Srinivasan, and Cricket South Africa's chief executive, Haroon Lorgat.

Not for the first time in the process that had begun when the Woolf report, commissioned by Lorgat during his ICC days, had landed on the executive board table, Edwards was the moderating voice between India, England and Australia – the 'big three', as they came to be described – and the rest of the world. Srinivasan had become an increasingly argumentative presence in the ICC, and the board ever more disconnected from ICC management in Dubai. The BCCI wanted a greater cut of ICC tournament revenue, the England and Wales Cricket Board a greater stake in decision-making and revenue-raising after being wrong-footed by the IPL and left out of the Champions League, and CA a better governance structure reflecting its own domestic reforms.

Edwards had gone to the ICC in 2012 hopeful of imparting the kind of change advocated by Woolf. Ultimately, he had to be content with the formalisation of the ICC as a members' organisation and assurances from India that they would take a more paternal leadership role in the game. At the Cape Town Test he had spoken with Cricket South Africa about agreements for future tours with Australia but also about the thawing of relations with the BCCI, who after Lorgat's appointment had demonstrated their opposition to the choice of chief executive by drastically downsizing a tour of South Africa and thus hobbling its board due to reduced television revenue. Edwards had tried his best to build relationships between all nations, his consultative approach contrasting with the more aloof Giles Clarke, chairman of the England and Wales board, and the forbidding Srinivasan.

In the middle, Australian tempers became frayed as the team felt their chance to win the match and the series begin to recede. This was

a series played to an exceptionally high standard, but it was also perhaps the most heated that Australia had been since the Monkeygate
summer of 2007–08. Sledging was frequent, and accusations of ball-
tampering were flung freely. As with Edwards' ICC negotiations in
the stands, Australia gained much on the Newlands field, but at a
price. Ryan Harris' late dismissals of Dale Steyn and Morné Morkel
delivered victory at last, though even in the moments of celebration it
was possible to wonder how fleeting it all might be.

South Africa offered Michael Clarke and Darren Lehmann a chance
to validate the Ashes victory by going on to defeat a hardened international team away from home. Lehmann's message to the team had
been simple enough: 'We can't afford to rest on our laurels,' he stated
in one of his emails to players and support staff. As ever, the conditions were the most similar to Australia's that a cricketer was likely to
find anywhere in the world – a fact that undoubtedly helped reduce
the impact of the squad's being forced out of its traditional stint in
Potchefstroom at the start of the tour by poor weather. Also helpful
was South Africa's relative lack of Test match sharpness, as they had
played only two matches against India in December and had then
gone into their domestic T20 tournament. Add to this the retirement of Jacques Kallis and Graeme Smith's growing resolve to join
his great all-rounder in exiting at the end of the series, and the hosts
found themselves in a position of decline and transition not shared
by Australia. Prolonged and satisfying as the Ashes celebrations had
been, Clarke's men were eager for more such hijinx in South Africa
before a long break from Test matches.

At Centurion it seemed as though England's harried cricketers
had simply swapped their blue helmets for the green headgear of the
South Africans, so similarly to those of the first match of the Ashes
series did events unfold. Steve Smith sculpted a high-quality century
in the company of Shaun Marsh (subbed in for Shane Watson) before

Mitchell Johnson bounced out Graeme Smith and Faf du Plessis with deliveries terrifying enough to drain away years of confidence. This ground had been South Africa's Gabba, but Australia's victory was sealed within four days. At the end of the match, no less an authority on fast bowling than Michael Holding sought out Johnson to offer his congratulations.

Certain images stuck in the mind. Smith's flinching response to a ball rearing at his face. Du Plessis not even having time to do that as the red leather flew at him, taking the shoulder of the bat on its way into the slips. Ryan McLaren being struck sickeningly on the side of the helmet and being treated for a swelling wound above the right ear. Robin Peterson jumping dramatically towards the off side to try to get out of the way of Johnson rockets launched with extreme prejudice from around the wicket. A first-ball bumper that reached Hashim Amla so quickly that it crashed into his helmet grille.

On what should have been the fifth day, Holding outlined Johnson's effect. 'We haven't seen too many people bowl with that sort of aggression and that sort of pace, and I think it's finding out some batsmen who have been quite comfortable over the past five or six years with the medium pacers they've had around. Dale Steyn has been quick . . . but Johnson has exhibited a great deal more pace and a lot more aggression. Pace is the game changer. A lot of bowlers are brilliant, Glenn McGrath was a fantastic bowler, but he didn't have the effect this man is having. With that much pace it's all about "This man can hurt me as well as get me out," and that changes the entire dynamic of the game.'

Graeme Smith found that his batsmen were unable to find an outlet to attack, meaning that when they weren't dodging Johnson they were also being starved of runs. He believed that the greatest difference between the Australian team of early 2014 and earlier editions was not Johnson but Nathan Lyon. 'I think Lyon has been the key factor in Australian cricket of late,' Smith says. 'I think he's added a lot of solidness around the bowling attack and I think his role in Australian cricket has been very important. Lyon allows Michael Clarke to use Mitch in an aggressive way.

'If your spinner's struggling and your quick bowlers keep having to come back again and again, eventually they're going to break. Tactically it is key to not have to do that with your quicks. It took a long time for Australian cricket to replace Shane Warne. Not with a world-beater, but with a role-player. A key man in our success was Paul Harris. He wasn't a world-beater but he filled a solid role for us, which allowed Steyn, Ntini, Morkel and others to go for it, be fresh for their next spell and make an impact. That's why Lyon has really added a lot of value. He allows the game to stand still so you can make an impact, instead of having to bring back fast bowlers when teams are going at five an over.'

About the only refuge that could be found from Johnson was in a slow pitch, which is precisely what was served up in Port Elizabeth for the second Test. Not known for offering much in the way of pace and bounce, St George's Park gave welcome relief to Smith's side, who were nevertheless distracted on match morning by last-minute doubts over the fitness of Vernon Philander. Winning the toss also afforded South Africa the chance to drive the direction of the game with first-innings runs, and over the next four days Australia's blind spot was exposed. Lacking helpful conditions in which to blast the South Africans out, none among Johnson, Ryan Harris or the flagging Peter Siddle could take wickets by other means, while Lyon's steadiness could never be mistaken for the unplayable.

Similarly, greater patience was required of the batsmen on a slow strip, as Smith set diligent ring fields and his bowlers worked on accuracy and subtle movement. A poor patch of batting on the second evening left too much for the tail to do, and after a large first-innings deficit had been conceded there was little Clarke could do about the skill of Hashim Amla and A B de Villiers. Chris Rogers was the only batsman left standing as Steyn and Morkel charged in on the fourth afternoon, helping bring about a rapid finish to a

match that had for the most part been fought at a far more deliber-
ate tempo.

The means by which Steyn and Morkel had so confounded
the touring batsmen was reverse swing, an art the Australians had
never quite mastered or even trusted. The fourth afternoon in Port
Elizabeth resembled nothing so much as the final morning of the
Mohali Test match in 2008, when a very different Australian batting
line-up had succumbed in similarly swift fashion to balls bending
around corners. Their bafflement was enhanced by the knowledge
that the Australian pacemen had been unable to extract anything like
the same movement. Whereas in 2008 questions had been thrown
around among the bowlers, this time the matter drew more pointed
glances at the opposition.

Clarke's players became convinced that the wicketkeeper, de Villiers,
was illegally changing the condition of the ball by rubbing it with his
gloves, thereby allowing Steyn and Morkel to gain sharp swerve. David
Warner, who had made a spectacular if chancy hundred at Centurion,
vented the team's concerns in public. 'We were actually questioning
whether or not A B de Villiers would get the ball in his hand and with
his glove wipe the rough side every ball,' Warner told Sky Sports Radio
between Tests. 'That's another thing we have to try and bring up with
the umpires.' It was a heavy accusation and resulted in an ICC fine for
Warner, even though du Plessis had been found guilty of ball-tampering
during an earlier series against Pakistan.

Australia's sense of underhand conduct increased when they
trained in Cape Town ahead of the third Test. Brad Haddin, following
up on Warner's allegation, decided to try the glove tactic for himself in
the nets and found that a few cursory rubs of glove on ball did indeed
result in the sort of scarifying effect that would get the ball curving.
The tactic was mentioned to the umpires, and early in the match de
Villiers was quietly counselled against handling the ball in the way he
had been doing previously. Coincidence or not, South Africa's bowlers
found precious little reverse swing at Newlands, and de Villiers faced

a hail of sledging from the Australians, spiced with liberal use of the word 'cheat'.

Warner's involvement in the episode was instructive, for he demonstrated the kinds of agitator qualities once used by Matthew Hayden and Andrew Symonds. During the match, du Plessis was asked by the press about the way in which he had been angrily rebuked by Australia's fielders when he picked up the ball while batting, and he said the response felt like he had been set upon by 'a pack of dogs'. On the final day, his dismissal was greeted by a chorus of woofing and howling from the Australian huddle, led primarily by Warner. Most pointedly, this rancour gave Warner a focus that he had seldom been able to capture in the past. His chanceless twin centuries – 135 and 145 – were the major reasons why Australia ultimately had time to bowl South Africa out.

The aggression embodied by Warner had one major flashpoint in the final session. The tourists' weary bowling attack was running out of firepower, and as the final hour ticked near even Johnson was losing some of his earlier pep in the hunt for South Africa's last two wickets. Summoning one final vicious bouncer, he struck Philander on the glove from around the wicket, and a catch at short leg was accompanied by umpire Aleem Dar's raised finger. Philander referred the decision, and the television arbiter, Richard Illingworth, decided that his glove had been off the bat handle when it was struck. The not out verdict blew the top off a boiling Australian kettle, and various squabbles broke out as the combatants took final drinks.

Chief among the arguments was that between Dale Steyn and James Pattinson, brought in for the final match in order to add the pace Siddle had lost over the course of nineteen consecutive Tests since December 2012. Before the match, Pattinson had asked Steyn to borrow a pair of bowling boots, as both men used the same brand. Pattinson bowled rapidly and well throughout, vitally removing Amla on the fourth evening with a sharp inswinger. But when he vented his frustrations at Steyn a little less then twenty-four hours later, South

Africa's spearhead responded with some fairly understandable incredulity. 'You're sledging me and you're wearing my boots?'

Into this argument stepped Clarke, hoping to make a similar impact to the one he had made on James Anderson in Brisbane a few months before. Clarke's contributions to the results had trailed off at the back end of the Ashes, and he had started poorly in South Africa. But in this Test he had made a bold and brave century ranked among his very best innings, despite Morkel's first-day battering with short balls, one of which was later revealed to have left Clarke with a fractured shoulder. It had taken place as Shane Warne watched approvingly from the team viewing area, having been hired by CA as a spin consultant. Clarke wanted to finish the summer on the best note possible. If he had to stir up Steyn, so be it.

Amid a flurry of expletives, Clarke twice referred to Steyn as a 'cheating ****'. Steyn was aggrieved and responded in kind. Eventually, Aleem Dar and Kumar Dharmasena stepped in to separate the players. For most of the previous seven years such scenes had been absent from Australian teams. The Ashes success had reminded all that this, for better or worse, was the way they won. When Harris ignored chronic knee and hip complaints once more to bowl Steyn and then Morkel, bringing Australia's Test summer to an exultant conclusion, the players on both sides shook hands with apparent warmth. But away from the cameras, the teams drank separately that night.

After a few years as popular losers, Australia had resumed their mantle of winners, respected but not always liked. In May, an ICC rankings adjustment briefly took Clarke's team back to number one in the world. By September, Steyn had publicly stated his distaste for what Clarke said to him at Newlands. 'I don't take many things personally, but what he did say to me I did take personally,' Steyn said after a limited-overs triangular series in Zimbabwe, in which South Africa gained some measure of revenge by taking the trophy. 'I know he apologised in the media and I should be playing this down. But the day he comes and shakes my hand and says, "I really mean what I said" and behaves like the way he should, maybe then I will [forgive him].' Everything old was new once more.

It cannot be disputed that between November 2013 and March 2014 Australia's Test side played the most powerful and compelling cricket mustered by the baggy green at any time since Shane Warne, Glenn McGrath and Justin Langer all bowed out on the same day in Sydney seven years before. But the achievements were those of the moment, and any groundwork for longer-term success remains some way from bedding down. After the travails of India in 2013, CA – its board, management, selectors and coaches – focused all its energies completely on regaining the Ashes. The victory in South Africa was a capstone on that achievement, proving that Australia had indeed reached a very high peak of proficiency, albeit in conditions that largely suited them.

Yet most of the players in those teams are the products of earlier times. All but one member of Australia's 2013 Ashes-winning team – George Bailey – were first chosen by the much-maligned panel of Andrew Hilditch. Michael Clarke, Brad Haddin, Ryan Harris, Shane Watson, Mitchell Johnson and Chris Rogers are all old enough to have played with or against Lehmann. Only David Warner and Steve Smith are young players likely to endure beyond the next summer or two. A fast-bowling arsenal that includes James Pattinson, Pat Cummins, Mitchell Starc and Josh Hazlewood should be enough to keep Australia competitive, provided their assorted injuries do not linger into full adulthood.

If Clarke has been able to champion an aggressive, inventive and attractive style of play, Australia's greatest on-field obstacle appears to be the fact that other teams have a fair idea of how to curtail it. Slow pitches, skilful spinners and patient reverse-swinging pacemen are all in plentiful enough supply to mean that the team may continue to struggle on tours of anywhere but South Africa. Domestic groundsmen are being coaxed into preparing drier surfaces after years of speedy, grassy and result-oriented wickets, but it may be a generation before the effects of that change are evident, in Australia's still-meagre spin-bowling stocks as well as in free-scoring but occasionally dunder-headed batsmen. The future is far from assured.

Clarke's body is growing more problematic with each series, as back and hamstring problems cross over with each other. His successor will be the tactically alert Steve Smith. His growing self-reliance and wise choices of mentors have served him richly so far, and his batting has taken on an air of authority that only the best players and captains can muster. By the time Smith assumes the role permanently, the game itself may have changed drastically once more. The new governance model championed by the 'big three' and their chairmen, Wally Edwards, Giles Clarke and N Srinivasan, has already shown signs of decay, from an ICC television rights dividend less than projected to the ruinous withdrawal of the troubled West Indies from an India tour. The BCCI's angry response to the latter event was anything but paternal.

A little like Haroon Lorgat, a passive spectator at the ICC's annual conference in Melbourne in June 2014 when the governing body adopted measures largely opposite to those Lord Woolf had recommended, CA's chief executive, James Sutherland, has stepped back from earlier attempts to influence the global direction of the game. His push for a World Test Championship has been derailed for at least the next eight years, and in recent times he has spoken most fervently of 'winning the war for talent' with other sports in Australia.

Thanks largely to the television rights deal that now includes lucrative free-to-air exposure for the Big Bash League, Australian cricket is in strong financial shape, and the board rewarded Sutherland by agreeing to make his role permanent, thirteen years after he began. His tenure has covered rich times and poor, wise decisions and foolish. From 2007 to 2014 Australian cricket made as many mistakes as it enjoyed successes, leaving in its wake plenty of lessons for those attentive and prudent enough to learn from them.

EPILOGUE

Hours after Australia's narrow defeat in the first Ashes Test of 2013 in Nottingham, I found myself in the town's Revolution nightclub. There seemed few other spots to venture for a post-match drink, and, as often happens, the touring journos chanced upon a handful of Australian cricketers equally keen to let off some steam after the intensity of the day's near miss.

Some were perched outside, others propped at the bar. But typically and fittingly, Phillip Hughes was busting a move or ten in the midst of the dancefloor. He'd had a good match, fashioning 81 in the first innings and looking as assured at Test level as I'd ever seen him. But for once a Hughes innings seemed to escape most attention, which was instead lavished on Ashton Agar and his dream score of 98.

There wasn't much that could distract Hughes from enjoying himself – certainly not a tired Australian correspondent getting his bearings in the club's garishly lit main room. Yet he spotted me, and wandered over to say what I expected would be a brief hello. Instead his previously merry expression turned serious, and earnest.

'Thank you for what you wrote, it meant a lot,' he said. 'I wasn't sure anyone had noticed me batting out there.'

My decision to write about Hughes on the day of his stand with Agar had been partly a matter of logic – my colleagues Jarrod Kimber, Tanya Aldred and David Hopps were all leaning heavily on Agar's performance in their pieces, leaving me to risk repetition if I did too. But I had also been drawn to the sight of Hughes finding a way to score runs against England, having struggled so much against them in 2009 and 2010–11.

The most exciting thing about Hughes that day to me was that he was happy to be inconspicuous, mature enough to let Agar's shooting star shine. England had not been able to find a way past him, and it seemed a preview of what we could expect from Hughes in years to come. The kid of South Africa in 2009 was becoming a man.

Eighteen months later and I found myself at the SCG when Hughes was felled by a bouncer, never to wake up again. The week that followed was harrowing, but the affection in which Hughes was held showed Australian cricket in a gentler and more genuine light than is often allowed by the brio of cricketers and the calculation of their handlers. Everyone from Ricky Ponting to Michael Clarke was revealed to be far more human than the projections we usually see.

Hughes was always that way. Through the hours at the ground, at the hospital and then in Macksville for the funeral, I kept thinking back to Nottingham, and to Revolution. Phillip hadn't needed to read that piece, let alone notice its author in a club full of far more enjoyable company. But he did, and I was grateful. He is missed.

STATISTICS

Australian Test team performance 2007–14
BATTING

Player	Mat	Inns	NO	Runs	HS	Ave	SR	100	50	0
MJ Clarke	78	139	15	6728	329*	54.25	55.68	23	22	9
MEK Hussey	63	111	10	4638	195	45.92	49.30	14	21	12
RT Ponting	58	104	4	4010	221	40.10	58.18	8	26	9
SR Watson	49	93	3	3327	176	36.96	53.64	4	22	5
BJ Haddin	57	96	10	3033	169	35.26	58.39	4	17	6
SM Katich	33	61	3	2928	157	50.48	49.33	8	17	2
DA Warner	30	56	3	2467	180	46.54	73.35	8	12	2
MG Johnson	59	88	14	1637	123*	22.12	58.29	1	8	16
PJ Hughes	26	49	2	1535	160	32.65	53.55	3	7	6
SPD Smith	20	38	4	1361	138*	40.02	51.69	4	6	2
MJ North	21	35	2	1171	128	35.48	48.14	5	4	5
CJL Rogers	14	27	0	1030	119	38.14	47.44	4	5	0
EJM Cowan	18	32	0	1001	136	31.28	41.27	1	6	2
A Symonds	13	22	5	944	162*	55.52	67.14	1	8	2
PM Siddle	53	76	11	926	51	14.24	46.72	0	2	14
ML Hayden	14	25	1	886	124	36.91	60.35	3	2	3
PA Jaques	9	16	0	806	150	50.37	53.41	3	5	1
MS Wade	12	22	4	623	106	34.61	50.08	2	3	0
SE Marsh	9	15	0	493	148	32.86	44.45	2	1	6
RJ Harris	24	35	10	483	68*	19.32	61.13	0	2	2
MA Starc	12	20	6	431	99	30.78	70.65	0	3	2
NM Hauritz	16	22	7	411	75	27.40	49.51	0	2	0
UT Khawaja	9	17	2	377	65	25.13	40.14	0	2	1
BW Hilfenhaus	27	38	12	355	56*	13.65	54.19	0	1	8
B Lee	17	25	5	353	63*	17.65	45.43	0	2	4
JL Pattinson	13	18	7	331	42	30.09	40.07	0	0	1

Player	Mat	Inns	NO	Runs	HS	Ave	SR	100	50	0
NM Lyon	33	41	21	323	40*	16.15	39.34	0	0	2
TD Paine	4	8	0	287	92	35.87	43.09	0	2	0
AC Gilchrist	6	8	1	217	67*	31.00	74.57	0	2	0
AJ Doolan	3	6	0	186	89	31.00	44.71	0	1	0
GJ Bailey	5	8	1	183	53	26.14	58.84	0	1	1
MC Henriques	3	6	1	156	81*	31.20	49.05	0	2	2
GB Hogg	3	5	2	148	79	49.33	61.66	0	1	0
CL White	4	7	2	146	46	29.20	44.24	0	0	0
SR Clark	15	16	5	132	32	12.00	70.58	0	0	3
AC Agar	2	4	0	130	98	32.50	63.10	0	1	0
AB McDonald	4	6	1	107	68	21.40	49.30	0	1	1
BJ Hodge	1	2	0	94	67	47.00	53.71	0	1	0
JJ Krejza	2	4	1	71	32	23.66	48.63	0	0	0
DE Bollinger	12	14	7	54	21	7.71	33.96	0	0	3
JW Hastings	1	2	0	52	32	26.00	59.09	0	0	0
XJ Doherty	4	7	3	51	18*	12.75	32.07	0	0	0
JP Faulkner	1	2	0	45	23	22.50	104.65	0	0	0
TA Copeland	3	4	1	39	23*	13.00	50.64	0	0	0
GJ Maxwell	2	4	0	39	13	9.75	52.70	0	0	0
GA Manou	1	2	1	21	13*	21.00	53.84	0	0	0
PJ Cummins	1	2	1	15	13*	15.00	68.18	0	0	0
SW Tait	1	2	0	12	8	6.00	63.15	0	0	0
B Casson	1	1	0	10	10	10.00	22.72	0	0	0
CJ McKay	1	1	0	10	10	10.00	66.66	0	0	0

* Not out

Australian Test team performance 2007–14
BOWLING

Player	Mat	Overs	Mdns	Runs	Wkts	BBI	BBM	Ave	Econ	SR	5	10
MG Johnson	59	2204.3	411	7240	264	8/61	12/127	27.42	3.28	50.1	12	3
PM Siddle	53	1870.3	486	5522	188	6/54	9/104	29.37	2.95	59.6	8	0
NM Lyon	33	1225.1	260	3695	112	7/94	9/165	32.99	3.01	65.6	5	0
RJ Harris	24	830.0	221	2324	103	7/117	9/106	22.56	2.80	48.3	5	0
BW Hilfenhaus	27	1013.0	258	2822	99	5/75	8/97	28.50	2.78	61.3	2	0
B Lee	17	708.4	137	2254	79	5/59	9/171	28.53	3.18	53.8	3	0
SR Watson	49	771.1	206	2082	67	6/33	6/51	31.07	2.69	69.0	3	0
NM Hauritz	16	673.0	139	2101	58	5/53	6/126	36.22	3.12	69.6	2	0
JL Pattinson	13	425.0	96	1381	51	5/27	8/105	27.07	3.24	50.0	3	0
DE Bollinger	12	400.1	78	1296	50	5/28	8/141	25.92	3.23	48.0	2	0
SR Clark	15	516.2	139	1406	47	5/32	8/91	29.91	2.72	65.9	1	0
MA Starc	12	408.2	74	1378	41	6/154	8/209	33.60	3.37	59.7	2	0
MJ Clarke	78	354.3	57	1024	23	5/86	5/104	44.52	2.88	92.4	1	0
MJ North	21	209.4	37	591	14	6/55	6/55	42.21	2.81	89.8	1	0
JM Bird	3	105.3	36	303	13	4/41	7/117	23.30	2.87	48.6	0	0
JJ Krejza	2	123.5	8	562	13	8/215	12/358	43.23	4.53	57.1	1	1
A Symonds	13	169.0	40	408	13	3/51	3/70	31.38	2.41	78.0	0	0
SPD Smith	20	137.0	18	527	11	3/18	4/83	47.90	3.84	74.7	0	0
SCG MacGill	4	171.0	21	651	10	2/43	4/143	65.10	3.80	102.6	0	0
SM Katich	33	63.2	11	229	9	3/34	3/44	25.44	3.61	42.2	0	0
AB McDonald	4	122.0	40	300	9	3/25	3/72	33.33	2.45	81.3	0	0
GB Hogg	3	125.0	15	481	8	2/51	4/133	60.12	3.84	93.7	0	0
PJ Cummins	1	44.0	8	117	7	6/79	7/117	16.71	2.65	37.7	1	0
XJ Doherty	4	153.0	36	548	7	3/131	3/131	78.28	3.58	131.1	0	0
MEK Hussey	63	93.0	11	283	7	1/0	2/2	40.42	3.04	79.7	0	0
GJ Maxwell	2	41.0	2	193	7	4/127	4/127	27.57	4.70	35.1	0	0
TA Copeland	3	108.0	34	227	6	2/24	3/87	37.83	2.10	108.0	0	0
JP Faulkner	1	27.4	4	98	6	4/51	6/98	16.33	3.54	27.6	0	0

Player	Mat	Overs	Mdns	Runs	Wkts	BBI	BBM	Ave	Econ	SR	5	10
CL White	4	93.0	8	342	5	2/71	3/119	68.40	3.67	111.6	0	0
DA Warner	30	49.0	1	218	4	2/45	2/45	54.50	4.44	73.5	0	0
MA Beer	2	67.4	13	178	3	2/56	2/66	59.33	2.63	135.3	0	0
B Casson	1	32.0	4	129	3	3/86	3/129	43.00	4.03	64.0	0	0
AC Agar	2	84.0	17	248	2	2/82	2/106	124.00	2.95	252.0	0	0
PR George	1	28.0	3	77	2	2/48	2/77	38.50	2.75	84.0	0	0
MC Henriques	3	53.0	12	155	2	1/48	1/48	77.50	2.92	159.0	0	0
JW Hastings	1	39.0	3	153	1	1/51	1/153	153.00	3.92	234.0	0	0
CJ McKay	1	28.0	5	101	1	1/56	1/101	101.00	3.60	168.0	0	0
BE McGain	1	18.0	2	149	0	-	-	-	8.27		0	0
RT Ponting	58	10.0	1	45	0	-	-	-	4.50		0	0
RJ Quiney	2	25.0	12	29	0	-	-	-	1.16		0	0
SW Tait	1	21.0	1	92	0	-	-	-	4.38		0	0
MS Wade	12	1.0	1	0	0	-	-	-	0.00		0	0

Australian Test team performance 2007–14
FIELDING

Player	Mat	Inns	Dis	Ct	St
BJ Haddin	57	110	233	228	5
MJ Clarke	78	150	105	105	0
MEK Hussey	63	121	77	77	0
RT Ponting	58	112	72	72	0
MS Wade	12	23	36	33	3
AC Gilchrist	6	12	35	35	0
SR Watson	49	93	35	35	0
EJM Cowan	18	35	24	24	0
SM Katich	33	63	24	24	0
DA Warner	30	59	24	24	0
MG Johnson	59	114	22	22	0
MJ North	21	40	17	17	0
TD Paine	4	8	17	16	1
PM Siddle	53	100	16	16	0
SPD Smith	20	38	16	16	0
PJ Hughes	26	48	15	15	0
NM Lyon	33	66	14	14	0
RJ Harris	24	46	11	11	0
GJ Bailey	5	10	10	10	0
ML Hayden	14	28	10	10	0
CJL Rogers	14	28	9	9	0
A Symonds	13	26	9	9	0
BW Hilfenhaus	27	50	7	7	0
PA Jaques	9	18	6	6	0
B Lee	17	34	6	6	0
SE Marsh	9	18	6	6	0
UT Khawaja	9	17	5	5	0
RJ Quiney	2	4	5	5	0

Player	Mat	Inns	Dis	Ct	St
JJ Krejza	2	4	4	4	0
MA Starc	12	24	4	4	0
AJ Doolan	3	6	3	3	0
GA Manou	1	1	3	3	0
DE Bollinger	12	23	2	2	0
B Casson	1	2	2	2	0
SR Clark	15	30	2	2	0
TA Copeland	3	6	2	2	0
XJ Doherty	4	6	2	2	0
NM Hauritz	16	31	2	2	0
AB McDonald	4	7	2	2	0
GJ Maxwell	2	3	2	2	0
MA Beer	2	3	1	1	0
JM Bird	3	6	1	1	0
PJ Cummins	1	2	1	1	0
JW Hastings	1	2	1	1	0
MC Henriques	3	5	1	1	0
GB Hogg	3	6	1	1	0
CJ McKay	1	2	1	1	0
JL Pattinson	13	25	1	1	0
SW Tait	1	2	1	1	0
CL White	4	8	1	1	0

SOURCES

Interviews

Adam Voges, Alex Kountouris, Andrew Jones, Belinda Clark, Bryce McGain, Chris Rogers, Craig McDermott, Ed Cowan, Gavin Dovey, Geoff Lawson, Graeme Smith, Graham Manou, Ian Chappell, James Hopes, James Sutherland, Jamie Cox, Jason Gillespie, John Inverarity, Justin Langer, Keith Bradshaw, Mark Taylor, Matthew Mott, Merv Hughes, Michael Brown, Michael Clarke, Michael Hussey, Mickey Arthur, Nathan Hauritz, Pat Howard, Paul Marsh, Phil Jaques, Ricky Ponting, Rodney Cavalier, Shane Warne, Shane Watson, Stephanie Beltrame, Steve Bernard, Stuart Clark, Stuart Karpinnen, Stuart Law, Stuart MacGill, Tim Nielsen, Trent Woodhill, Wally Edwards.

Books

Arthur, Mickey and Manthorp, Neil. *Taking the Mickey: The Inside Story*. Johannesburg: Jonathan Ball Publishers, 2010.

Astill, James. *The Great Tamasha: Cricket, Corruption and the Turbulent Rise of Modern India*. London: Wisden, 2013.

Atherton, Mike. *Glorious Summers and Discontents*. London: Simon & Schuster, 2011.

Baum, Greg. *The Waugh Era*. Sydney: ABC Books, 2004.

Buchanan, John. *The Future of Cricket*. Melbourne: Hardie Grant, 2009.

Clarke, Michael. *The Ashes Diary*. Sydney: Pan Macmillan, 2013.

Clarke, Michael. *The Captain's Diary*. Sydney: Pan Macmillan, 2014.

Gilchrist, Adam. *True Colours*. Sydney: Pan Macmillan, 2008.

Haigh, Gideon. *All Out: The Ashes 2006–07*. Melbourne: Black Inc, 2007.

Haigh, Gideon. *Good Enough: The Ashes 2009.* Melbourne: Victory Books, 2009.

Haigh, Gideon. *Sphere of Influence: Writings on Cricket and Its Discontents.* Melbourne University Publishing, 2009.

Haigh, Gideon. *Out of the Running: The 2010–11 Ashes Series.* Melbourne: Penguin, 2011.

Haigh, Gideon. *Uncertain Corridors: Writings on Modern Cricket.* Melbourne: Penguin, 2013.

Haigh, Gideon. *Ashes to Ashes: How Australia Came Back and England Came Unstuck, 2013–14.* Melbourne: Penguin, 2014.

Haigh, Gideon and Frith, David. *Inside Story: Unlocking Australian Cricket's Archives.* Sydney: News Custom Publishing, 2007.

Hayden, Matthew. *Standing My Ground.* Melbourne: Penguin, 2010.

Hussey, Michael. *Underneath the Southern Cross.* Melbourne: Hardie Grant, 2013.

James, Steve. *The Plan: How Fletcher and Flower Transformed English Cricket.* London: Transworld Publishers, 2012.

Knox, Malcolm. *Taylor and Beyond.* Sydney: ABC Books, 2000.

Knox, Malcolm. *The Greatest.* Melbourne: Hardie Grant, 2010.

Lee, Brett and Knight, James. *My Life.* Sydney: Random House, 2011.

Lehmann, Darren. *Worth the Wait.* Melbourne: Hardie Grant, 2004.

McGrath, Glenn and Lane, Daniel. *Line and Strength: The Complete Story.* Sydney: Random House, 2007.

McGregor, Malcolm. *An Indian Summer of Cricket.* Canberra: Barrallier Books, 2012.

Pietersen, Kevin. *KP: The Autobiography.* London: Sphere, 2014.

Ponting, Ricky. *Captain's Diary 2008.* Sydney: HarperCollins, 2008.

Ponting, Ricky. *Captain's Diary 2009.* Sydney: HarperCollins, 2009.

Ponting, Ricky. *The Captain's Year.* Sydney: HarperCollins, 2010.

Ponting, Ricky. *At the Close of Play.* Sydney: HarperCollins, 2013.

Ray, Mark. *Border and Beyond.* Sydney: ABC Books, 1995.

Ryan, Christian. *Australia: Story of a Cricket Country.* Melbourne: Hardie Grant, 2011.

Smith, Graeme and Manthorp, Neil. *A Captain's Diary*.
 Johannesburg: Jonathan Ball Publishers, 2009.
Speed, Malcolm. *Sticky Wicket: A Decade of Change in World Cricket*.
 Sydney: HarperCollins, 2011.
Strauss, Andrew. *Driving Ambition: My Autobiography*. London:
 Hodder & Stoughton, 2013.
Symonds, Andrew and Gray, Stephen. *Roy on the Rise: A Year of
 Living Dangerously*. Melbourne: Hardie Grant, 2008.
Taylor, Mark. *Time to Declare*. Sydney: Pan Macmillan, 1999.
Warne, Shane and Hobson, Richard. *My Illustrated Career*. London:
 Cassell Illustrated, 2007.
Watson, Shane and Thompson, Jimmy. *Watto*. Sydney: Allen &
 Unwin, 2011.

Magazines and annuals

Between Wickets
Inside Cricket
Wisden 2007, 2008, 2009, 2010, 2011, 2012, 2013, 2014.
Wisden Australia 2004–05
The Wisden Cricketer

Newspapers

The Advertiser, Adelaide
The Age, Melbourne
The Australian
Courier-Mail, Brisbane
Daily Mail, London
Daily Telegraph, Sydney
The Guardian, London
Herald Sun, Melbourne
Hindustan Times, Delhi

Sydney Morning Herald
The Telegraph, London
The Times, London
West Australian, Perth

Websites

backpagelead.com.au
cricket.com.au
cricketarchive.com
espncricinfo.com

ACKNOWLEDGEMENTS

I had thought about the possibility of this book well before the start of its seven-year timespan. That was because as a teenager I read *Border and Beyond* by Mark Ray then *Taylor and Beyond* by Malcolm Knox, a pair of invaluable, insightful and clear-headed accounts of contemporary Australian cricket. My first thanks must then go to Mark and Malcolm for showing me that long-form writing on the game can be written frankly and fearlessly by the journalists who cover it, without the ghostwriter's cloak.

Gideon Haigh and Christian Ryan have each been wonderful sources of inspiration, advice, encouragement and direction. Gideon tore strips off the first piece I summoned the courage to send him when still a journalism student, and I will be forever grateful that he did. Christian was similarly exacting as the editor of *Inside Edge* and *Wisden Australia*, while also serving as an embodiment of how uncompromising a writer should be. I'm proud to call them friends.

The Advertiser and Australian Associated Press gave me my start in journalism and cricket writing respectively, and I am indebted to both for offering me that chance. Mike Osborne, Neil Harvey and Steve Larkin were grand mentors at AAP. The tours Mike and Neil assigned to me led ultimately to work for ESPNcricinfo, which is the best place in the world to work. From the editor-in-chief Sambit Bal down, all have provided me with great help since I joined. Nagraj Gollapudi, Brydon Coverdale, Melinda Farrell, George Dobell, David Hopps, Sharda Ugra, Jayaditya Gupta, Sidharth Monga, Leslie Mathew, Osman Samiuddin, Rahul Bhattacharya and S Rajesh are just a few of the brilliant folk who have worked alongside me. To Jarrod Kimber, thanks for the massages.

Past and present colleagues in the press box have all been a great help over the years and as I wrote this work, as friends and sources of advice, humour or even the occasional harsh word when I needed it. Special thanks to Peter English, Mike Coward, Malcolm Conn, Peter Lalor, Alex Brown, Ben Horne, Will Swanton, Jim Maxwell, Ben Dorries, Andrew Wu, Greg Baum and John Townsend for chats about this book, Australian cricket or writing in general. Overseas compatriots have also provided tremendous company, especially Nick Hoult, Lawrence Booth, Scyld Berry, Anjali Doshi, Anand Vasu and Dileep Premachandran. Harsha Bhogle's interview with Andrew Symonds was exceptionally useful.

Cricket Australia has been a great help, particularly the team media managers and public affairs staff. Peter Young, Phillip Pope, Lachy Patterson, Matt Slade, Matt Cenin and Kate Hutchison all offered recollections and assistance. So too did Queensland Cricket's unflappable Stephen Gray . I am particularly indebted to Jonathan Rose, who worked as something of an advocate for the project and facilitated most of my interviews with current CA staff, management, the chief executive James Sutherland and the chairman Wally Edwards. He has also shown a rare ability to understand my verbal directions around Adelaide.

Other folk around Australian cricket gave me considerable encouragement as well as time for interviews or more general discussions. Ian Chappell, Andrew Jones, Tim Nielsen, Mickey Arthur, Steve Bernard and Michael Brown were all particularly generous with their time and observations. I am grateful to every interviewee for being unfailingly frank, and for trusting me to render events faithfully.

In addition to their courage in taking on the book in the first place, Penguin have provided an enjoyable entry into the world of publishing. Ben Ball's confidence in the idea was vital, while Rachel Scully kept the ship on course, even as it entered the choppier waters of summer. Penny Mansley provided a fresh pair of eyes and a constructive sifting through the manuscript. John Canty brought his design flair to the book. A few good friends doubled as thorough readers of chapters or sections – Patrick Bour, Adam Collins, Russell Jackson, Siddhartha Vaidyanathan and Alex Malcolm reassured me that the words they read made sense. Vital early readings, thinking and planning for the story took place in the tiny New South Wales south coast community of Congo, at the family beach house of Leo Shanahan. Alex and his partner Gemma Court were also the most generous of hosts when I visited Perth.

Most of all I'd like to thank Chloe Saltau, who agreed to serve as something of an accomplice on the project. She helped me reach a state of clarity about the overall idea, assisted in gathering interviews, read each fragment of the book as I finished it, and helped enormously in shaping the television rights chapter. We first toured together to India in 2008; a better comrade-in-arms one could not hope to find.